Somerset County Maryland

MARRIAGE RECORDS

1796–1871

Roy C. Pollitt

HERITAGE BOOKS
2021

HERITAGE BOOKS
AN IMPRINT OF HERITAGE BOOKS, INC.

Books, CDs, and more—Worldwide

For our listing of thousands of titles see our website
at
www.HeritageBooks.com

Published 2021 by
HERITAGE BOOKS, INC.
Publishing Division
5810 Ruatan Street
Berwyn Heights, Md. 20740

International Standard Book Number
Paperbound: 978-1-68034-509-4

CONTENTS

PREFACE

This book is a compilation of the marriage records for Somerset County, Maryland for the period of 1 November 1796 to the end of December 1871. The researcher should be cautioned that the dates given are, in most cases, the dates that the licenses were purchased and recorded.. The actual marriage usually did not take place until 1-5 days later, if at all. The source for these marriage records is as follows:

Marriages 1796 to 30 Apr 1831: (1805 to 1807 marriages excluded, as these have been lost). From a typescript on file in the Genealogical Library at the North Carolina State Archives, Raleigh NC. (This typescript is also found at the Maryland Historical Society, and probably elsewhere as well.)

Marriages 1 May 1831 to 1871 Microfilmed marriage registers, Somerset County MD. (Maryland State Archives, Annapolis MD)

There are three duplicate entries recorded in this book due to the fact that they are recorded in the typescript and the microfilmed registers. This is, in effect, an overlap of the typescript and the microfilmed registers --an overlap of one month (May 1831). The three duplicate entries are:

Jackson, Henry to Huston, Allifair 20 May 1831
Lankford, Thomas to Boston, Mary 10 May 1831
Leatherbury, John to Jones, Mary 10 May 1831

All things considered, the original registers are in satisfactory condition. However, parts of some pages are torn out, badly stained, etc. At any rate, I have attempted to reproduce as many of the original entries as possible, as accurately as possible, even where a partial entry could be deciphered.

As for the handwriting in the original records I have tried to reproduce the names exactly as found. No attempt to correct the spelling of either the surnames or the Christian names has been made. Therefore, the researcher is urged to consult all possible spelling variations before drawing conclusions. One must also remember that the handwriting of the day, even at its best, is at times difficult to decipher. The letters "I" and "J" are especially puzzling, if not outright impossible to differentiate. Thus a "Mary J. Jones" could have been "Mary I. Jones." I have recorded most of these middle initial I's and J's as J's, on the theory that more people had middle names beginning with a J. than had middle names beginning with an I.

Many "colored" marriages are found in these records. This is especially true for the period of 1831 to 1871. The original entries designated these marriages as fn" (free negroes), "color", or "colored." I have identified these marriages as "C" at the end of the entry.

There are 7,903 marriage records found in this volume (plus the previously mentioned three duplicates). I am sure that there were more marriages in Somerset County than those recorded here. The author suggests additions, corrections, and/or deletions be submitted to the publisher, Colonial Roots, for possible inclusion if future reprints of this book, if any.

This volume is dedicated to my mother, Mrs. Doris S. Pollitt, for her patience and help, and to my father, the late Alton Fisher Pollitt, whose interest in his family's history was intense and genuine.

Roy C. Pollitt
June 1986

SOMERSET COUNTY, MARYLAND MARRIAGE RECORDS
1796 - 1871

________ _______ to ________ _______21 Jul 1840
________ _____ to Collins Nancy Dec 1871
________Calvin to ___________ 6 Jul 1840
________ Edward L. to Gibbons Sarah E. 10 Oct 1871
________ Elijah to ____ ______ 7 Jul 1840
________ Isaac to ____ ____ 30 Jon 1840
________ James to Evans Mary 21 Mar 1870
________ Jo _____ to ____14 Jul 1840
________ John Bo____ to _____ _____ 30 Jun 1840
________ Levin D. to _____ _____20 Jun 1840
________ Levin H. to _____ _____ 24 Jun 1840
________ Raymand to Street Jane 3 Dec 1850
________ Scott to ______ _____ 17 Jun 1840
________ Step _____ to ___ __ _____7 Jul 1840
________ William to Evans Rachel 11 Aug 1819
Abbot Jabez to Webster Adeline 28 Mar 1848
Abbot Mason to McGrath Elizabeth 29 Jul 1809
Abbott Alexander to Hall Sophia 31 Oct 1838
Abbott Curtis to Crouch Betsy 20 Dec 1820
Abbott Edward to Jones Louisa 2 Jan 1861
Abbott George W.D. to Webster Louisa E. 14 Sep 1870
Abbott James Thomas to Webster Lucinda 19 Dec 1841
Abbott Lloyd to Wallace Harriett 30 Oct 1821
Abbott Lloyd to Webster Susan 23 Aug 1825
Abbott Major to Jones Rebecca 14 Oct 1853
Abbott Mason to Turner Sally 11 Oct 1808
Abbott Samuel J. to Langrall Celestine C. 16 May 1871
Abbott Wesley C. to Jones Virginia S. 20 Dec 1870
Abbott William to Webster Levina 29 Jan 1835
Abbott William to Bounds Elizabeth 23 May 1840
Abbott William to Webster Victoria 27 Feb 1855
Abbott William George to Bedill Julia 14 Jul 1858
Abdail Jacob to Brinkley Eleanor 24 Jan 1832
Abdel Robert D. to Turner Sarah Ann 11 Dec 1850
Absolom Henry to Robertson Anne 19 Jan 1830
Ackinson Robert to Trehearn Alvina 23 Jan 1857
Ackworth Train to Hull Nancy 10 Dec 1822

Acworth Albert E. to Dougherty Charlotte E. 23 Apr 1855
Acworth Beacham to Crockett Jane 13 Jul 1815
Acworth Columbus to Jenkins Mary 2i Feb 1851
Acworth James to Smith Eliza 29 Jan 1822
Acworth James to Hillman Lydia 13 Jan 1829
Acworth James to Turner Juliet 5 Aug 1851
Acworth Richard to Wright Sarah 27 Feb 1815
Acworth Samuel to Harris Kitty 3 May 1803
Acworth Samuel to Moore Elizabeth 31 Dec 1816
Acworth Terry to Marshall Caroline 20 Feb 1850
Acworth William to Polk Mary T. 1 May 1866
Acworth William B. to Goslee Ellen 1 Feb 1831
Acworth William H. to Waller Mary Ann 6 Apr 1847
Adams Andrew to Taylor Mary 25 Jan 1797
Adams Andrew to Moore Amelia 20 Feb 1828
Adams Beauchamp D. to Moore Sally 9 Apr 1816
Adams Benjamin F. to Sudler Elizabeth 16 Feb 1864
Adams Charles to Miles Leah 31 Dec 1867 C
Adams Collins to Tilghman Peggy 23 Jul 1810
Adams Collins to Boston Charlotte 16 Jan 1816
Adams Colmore to Holland Emeline 22 Oct 1839
Adams Daniel D. to Layfield Elizabeth J. 18 Dec 1833
Adams Edward to Cox Ann 1 Feb 1842
Adams Edward H. to Anderson Julia A. 12 Jul 1831
Adams Edward J. to Powell Emily F. 29 Jul 1856
Adams Edward M. to Ewall Elizabeth 6 Feb 1845
Adams Elijah B. to Dashiell Anna M. 8 Sep 1849
Adams Elijah T. to Miles Elizabeth E. 15 Jan 1856
Adams Festus to Purnell Elizabeth 26 Oct 1869 C
Adams Frederick A. to Hayman Sarah W. 4 Nov 1868
Adams George to Beauchamp Eleanor L. 6 Mar 1832
Adams George to Sterling Mary 1 Jun 1837
Adams George to Goslee Mary E. 17 Jan 1844
Adams George to Handy Susan J. 19 May 1853
Adams George L. to Adams Sallie P. 14 Jun 1869
Adams George W. to Dougherty Patty 15 Apr 1863
Adams George W.S.D. to Insley Mary Jane Victoria 16 Aug 1859
Adams Henry to Marshall Jane 3 Feb 1801
Adams Henry to Blake Sarah Underwood 3 May 1804
Adams Henry to Gibbons Elizabeth 3 Jan 1827

Adams Henry to Anderson Nancy 27 Jan 1829
Adams Henry J. to Benson Elizabeth J.D. 20 Jan 1840
Adams Hope to Moore Peggy 2 Aug 1815
Adams Hope to Wilson Polly 12 Dec 1826
Adams Hopewell to Long Dalia 22 Sep 1835
Adams Isaac to Wood Leah 19 Sep 1797
Adams Isaac to Beauchamp Nancy 15 Nov 1803
Adams Isaac H. to Pruitt Virginia F. 3 Mar 1863
Adams James to Palmer Elizabeth Susan 26 Apr 1831
Adams James to Walker Eleanor 20 Jan 1852
Adams James to McDaniel Sally 13 Oct 1870
Adams James D. to Mezick Leah W. 3 Feb 1829
Adams James F. to Wilson Elizabeth E. 26 Feb 1839
Adams James O. to Marain Vashti 11 Jan 1842
Adams James T. to Adams Elizabeth Ann 9 Nov 1847
Adams James T.M. to Furniss Mary E. 23 Apr 1860
Adams Jesse to Marshall Esther 9 Dec 1812
Adams Jesse to Silverthorn Elizabeth 20 Jan 1829
Adams Jesse (of Hope) to Aires Maria 6 Aug 1811
Adams John to Webster Milcah 28 May 1810
Adams John to Dryden Eliza Ann 11 Mar 1820
Adams John to Robertson Anne D. 3 Mar 1835
Adams John to Brown Margaret T. 14 Jun 1843
Adams John to Hall Margaret 4 Mar 1851
Adams John (of Peter) to Jones Nancy 8 Mar 1803
Adams John A. to Beauchamp Sarah A. 2 Jan 1867
Adams John C. to Paradise Annie 30 Jul 1867
Adams John D. to Winright Biddy 4 Jan 1820
Adams John D. to Walter Esther D. 20 Nov 1838
Adams John H. to Cottman Araminta Matilda 11 Oct 1821
Adams John H. to Curtis Susan A. 22 Dec 1835
Adams John H. to Curtis Sarah T. --(?) 1838
Adams John Henry to Williams Elizabeth Ellen 21 May 1849
Adams John T. to Broughton Mary Anne T. 29 Oct 1834
Adams John W. to Adams Elizabeth 8 Dec 1801
Adams John W. to Smith Sophia 1 Nov 1808
Adams John Whit to Disharoon Sally 16 May 1797
Adams Joseph to Robert Eleanor T. 9 Nov 1824
Adams Joseph to Robertson Eleanor J. 9 Nov 1824
Adams Joseph W. to Handy Catherine J. 27 May 1856

Adams Joshua B. to Matthews Margaret A. 21 May 1861
Adams Lazarus to Schoolfield Betsy Williams 8 Sep 1807
Adams Lazarus to Cane Anne 22 Feb 1820
Adams Levi to Johnson Sophia C. 12 Apr 1836
Adams Levi W. to Mister Emily J. 14 Dec 1848
Adams Littleton to McCready Elizabeth 26 Dec 1843
Adams Nathan to Howard Charity 28 Jul 1797
Adams Nehemiah to Jones Gatty 10 Dec 1842
Adams Peter to Phillips Amelia 22 Sep 1812
Adams Philip to Adams Elizabeth 26 Jun 1826
Adams Philip C. to Fruce Polly 18 Jun 1823
Adams Phillip C. to Taylor Leah 19 Oct 1821
Adams Phillips to Prior Esther 12 Feb 1799
Adams Rayman to Irving Eleanor 19 Aug 1833
Adams Revill J. to Cox Matilda 16 May 1857
Adams Richard to Beal Susan R. 8 Nov 1869
Adams Rodger to Hitch Catharine A. 13 Aug 1842
Adams Sampson to Tull Rachael 11 Feb 1823
Adams Sampson to Miles Jane 13 Sep 1831
Adams Samuel to Whittingham Nancy 8 Sep 1801
Adams Samuel to Collins Anne 26 Jul 1802
Adams Samuel to Dryden Mary 25 May 1813
Adams Samuel to Wilson Mary Anne 7 Jun 1825
Adams Samuel to Harris Sarah 3 Feb 1840
Adams Samuel H. to Riggin Zipporah 26 Feb 1833
Adams Samuel T. to Whittington Mary A. 13 Nov 1860
Adams Stephen to Dryden Ellender N. 29 Nov 1808
Adams Stephen to Cottman Amanda 28 Sep 1864
Adams Stephen H. to Hobbs Mides 3 Feb 1829
Adams Sydney to Dashiell Cinderella 30 May 1864
Adams Theodore F. to Jones Jane 17 Jan 1867 C
Adams Thomas to Rounds Mary 16 Oct 1798
Adams Thomas to Landen Nelly 27 Oct 1801
Adams Thomas J. to Jenkins Nancy 3 Jul 1849
Adams Thomas P. to Cottingham Anne 20 Dec 1825
Adams William to Hall Rebecca 4 Dec 1798
Adams William to Broughton Esther 2 Jan 1810
Adams William to Prior Nelly 19 Feb 1822
Adams William to Milbourne Sally 28 Jul 1829
Adams William to Johnson Susan J. 6 Dec 1842

Adams William to Cluff Sarah 14 Mar 1848
Adams William to Coulbourn Holly O. 24 Dec 1849
Adams William to Howard Nancy 25 Jun 1853
Adams William to Stevens Mary Jane 13 Nov 1855
Adams William (Capt} to Furniss Margaret 28 0ct 1834
Adams William Carey to Hall Polly 3 Apr 1804
Adams William D. to Gibbs Eliza Anne 18 Oct 1860
Adams William F. to Mitchell Mary 27 May 1828
Adams William H. to Sturgis Priscilla 19 0ct 1821
Adams William How to Cottingham Sally 21 Feb 1804
Adams William J.F. to Brereton Maria L. 18 Sep 1849
Adams William L. to Green Mary E.W. 28 Mar 1853
Adams William T. to Milbourn Margaret 13 Mar 1849
Adams William T. to Lankford Cinderella 24 Mar 1863
Addams Noah to Lambden Zipporah 17 Feb 1801
Adkins Robert H. to Calloway Hester E. 24 Jun 1853
Aikman George to Smith Nancy 23 Jun 1803
Aikman Wesley R. to Moore Sallie E. 19 Mar 1862
Aires George to Leatherbury Amelia 14 May 1803
Aires George (Sr.) to Irving Betsy 23 Oct 1804
Aires Moses to Wright Priscilla 2 May 1843
Aires Thomas I. to Somers Mary Anne 12 Feb 1828
Airs Littleton to Hitch Sally 29 Jan 1799
Allen Albert J. to Twilley Elizabeth E. 17 Apr 1866
Allen Benjamin to Pollitt Tamar 31 Dec 1862
Allen Benjamin to Welsh Anna 8 May 1865
Allen John to McCurdy Elizabeth 9 Apr 1799
Allen John to Fontaine Eleanor A. 30 Apr 1814
Allen John to Fountaine Henrieitta 28 Nov 1848
Allen John G. to Davis Ellen B. 10 Mar 1841
Allen Joseph S. C. to Phoebus Mary C. 3 Jul 1866
Allen William W. to Whittington Mary 19 May 1819
Alpha Mitchell to Parramore Sarah 10 Jan 1815
Alpha William. to Horseman Caroline 23 Apr 1844
Ames Theodore E. to Jones Virginia C. 24 Jan 1854
Anderson Andrew W. to Fletcher Elizabeth C. 30 Oct 1827
Anderson Augustus Henry to Davis Elizabeth 24 May 1814
Anderson Ebenezer to Hopkins Priscilla 24 Jul 1827
Anderson Edward to Daniel Sarah A. 20 Dec 1852
Anderson George to Lankford Elizabeth 22 Feb 1820

Anderson Gillis to Barkley Eliza Jane G. 30 Apr 1834
Anderson Gilliss to Anderson Elizabeth 11 Jan 1827
Anderson Henry to Winkle Patsy 27 Apr 1867 C
Anderson Henry W. to Price Martha J.W. 10 Jan 1860
Anderson Isaac to Daley Mary 21 Dec 1824
Anderson Isaac to Walston Anne M.E. 5 Feb 1857
Anderson James to Mitchel Maria 19 Dec 1820
Anderson James S. to Stanford Clementine 4 Oct 1836
Anderson John to Hayman Louisa 3 Jan 1849 C
Anderson John (Jr.) to Connaway Sally 7 Sep 1802
Anderson John Adams to Wallace Santa --(?) 1838
Anderson John D. to Adams Leah Jane 16 Mar 1831
Anderson John H. to Jones Anne Maria M. 24 Dec 1810
Anderson John W.D. to Porter Sarah E. 9 Dec 1851
Anderson Martin to Dunn Sarah 31 Mar 1835
Anderson Peter to Wilson Hannah 29 Apr 1808
Anderson Peter to Wilson Polly 25 Dec 1834
Anderson Stephen G. to Weatherly Anne M. 19 Jan 1854
Anderson Thomas B. to Street Hannah 15 Dec 1846
Anderson William to Humphris Matilda 12 Sep 1804
Anderson William to Moore Betsy 5 Apr 1814
Anderson William to Rencher Sally M. 21 Jan 1829
Anderson William to Polk Louisa J. 31 Oct 1837
Anderson William H. to Morris Emeline 17 Sep 1834
Anderson William J. to Langford Sarah H. 23 Jan 1867
Anderson Zededee to Greene Mary 26 Mar 1827
Andress Robert to Stant Elishey Ann 24 Apr 1849
Andrew Robert to Hughes Sarah E. 3 Jun 1862
Andrews Thomas to Smith Myrandy 8 Jun 1849
Andrews William to Milbourn Anne 12 Jan 1802
Annis William to Young Elizabeth 15 Jul 1847
Ansley William to Carsey Polly 5 Aug 1800
Armiger Joseph to Willing Mary 11 Feb 1864
Armstrong James B. to Bounds Elizabeth J. 26 Oct 1858
Armstrong Wm. to Parmer Harriet 3 Aug 1827
Armwood Angelo to Polk Esther 25 Oct 1871 C
Armwood James to Fooks Permelia A. 25 Aug 1863 C
Arvey George G. to Brinkley Mary Jane 25 Dec 1841
Arvey Napoleon to Taylor Elizabeth 17 Jun 1834
Arvey William to Hopkins Unice 5 Mar 1835

Arvey William to Anderson Margaret 4 Oct 1837
Ashmead Joseph to Evans Nancy 14 Aug 1849
Askins Samuel to Huffington Betsy 2 Aug 1802
Atkinson George S. to Jones Elizabeth 30 Apr 1851
Atkinson Irving W. to Mason Sarah E. 1 Mar 1864
Atkinson Joseph to Scott Henrietta 13 Aug 1867 C
Atkinson Samuel to Miller Adaline E. 9 Dec 1847
Atkinson Thomas D. to Long Mary 17 Feb 1829
Austen George B. to Wailes Sarah Ellen 25 Oct 1842
Austen George P. to Ritchie Mary E. 31 May 1852
Austen Levin to Anderson Julian 25 May 1839
Austen William to Clark Milly 5 Sep 1800
Austin Edward to James Teresa 23 Oct 1811
Austin Edward to James Susan 3 Dec 1816
Austin Fielder to Adams Sarah Anne 30 Sep 1829
Austin Fielder to Adams Lovey 1 Jun 1831
Austin Fielder to Collier Mary Jane 7 May 1850
Albtin Isaac M. to Furniss Elizabeth C. 3 Dec 1861
Austin Isaac M. to Reed Harriet 20 Dec 1865
Austin Isaac R. to Malcomb Martha G. 16 Dec 1797
Austin John to Bedsworth Sally 8 May 1850
Austin John (Dr.) to Handy Jane 25 Oct 1834
Austin Nathaniel B. to Dashiell Mary E.E. 6 Apr 1841
Avery Josiah (Capt.) to Mure Martha Ann 7 Jan 1851
Aydelotte Joseph to Ryder Mary 13 Nov 1810
Backett Joshua H. to Bowser Mary A. 10 Dec 1861 C
Badley Clement to Jackson Nancy 28 Oct 1834
Badley Elijah to Darby Eliza 19 May 1829
Badley Gideon (Jr) to Cooper Mary B. Sep 1830
Badley John to Jackson Louisa Eleanor 1 Jun 1832
Badley John to Henderson Mary 10 Mar 1858
Badley John (Senr.) to Taylor Nancy 23 Oct 1844
Badley Perry W. to Dashiell Mary 13 Apr 1847
Badley Samuel T. to Bennett Emaline 5 Jan 1848
Badley Severn to Gilliss Elizabeth 5 Aug 1829
Badley Thomas J. to Taylor Leah E. 21 May 1856
Baefford Thomas to Layfield Margaret E. 16 Jan 1850
Bagwell John H. to Sterling Harriet F. 17 Jan 1865 C
Bailey Benjamin to Dashiell Sally R. 16 Apr 1853
Bailey Benjamin to Fleming Mary G. 14 Feb 1855

Bailey Elias to Roberts Caroline 2 Jul 1850
Bailey Hosias to Smith Sally Ann 16 May 1865
Bailey Isaiah to Kirwan Rachael 30 Oct 1833
Bailey James to Pinkett Ellen 2 Mar 1870 C
Bailey James E. to Bloodsworth Susan A. 2 Mar 1847
Bailey John H. to Jones Anne R. 10 Sep 1867
Bailey Joshua to Wright Mary 23 Jan 1854 C
Bailey Josiah to Weatherly Margaret K. 6 Dec 1842
Bailey Levin to Russel Elizabeth 24 Feb 1852
Bailey Levin H. to Conoly Amanda W. 21 Jan 1864
Bailey Marcellus W. to Bradley Mary F. 30 Oct 1855
Bailey Oliver A. to Marsh Eliza A. 25 Apr 1865
Bailey Robert to Covington Sally A. 9 Feb 1847
Bailey Thomas J. to Brown Cora T. 25 Nov 1856
Bailey William to Taylor Frances 16 Dec 1868
Bailey William A. to Covington Susan W. 6 May 1846
Bailey William H.H. to Robertson Mary E. 2 Mar 1863
Baily Levin to Taylor Nancy 20 Dec 1814
Baker Riley to Carmichael Priscilla 19 Jun 1797
Baker William to Shores Mary 19 Jan 1866
Ball Jacob to Mills Mollie 3 Sep 1799
Ballard Arnold H. to Ballard Ruth M. 18 Feb 1829
Ballard Daniel to Waters Dorothy 6 Jul 1797
Ballard Daniel to Bowen Nancy 7 Jan 1840
Ballard Daniel J. to Waters Eleanor G. 10 Oct 1836
Ballard Daniel J. to Maddux Elizabeth A. 5 Apr 1853
Ballard Daniel Washington to Rupel Henrietta 9 Feb 1864
Ballard David to Maddux Keziah 8 Dec 1848 C
Ballard Edward to Beauchamp Hannah 16 Sep 1823
Ballard Edward to Hall Mary H. 20 Feb 1867
Ballard Elijah to Stone Jane 24 Aug 1866 C
Ballard George to Garretson Mary 2 Jan 1821
Ballard George to Church Nelly 21 Dec 1838
Ballard George to Miles Julia 29 Nov 1871 C
Ballard George to Cottman Louisa 3 Mar 1871 C
Ballard George (of Levin) to Brown Sally 7 Mar 1844
Ballard Henry to Hayward Lucy 4 Apr 1867 C
Ballard Henry U. to Townsend Maria 6 Sep 1830
Ballard Isaac G. to Lang Mary 15 Aug 1871
Ballard James E. to Black Sally M. 17 Dec 1861 C

Ballard John to Miles Esther 4 Feb 1868 C
Ballard Levi to Covington Mary 27 Jul 1816
Ballard Levin to Willing Sally 23 Aug 1808
Ballard Levin (Sr) to Elzey Anne C. 15 Jun 1814
Ballard Levin Henry to Dashiell Ellen 6 Jan 1865 C
Ballard Levin W. to Cottman Charlotte 31 Jan 1821
Ballard Levin W. to Dashiell Eliza Anne 27 Apr 1826
Ballard Robert R. to Waters Sarah D. 2 Nov 1826
Ballard Severn to Foxwell Annice 18 Jun 1832
Ballard Theodore to Collins Matilda 24 Aug 1871 C
Ballard Thomas E. to Maddux Kitturah H. 30 Oct 1827
Ballard Thomas E. to Turpin Rozina 21 Sep 1857
Ballard William to Adams Sarah 10 Apr 1827
Ballard William to Insley Lovey 6 Aug 1828
Ballard William to Parks Mary E. 13 Nov 1867
Ballard William J. to Fisher Mary C. 17 Sep 1839
Ballard William J. to Bailey Susan 3 Sep 1855
Ballard William R. to Hyland Harriet Elizabeth 27 Mar 1865
Banker Nelson to Maddux Harriet 28 Apr 1870 C
Banker Rufus to Horsey Keziah Jane 5 Dec 1865
Banks Emory to Whelon Anne 16 Jun 1858
Banks Gabriel to Jenkins Rebecca 4 Aug 1818
Banks Gamale to Disharoon Leah E. 13 Apr 1858
Banks Henry to Messick Polly 19 Nov 1799
Banks Henry to Ray Betsy 20 Dec 1808
Banks Henry to Cheatham Hetty 24 Jul 1821
Banks John W. to Anderson Margaret E. 9 Dec 1856
Banks John W. to Malone Sarah A. 21 Oct 1858
Banks Thomas to Mazick Sally 29 Jul 1802
Banks Thomas to Norris Elizabeth 13 May 1828
Banks Thomas to Conway Priscilla 28 Mar 1842
Banks Thomas J. to Bounds Leah Jane 5 Feb 1856
Banks Thomas W. to Smith Mary L. 9 Jun 1858
Banks William to Hewman Margaret 15 Mar 1825
Barbon Levin to Hitch Sarah Jane 17 Dec 1850
Barbon Soren to Hitch Elizabeth 1 Apr 1863
Barclay Alexander P. to Disharoon Martha W. 4 Apr 1860
Barkley Alfred to Stewart Betsy Ann 15 Nov 1865 C
Barkley David to Collier Hetty 9 Nov 1813
Barkley David to Larmore Sarah Ann 7 May 1822

Barkley David to Hayman Eliza 9 Dec 1823
Barkley David to Heath Margaret T .W. 17 Dec 1827
Barkley David to Nutter Priscilla Jane 23 Dec 1853 C
Barkley Eliphalet to Cordray Maria S. 6 Jan 1846
Barkley Esme to Anderson Esther W. 25 Sep 1840
Barkley Henry to Cordry Sarah 19 Feb 1819
Barkley Isaac to Evans Rebecca 11 Feb 1843
Barkley Isaac to Smith Mary Jane 3 Jun 1851
Barkley Jacob to Nutter Delia 2 Dec 1862 C
Barkley John to Robertson Milky 13 Jan 1840 C
Barkley John C. to Smith Elenora S. 27 Mar 1860
Barkley John H. to Nutter Henrietta 30 Oct 1866
Barkley Joseph to Gilliss Eliza 12 Jan 1808
Barkley Joseph to Gilliss Polly 17 Feb 1816
Barkley Joseph to Heath Sally D. 5 May 1825
Barkley Orrick to Graham Hester 8 Jan 1868 C
Barkley Samuel to Cox Mary 1 Nov 1837
Barkley Stephen to Nutter Matilda 22 Nov 1850
Barkley William to Jones Susan 24 Dec 1866 C
Barley Osias to Cooper Elizabeth E. 14 Mar 1849
Barnes Francis J. to Lankford Emma F. 22 Oct 1866
Barnes Isaac T. to King Laura E.W. 17 Feb 1849
Barnes James to Scott Leah E. 8 Dec 1869
Barnes James A. to Adams Sarah Eleanor 12 Mar 1833
Barnes Levin P. to Lankford Marcilla 18 Jul 1866
Barnes Parker to Broughton Peggy 3 Jun 1817
Barnes Richard to Denwood Anne 6 Nov 1810
Barnes Samuel to Wingate Molsey 25 Dec 1809
Barnes Wheatly D. to Adams Elizabeth M.J. 4 Dec 1841
Barnes William to Givans Eleanor 20 Jul 1813
Barnett John W. to Martin Sarah J. 19 Sep 1865
Barnett Oliver P. to Wilson Mary A.E. 21 Sep 1852
Barret Joseph to Schoolfield Leah 25 Jul 1820
Barry Charles F. to Somers Mary S. 10 Sep 1861
Barttan Anthony to Huffington Eleanor 22 Jun 1830
Bassett William to Bayne Rosey 9 May 1821
Bassit Samuel to Taylor Nancy 24 Sep 1816
Batts Lemuel to Monroe Nancy 31 Aug 1802
Batts William to Sterling Bernetta 4 Sep 1866
Bayly Benjamin to Anderson Mary 19 Nov 1818

Bayly Henry E. to Nutter Sarah I 16 Mar 1802
Bayly Jacob W. to Denson Mary D. 10 May 1825
Bayly John to Dikes Sylvia 17 Oct 1818
Bayly Richard to Upshur Sally 8 Dec 1801
Bayly Stephen to Waller Priscilla 18 Dec 1799
Bayly Stephen to Adams Elizabeth 4 Dec 1801
Bayly Stephen to Glasgow Peggy 7 Mar 1821
Bayly Theodore T. to Bennett Sarah E. 8 May 1860
Bayly Thomas to Cooper Betsy 17 Nov 1800
Bayne Edward I. to Bell Lovy 4 Jan 1870 C
Beathard Jonathan A. to Rhodes Anne Maria 3 Jan 1857
Beaucham Levin to Reynon Susan A. 27 Sep 1849
Beauchamp Arthur to Boyer Henrietta 17 Jul 1867 C
Beauchamp Benjamin to Jones Nelly 21 Feb 1811
Beauchamp Benjamin to Matthews Mary James 14 Aug 1845
Beauchamp Charles Q. to Howarth Sadonia S. 27 Mar 1866
Beauchamp Daniel to Moore Anne 18 Feb 1797
Beauchamp Edward to Williams Mary 21 Dec 1853
Beauchamp Elijah to Dougherty Leah 5 Feb 1835
Beauchamp Elisha to Bedsworth Milly 16 May 1804
Beauchamp Elisha to McDaniel Leah Jane 19 Jan 1841
Beauchamp Fountain to Beauchamp Anne 2 May 1807
Beauchamp George H.J. to Waters Anne 5 Jan 1841
Beauchamp Henry to Adams Peggy 8 Feb 1803
Beauchamp Henry to Jordan Jane 15 Jul 1807
Beauchamp Henry to Johnson Anne 23 Apr 1834
Beauchamp Humphreys to Swift Jane 22 May 1849
Beauchamp Isaac to Lankford Peggy 3 Sep 1811
Beauchamp Isaac T. (Col.) to Gibbons Margaret Priscilla 15 Feb 1858
Beauchamp Isaiah to Anderson Betsy 4 Nov 1818
Beauchamp James to Cullen Amelia 28 Oct 1816
Beauchamp Jesse to Baker Lydia 14 Aug 1799
Beauchamp Jesse to Carroll Polly 11 Feb 1817
Beauchamp John to Lamberson Leah 31 Jan 1812
Beauchamp John to White Sally 16 Nov 1815
Beauchamp John H. to Abbott Jane 22 Feb 1849
Beauchamp John H. to Ford Mary J. 21 Aug 1855
Beauchamp Joseph to More Betsey 2 Dec 1796
Beauchamp Joseph to Hubbert Caroline 13 Mar 1841
Beauchamp Josiah to Schoolfield Polly 26 Jan 1802

Beauchamp Levi to Jones Ardelia 17 Apr 1860
Beauchamp Levin H. to White Margaret E. 19 Oct 1857
Beauchamp Luther J. to Ford Mary R. 7 May 1861
Beauchamp Matthias T. to Whealton Anne 7 Jan 1840
Beauchamp Nathan to Catlin Betsey 1 Apr 1812
Beauchamp Richard to Adams Zipporah 21 Nov 1826
Beauchamp Samuel to Beauchamp Ann 25 Jan 1817
Beauchamp Samuel to Bunce Hetty 12 Dec 1833
Beauchamp Samuel W. to Parks Virginia U. 23 May 1860
Beauchamp Selby to Reece Nancy 19 May 1818
Beauchamp Selby to Wingate Eleanor 18 Feb 1854
Beauchamp Stephen to Hitch Nally 8 Dec 1801
Beauchamp Stephen to Jones Zipporah 10 Jul 1815
Beauchamp Theodore F. to Parks Elizabeth J. 23 Apr 1855
Beauchamp Theodore F. to Croswell Priscilla F. 3 Nov 1863
Beauchamp Thomas to Lockwood Anne 13 Feb 1798
Beauchamp Thomas to Silverthorn Leah 19 Apr 1803
Beauchamp Thomas G. to Long Maria 24 Mar 1827
Beauchamp Thomas G. to King Leah A. U. 24 Sep 1828
Beauchamp Thomas H. to Millbourn Margaret J. 4 Jul 1848
Beauchamp Tubman T. to Powell Arianna 20 Sep 1870
Beauchamp Whittington to Moore Duley Ann 12 Feb 1850
Beauchamp Whitty to Adams Harriet 17 Apr 1827
Beauchamp William to Adams Minty 16 Feb 1798
Beauchamp William to Cottingham Mary G. 6 Mar 1832
Beauchamp William to Bozman Susan 21 Feb 1859
Beauchamp William D.W. to Marriner Eliza 26 Dec 1842
Beauchamp William D.W. to Tar Nancy M. 12 Jul 1854
Beauchamp William H. to Tull Mary 19 Sep 1836
Beauchamp William H. to Adams Elizabeth 10 Dec 1839
Beauchamp William H. to Robertson Susan P. 6 Jun 1868
Beauchamp William H. to Landing Josephine 15 Jan 1870
Beauchamp William W. to Handy Margaret A. 18 May 1842
Beauchamp Wm. N. to White Margaret C. 10 Mar 1835
Beckett Benjamin to Denson Mahala 6 Feb 1821
Bedsworth Benjamin to Moore Nancy 11 Jan 1804
Bedsworth Benjamin to Wilson Rebecca 13 Mar 1813
Bedsworth Franklin to Dougherty Elvira 24 Dec 1839
Bedsworth George to Wilson Emeline S. 27 Jul 1855
Bedsworth John F. to Bedsworth Emana F. 31 May 1870

Bedsworth John H. to Sterling Permelia 5 Nov 1819
Bedsworth John W. to Phoebus Mary 7 Feb 1854
Bedsworth Noah to Bownds Rachel W. 4 Sep 1849
Bedsworth Solomon E. to McDaniel Sally 3 Jan 1871
Bedsworth Thomas to Brown Sally 12 Jun 1810
Bedsworth Thomas to Todd Jane 8 Jul 1863
Bedsworth Tubman to Lowe Anna 12 Aug 1813
Bedsworth Whitty to Linton Fanny 7 Feb 1820
Bedsworth Whitty to Parks Ann Eliza 1 Dec 1866
Bedsworth William H. to Riggin Emily F. 8 Apr 1862
Bedsworth William Henry to Riggin Sally Anne 22 Nov 1853
Bedsworth William J. to Weatherly Rachel W. 30 Jul 1836
Bedue John P. to McColister Sarah C. 26 Apr 1860
Bell Francis to Cottman Rosetta 4 Feb 1869 C
Bell Francis A. to Carter Louisa A. 20 Mar 1867
Bell George E. to Waters Esther E. 26 Dec 1866 C
Bell George W. to Brittingham Annie E. 29 May 1865
Bell Henry to Davis Clarissa 22 Mar 1830
Bell Jacob to Boston Susan 16 Nov 1843
Bell John to Marshall Polly 10 Jan 1797
Bell John to Gibbons Amelia 23 Jan 1808
Bell John to Horsey Elizabeth 3 Dec 1844
Bell John H. to Cottman Ann Maria 3 May 1808
Bell John H. to Stewart Eleanor 4 Jan 1821
Bell John H. to Polk Mary W. 3 Dec 1846
Bell Joshua to Handy Levitha 14 Nov 1871 C
Bell Nathaniel to Tull Caroline 19 Dec 1831
Bell Nathaniel T. to Hawkes Julia F. 8 Mar 1859
Bell Robert to Broughton Polly 26 Jun 1807
Bell Robert to Bell Elizabeth 18 Jun 1834
Bell Robert J. to Moore Mary A. 14 Dec 1869
Bell Thomas to Hughes Retta 13 Jan 1829
Bell Thomas M. to Taylor Sarah A. 15 Feb 1859
Bell William to Gunby Jane W. 22 Apr 1823
Bell William A. to Sanders Amanda 22 Dec 1842
Bell William C. to Horsey Margaret W. 14 Jan 1851
Bell William Charles to Wilson Hannah Q. 4 Oct 1857
Bell William H. to Pollitt Harriet 16 May 1822
Bennett Charles B. to Vance Anne D.E. 23 Feb 1836
Bennett Eben T. to Taylor Sally E. 21 Dec 1847

Bennett Elisha P. to Elliott Mary Jane 15 Jan 1857
Bennett George P. to Marain Sarah Ann 30 Jun 1849
Bennett Gilliss to Bennett Mary E.T. 12 Apr 1836
Bennett Hamilton to Vincent Anne 5 Dec 1823
Bennett Hazard T. to Wright Margaret J. 5 Aug 1853
Bennett Henry to Green Polly 7 Jun 1814
Bennett James to Gravner Elizabeth 1 Nov 1847
Bennett James Edmond (Dr.) to Taylor Martha Ann 15 Nov 1854
Bennett James T. to Taylor Elizabeth 30 Jul 1822
Bennett John to Shores Sarah 18 Jan 1854
Bennett John B. to Stanton Nancy 28 Jan 1840
Bennett John H. to Shockley Sarah C. 27 Jun 1864
Bennett John T. to Smith Annie B. 14 Jun 1866
Bennett John T. to Jones Virginia Emily -- Jul 1867
Bennett Jonathan to Graham Hetty 15 Feb 1848
Bennett Jonathan to English Sarah Eleanor 16 Dec 1850
Bennett Jonathan P. to Adams Nancy M.E. 13 Feb 1862
Bennett Lambert to Baker Brittana 26 Jan 1849
Bennett Levin to Goslee Elizabeth 9 Oct 1810
Bennett Levin to Bradley Sally 26 Oct 1819
Bennett Matthias to Russell Sarah 23 Apr 1822
Bennett Richard to Tully Sally 20 Feb 1798
Bennett Robert S. to Hopkins Emily Jane 6 Mar 1855
Bennett Swain to Bennett Mary 30 Dec 1828
Bennett Thomas B. to Gravener Mary Anne 12 Apr 1853
Bennett William to Gravener Leah 21 Jan 1845
Bennett William to Wilson Maria 9 Jun 1847
Bennett William to Revill Sarah J. 23 Jul 1857
Bennett William D. to Shockley Mary E. 30 Mar 1852
Bennett William E. to Bailey Mary E. 6 Mar 1856
Bennett William J. to Ballard Caroline 8 Jan 1857
Bennett William T. to Robertson Rachael 10 Nov 1852
Bennett William W. to Riggin Elizabeth A. 1 Mar 1864
Benson Benjamin to Betsworth Mary 28 Jun 1809
Benson Daniel to Dakes Sally 4 Jun 1816
Benson Elijah to Adams Eliza 31 Jul 1824
Benson George to Hopkins Sally 14 Sep 1820
Benson Henry to Heath Fanny D.W. 17 Oct 1816
Benson James to Millikin Peggy 30 Sep 1817
Benson James to Milligan Eliza 31 Jan 1823

Benson John to Howard Sally 8 Dec 1841
Benson Jonathan W. to Robertson Sabrala 20 Jan 1840
Benson Michael to Hall Betsey 26 Nov 1811
Benson William to Long Matilda 14 Apr 1830
Benson Wm. James to Benson Rhoda 12 Jan 1831
Benston Ephraim to Roberts Sukey 11 Mar 1800
Benston Jesse to Johnson Nancy White 5 Aug 1812
Benston William to Robertson Nancy 11 Aug 1807
Benton Alexander W. to Webster Mary W. 10 Oct 1867
Benton Samuel J. to Evans Josephine 26 Jan 1865
Benton Thomas W. to Lankford Susan F. 15 Nov 1867
Berlemann Henry to Horner Mary E. 8 Mar 1871
Betsworth John to Ballard Amelia 5 Jul 1814
Betts Henry to Jones Elizabeth 18 Aug 1858
Betts John to Bethards Mary A. 5 Apr 1870
Bevans Columbus to Dashiell Esther 20 Dec 1871 C
Bevans John to Smullin Sarah A. 15 Dec 1829
Bevans Sheppard to Cottingham Caroline 8 Sep 1871 C
Bevans Theodore T.P. to Wilson Mary E. 15 Dec 1863
Bevans William to Marshall Dianna 14 Dec 1803
Bevans William to Marshall Patty 26 Apr 1827
Bevans William to Wallace Mary C. 12 May 1852
Bevans William to Cottman Hester Anne 30 Sep 1854 C
Bird Gilbert to Milligan Sally 8 Apr 1823
Bird Henry S. to Miles Sarah A. 3 Jan 1866 C
Bird Isaac J. to Ayres Rachil 22 Nov 1864
Bird Jacob to Sterling Absey 13 Jun 1848
Bird John to Conner Lovey 22 Feb 1820
Bird John to Jones Sarah 4 Sep 1849
Bird John H.W. to Windsor Mary 2 Mar 1858
Bird Joseph to Sterling Hannah Elizabeth 31 May 1848
Bird Joshua H. to Walter Elizabeth A. 1 Mar 1842
Bird Littleton to Tyler Sally 13 Jan 1800
Bird Stephen to Sterling Esther Anne 13 Jun 1843
Bird Stephen to Moore Mary 9 Jun 1846
Bird Stephen to Cullin Mary A. 28 Jun 1860
Bird Stephen W. to Sterling Louisa 7 Jul 1857
Bird Thomas to Records Sarah 19 Mar 1799
Bird Thomas J. to Leatherbury Maria 10 Dec 1839
Birding Ernest W. to Tull Martha H. 12 Oct 1836

Birk John to Wright Denny 20 Apr 1798
Birkhead William to Weatherly Sally 21 Oct 1797
Black Cornelius to Reed Sally 27 Dec 1810
Black Henry to Wright Betsy 10 Apr 1822
Black Hezekiah to Dashiell Caroline V. 19 Apr 1842
Black James to Black Angeline 1 Jul 1862 C
Black John to Wright Henrietta 9 Jan 1849
Black Samuel V. to Black Elizabeth 11 Jan 1853 C
Black Severn to Pucham Hetty 2 Sep 1829
Black William to Hutt Alexine 4 Jul 1854
Blades James to Somers Elizabeth 17 Feb 1827
Blades L.R. to Sterling Virginia 30 Dec 1862
Blades Luther R. to Ward Elizabeth 16 Jun 1860
Blades Samuel to Burch Nancy 2 May 1820
Blades Seth to Sterling Emily 7 Oct 1854
Blaine James to Beauchamp Sally 30 Oct 1821
Blake Edward to Horsey Sally 7 Nov 1815
Blake George to Parks Alcey 29 Jul 1822
Blake George to Parks Rettana 24 Feb 1835
Blake George Wesley to Beauchamp Mary J. 2 Aug 1864
Blake James H. to Howeth Margaret 23 May 1871
Blake John to Henry Mary 20 Jul 1852 C
Blake John S. to Tyler Margaret E. 5 Jul 1864
Blake Thomas J. to Hewitt Elizabeth A. 8 Jul 1870
Blake William to Marsh Charlotte 21 Sep 1857
Blake William to Parker Harriet 26 Jan 1858
Blinker James to Tyler Amanda J. 7 Jul 1862
Blizzard John to Boon Melissa 2 Apr 1868
Blockston Edward to Lawson Nancy 21 Aug 1861
Bloodsworth Andrew to Murphy Mary E. 7 Aug 1868
Bloodsworth Jacob to Benson Arianna C. 16 Jan 1860
Bloodsworth Jesse to Todd Eleanor 15 Aug 1837
Bloodsworth John R. to Kirwan Virginia K. 16 Feb 1858
Bloodsworth Littleton to Sims Sally 18 Dec 1810
Bloodsworth Littleton to Murrill Lucretia Anne 24 Feb 1847
Bloodsworth Nathan to Wingate Margaret 14 Jan 1826
Bloodsworth Risdon to Blake Sarah 13 Apr 1833
Bloodsworth Risdon to Marsh Anne M. 22 Mar 1853
Bloodsworth Rizdon to Kirwin Susan 10 Feb 1818
Bloodsworth Robert to Jones Julianna 30 Jun 1846

Bloodsworth William to Redding Elizabeth Dorsey 18 Apr 1812
Bloss John to Grant Leah 23 Jan 1819
Bloxom Edward to Hayman Letitia 28 Mar 1821
Bloyd James to Tull Lizzy 13 Jan 1829
Blundon Henry to Nelms Margaretta F. 27 May 1848
Bock Thomas H. to Lawson Angie 2 Oct 1871
Boddy Waitman to Gould Susan A. 18 Jan 1815
Boggs Francis to M.K. Waters Sarah E. 13 Jun 1848
Boggs Hiram to Burnett Anne 21 Dec 1864 C
Boggs John to Waters Mary 11 Jan 1853 C
Boggs Robert to Waters Leah 21 Jan 1862 C
Boggs Samuel S. to Brinkley Sarah A. 20 Jun 1838
Boggs William to Thomas Mary E. 8 Sep 1868 C
Bonewell Henry D. to Adams Hester Anne 20 Mar 1850
Bonewell Samuel to Ford Anne 16 Oct 1826
Bonnawell Andrew to Maddux Harriet 31 Dec 1827
Bonnawell George P. to Linton Anne 17 Feb 1851
Bonnawell James to Spencer Priscilla 26 Oct 1847
Bonnawell James to Jones Elizabeth 28 Jan 1851
Bonnawell Tubman F. to Veazey Elizabeth G. 8 Dec 1859
Bonne Anthony De to Lang Sally 18 Nov 1796
Bonne Anthony De to Dorsey Sally 30 Dec 1820
Bonne Tubman De to Walston Sally 10 Sep 1825
Bonneville James S. to Johnson Catherine S. 26 Mar 1868
Bonnewell Thomas to Tull Nancy 25 Dec 1820
Booth Benjamin T. to White Martha 6 Jun 1866
Booth William to Benson Susan 14 Feb 1837
Borton John to Beauchamp Grace 20 Dec 1810
Boston Edward to Handy Mary J. 8 Jan 1868 C
Boston Elijah to Rounds Nancy 13 Mar 1804
Boston Esau to Beauchamp Agusta 19 May 1807
Boston Esau to Bell Molly 22 Mar 1831
Boston James to Adams Nancy 16 Jan 1821
Boston Jesse to Peden Polly 4 Jan 1803
Boston John to Vessels Sarah 1 Sep 1830
Boston Samuel J. to Henderson Emeline 7 Dec 1865
Boston Solomon C. to Nock Mary Ann 31 Mar 1840
Boston Thomas W. to Adams Amelia 3 Dec 1816
Boston William A. to Lankford Sarah E. 28 Apr 1869
Boston William S. to Larmore Janus Anna 19 Jun 1860

Botham Levin to Whayland Anne 22 Jan 1799
Botham Levin D. to Langsdale Eleanor 4 Feb 1835
Botham Thomas to Whittington Margaret 24 Apr 1824
Bounds Edward P. to Puzey Emily A. 20 Nov 1861
Bounds Francis to Pusey Mahaley J. 18 May 1864
Bounds George to Huffington Hetty 12 Aug 1825
Bounds George to Price Margaret 22 Dec 1856
Bounds George to White Elizabeth 30 May 1868 C
Bounds George T. to Curtis Mary A. 26 Nov 1861
Bounds George W. to Bedsworth Richard W. 3 Dec 1844
Bounds Henry J.E. to Hughes Henrietta J.E. 19 Feb 1857
Bounds James to Wailes Betsy 5 Apr 1802
Bounds James to Crawford Elizabeth 18 Apr 1818
Bounds James to Malone Esther 21 Aug 1832
Bounds James to Collier Mary Jane 30 Sep 1846
Bounds James to Collier Martha 17 Sep 1849
Bounds James A. to Puzey Susan E. 19 Nov 1861
Bounds James R. to Lowe Margaret 11 Feb 1851
Bounds John to Mezick Elizabeth 8 Jan 1839
Bounds John to Brewington Margaret 22 Jan 1862
Bounds John S. to Lankford Louisa P. 12 Aug 1857
Bounds Jones to White Anne Maria 11 Mar 1856
Bounds Levin to Fontain Virginia A.C. 27 May 1856
Bounds Marcellus to Crawford Hetty 11 Dec 1832
Bounds Marcellus to Twilley Anne Maria 8 Mar 1842
Bounds Marcellus to Bacon Mary J. 28 Feb 1854
Bounds Monelus to Brady Sally Anne 19 Apr 1843
Bounds Richard to Malone Elizabeth 24 Dec 1833
Bounds Samuel D. to Noble Sarah E. 16 Apr 1867
Bounds Samuel T. to Disharoon Anne 31 May 1825
Bounds Stephen to Ward Elizabeth 7 Oct 1822
Bounds Thomas to Purnell Hetty 11 Nov 1823
Bounds Train A. to Windsor Elizabeth J. 30 Oct 1854
Bounds William to Leatherbury Zipporah 22 Aug 1801
Bounds William to Hebble Sally 2 Jan 1810
Bounds William to Morris Sally 22 Mar 1825
Bounds William to Banks Jane 23 Jun 1846
Bounds William to Culver Miranda 9 Jan 1867
Bounds William (Jr.) to Wailes Peggy 8 Sep 1798
Bounds William A.D. to Harris Temperance 16 Feb 1836

Bounds William I. to Hasting Hester E. 29 Dec 1866
Bounds William J. to Lowe Elizabeth J. 17 Nov 1854
Bounds William J. to Pusey Elizabeth 13 Oct 1859
Bourbon Charles to Fletcher Mary 9 Jul 1835
Bowen Martin to Gibbons Maria W. 14 Dec 1825
Bowen William J. to Ford Nancy 27 Nov 1855
Bowen Zacheus to Parks Emeline 4 Apr 1861
Bowland Denard to Logy Maria 28 Jun 1866 C
Bowland John R. to Coulbourn Indiana 4 Jun 1851
Bowland Levin P. to Dale Elizabeth C. 17 Jan 1850
Bowland Levin P. to Cooper Ann W. 23 Feb 1859
Bowland Sandy to Bell Elizabeth 30 Mar 1865 C
Bowser John to Johnson Mary 23 Oct 1869 C
Bozman Alexander to Ballard Sarah E. 4 Jan 1824
Bozman Alexander to Winder Ellen 26 Oct 1867 C
Bozman Alfred to Webster Sarah 25 Apr 1849
Bozman Ballard to Milligan Rachel Sep 1821
Bozman Caleb Washington to Melson Milcah Anne 4 Sep 1855
Bozman David to Martin Anne 2 Oct 1809
Bozman Edward to Carew Anne Eliza 30 Nov 1852
Bozman George to Colbert Nancy 7 Jan 1828
Bozman George to Mariner Sally 25 Jan 1848
Bozman George to Bedsworth Margaret 6 Feb 1860
Bozman Hargis to Bozman Esther 20 Dec 1865
Bozman Henry to Glascow Mary Jane 5 Jun 1855
Bozman Henry to Bozman Charlotte 7 Nov 1861
Bozman Henry to Bozman Sarah 27 Aug 1868
Bozman Isaac to Dorsey Mary 16 Dec 1828
Bozman Isaac to Wallace Charlotte A. 5 Jun 1862
Bozman Isaac H. to Killman Anne S. 9 Sep 1856
Bozman Isaac W. to Beauchamp Maria 25 Sep 1847
Bozman Isaac W. to Brewington Jane 25 Jan 1859
Bozman John to Shores Anne 12 Jun 1826
Bozman John B. to Jones Mary E. 30 May 1861
Bozman John R. to Shores Louisa A. 22 May 1861
Bozman John Samuel to Jackson Martha Washington 21 Sep 1853
Bozman John William to Dorman Mary Rebecca 9 Feb 1859
Bozman Levin R. to Dorman Sarah E. 22 Jul 1863
Bozman Mitchell to Shores Rebecca 18 Jul 1828
Bozman Mitchell to Wallace Margaret 29 Jun 1858

Bozman Nehemiah to Shores Marjurah 21 Nov 1812
Bozman Risdon to Schoolfield Elizabeth 15 Jun 1802
Bozman Robert to Shouz Margaret 17 Jun 1834
Bozman Samuel to Hurley Lanta 9 Sep 1851
Bozman Sandy to Lord Harriet 6 Apr 1864
Bozman Sandy J. to Bozman Anne 3 Jul 1861
Bozman Thomas to Scott Rachel 11 Feb 1800
Bozman Thomas to Austin Mary 8 Nov 1830
Bozman Thomas to Shores Sally 8 Aug 1836
Bozman Thomas to Webster Anne 25 Jan 1844
Bozman Thomas A. to Lawrence Mary A. 2 Jun 1869
Bozman Thomas E. to Beauchamp Elizabeth E. 17 Jan 1843
Bozman Thomas J. to Somers Frances 27 Feb 1871
Bozman William to Milligan Charity 4 May 1826
Bozman William T. to Shores Harriet S.B. 8 Aug 1853
Bozman Wm. H. to Bozman Mary L. 3 Apr 1863
Bradford Avery to Riggin Sophia 8 Jan 1799
Bradford George H. to Parks Nancy E. 17 Jan 1861
Bradford John H. to Ward Matilda A. 9 Jun 1857
Bradley Charles D. to Taylor Sarah Anne 28 Oct 1845
Bradley Charles D. to Hobbs Sarah E. 6 May 1856
Bradley Daniel D. to Byrd Sallie S. 30 Aug 1859
Bradley David to Wright Sally 28 May 1804
Bradley Eli to Collier Eliza A. 3 Feb 1824
Bradley James to Scovemount (?) Anne 21 Mar 1821
Bradley James to Gill Mary 22 Nov 1843
Bradley James W. to English Rirtta 5 Mar 1867
Bradley Jeremiah to Dougherty Julia A. 13 Nov 1866
Bradley John to Gravener Charlotte 30 Nov 1846
Bradley John to Crosby Rachel J. 2 Sep 1856
Bradley Lemuel to Bennett Margaret 20 Mar 1855
Bradley Levin to Melson Hannah 6 Nov 1804
Bradley Levin D. to Hill Mary R. 21 Jan 1833
Bradley Lucien M. to Wilson Josephine 1 Mar 1867
Bradley Noah J. to Bradley Eliza 29 Nov 1861
Bradley Peregrine to Philips Elizabeth 10 Feb 1827
Bradley Richard to Allen Phoebe 4 Feb 1828
Bradley Samuel to Handy Eliza 29 Dec 1812
Bradley Samuel to Hurley Rachel 8 Mar 1831
Bradley Stephen to Elliott Mary Ann 22 Dec 1831

Bradley Thomas S.C. to Dennis Sarepta C. 26 Mar 1856
Bradley William to Jackson Sally 1 Apr 1828
Bradley William to Abbott Virginia 13 Oct 1863
Bradley William to Covington Margaret N. 13 Feb 1866
Bradshaw Aaron to Cox Arabella 1 Jun 1833
Bradshaw David to Knox Elizabeth 1 Jun 1840
Bradshaw Elisha T. to Crockett Theresa M. 23 May 1871
Bradshaw Hamilton to Evans Nelly 7 Jan 1811
Bradshaw John to Lambden Ellen 31 Jul 1866
Bradshaw Littleton to Evans Julany 8 Jul 1839
Bradshaw Richard to Hopman Racheal 20 Dec 1838
Bradshaw Solomon to Mezick Elizabeth A. 23 Jun 1868
Bradshaw Thomas to Price Elizabeth E. 20 Jul 1858
Bradshaw Tyler to Duncan Sidney 14 Feb 1843
Bradshaw William A. to Evans Priscilla A. 24 May 1871
Bradshaw William J. to Betts Mary V. 9 Aug 1867
Brady Francis to Twig Lucretia 19 Jul 1819
Bramble John to McGee Polly 20 Jan 1840
Branch James C. to Coulbourn Leah 25 Dec 1816
Brannagan Sylvester to Bozman Kate 18 Jan 1871
Bratcher William to Ford Mary Anne 3 Jun 1823
Braterson John to Williams Anne 8 Aug 1868 C
Brattan Anthony to Porter Sarah Anne 30 May 1837
Brattan Franklin to Taylor Mary Anne 19 Nov 1839
Brattan Joseph to Venables Elizabeth H. 6 Mar 1843
Brattan Lemuel R. to Whittington Eliza Jane 22 Dec 1847
Brattan Samuel to Weatherly Margaret Ellen 1 Apr 1845
Brereton George to Weatherly Peggy 2 Jan 1827
Brereton Henry to Jenkins Henriatta 13 Aug 1808
Brewington Edward A. to Pryer Charlotte 6 Jan 1846
Brewington George to Crouch Nancy 9 Jan 1833
Brewington George to Pollitt Martha 14 Dec 1859 C
Brewington George L. to Townsend Elizabeth S. 19 Feb 1867
Brewington Henry to Davis Eleanor 27 Feb 1834
Brewington Henry to Denson Sally H. 4 Nov 1851
Brewington Henry Scott to Hayman Edwina C. 23 Nov 1871
Brewington Isaac W. to Dorman Anne M. 15 Feb 1855
Brewington James to Hayman Susan R. 22 Nov 1853
Brewington John to White Clarissa 25 Oct 1820
Brewington John to Dashiell Casey Anne 22 Oct 1857 C

Brewington John T. to Carvin Milly Anne 20 Oct 1834
Brewington Joseph to Hillman Elizabeth 30 Jan 1821
Brewington Richard I. to Waller Biddy E. 27 Nov 1867
Brewington Thomas to Taylor Amanda 15 Oct 1839
Brewington William H. to Robertson Anne Maria 8 Dec 1863
Brewington William H. to Cooksey Martha J. 2 Mar 1864
Brickhead Alexander to Hubbard Susan A. 20 Dec 1865
Brickhead William to Jones Elizabeth 10 Jan 1843
Briddle Francis A. to Powell Matilda J. 14 Mar 1855
Briddle John J. to Howard Eleanor D. 7 Dec 1859
Briddle Joshua to Johnson Anne Elizabeth 12 Feb 1867
Briddle Luther A. to Jones Mary Anne 6 Jul 1852
Bridell David H. to Bridell Ellen D. 5 Dec 1866
Brindle James A. (Rev.) to Hall Sarah M. 6 Feb 1855
Brinkley Joseph B. to Miles Betsy 23 Aug 1808
Brinkley Thomas to Gunby Emily W. 10 Nov 1852
Briscoe Henry to Cottman Esther H. 11 Oct 1865
Brittingham Edward J. to Gibbons Susan E. 10 Jan 1871
Brittingham Elijah to Catlin Julian 30 Sep 1828
Brittingham James to Wainwright Rosanna A.W. 4 Jul 1833
Brittingham James M. to Shay Elizabeth 6 Feb 1849
Brittingham John to Maddux Charlotte 2 Jun 1846
Brittingham John E. to Sterling Mary S. 21 Sep 1858
Brittingham Joseph to Cottman Sarah 25 Dec 1860
Brittingham Joshua M. to Bonabell Virginia 7 Dec 1852
Brittingham William to Richards Emeline 7 Dec 1841
Brittingham William J. to Lawrence Henrietta C. 5 Jan 1847
Brittingham William J. to Gardner Henrietta S. 26 Jul 1865
Broadwater Caleb to McGrath Sally Ann 22 Oct 1845
Broadwater Richard to Wilson Sally E. 14 Jan 1845
Brodwater William M. to Brewington Miranda 19 Feb 1867
Brodwater William M. to Lewis Narcissa E. 13 Apr 1868
Bromley David to Marshall Nancy 9 Sep 1817
Bromley Jesse to Willing Aurelia 13 Sep 1864
Bromly Warren to Jones Eliza Jane 23 Jun 1846
Brooks Caleb T. to Riggin Margaret A. 22 Jan 1862
Brooks Isaac to McGrath Elizabeth 9 Jun 1812
Brooks Thomas to Dear Betsy 8 Dec 1808
Brooks Thomas to Snelling Serienda 15 Dec 1835
Brooks William to Matthews Nancy 30 Jun 1802

Brosworth Elisha J. to Sterling Hetty 3 Dec 1852
Broughton Charles to Hitch Matilda Jane 15 Feb 1865 C
Broughton Elijah to Coulbourn Grace 21 Dec 1819
Broughton Henry to Givans Sally 17 Dec 1816
Broughton Isaac A. to Conner Zipporah 10 Jun 1840
Broughton Isaac M. to Adams Anne 27 Jul 1813
Broughton James to Adams Betsy 10 Sep 1816
Broughton James to Stevens Henrietta 23 Jan 1860
Broughton Joshua to Porter Nancy 5 Sep 1804
Broughton Josiah to Scott Esther 1 May 1798
Broughton Kellen to Aaron Sally J. 22 May 1849
Broughton Kellum to Stevens Mary A. 1 Oct 1851
Broughton Killum to Tull Leah 12 Nov 1822
Broughton Samuel to Kersey Sarah Ann 30 Aug 1844
Broughton William to Handy Sally 22 Mar 1803
Broughton William to Matthews Mary 28 Apr 1807
Broughton William to Milbourn Betsy 13 Feb 1818
Broughton William to Polk Mary A. 22 Jan 1840
Broughton William S. to Coulbourn Betsy 20 Dec 1824
Brown Adolphus to Pruitt Louisa 6 Jun 1871
Brown David H. to Dailey Mary Anne 21 Aug 1837
Brown Elisha to Wheatley Mary 2 Nov 1858
Brown Emanual to Game Betsy 18 Mar 1798
Brown Emanuel to Wooden Nancy 20 May 1800
Brown Francis R.W. to Ross Sarah Jane 26 Feb 1840
Brown George T. to Harris Jane 11 Mar 1829
Brown Hezekiah to Marsh Margaret 10 Jan 1871
Brown James to Hopkins Sarah 1 Dec 1841
Brown James to Parsons Levinia 6 Aug 1868 C
Brown James C. to Coulbourn Mary A. T. 10 Jul 1845
Brown John to Walter Sarah Jane 17 Oct 1840
Brown Marcellus to Dorman Elizabeth 30 Aug 1847
Brown Robert to Lloyd Peggy 26 Nov 1811
Brown Samuel to Adams Henerietta 5 Dec 1816
Brown Samuel to Wilson Mary Jane 5 Apr 1853
Brown Thomas to Waters Rose Ann 26 Mar 1804
Brown Thomas to Bounds Betsy 27 Dec 1810
Brown Thomas to Price Betsy 27 Nov 1827
Brown Thomas to Maddux Caroline 12 Jun 1866 C
Brown Tubman to Matthews Polly 13 Sep 1803

Brown William E. to Sampson Sarah J. 19 Aug 1864 C
Brown William H. to Robertson Eliza Ann 11 May 1859
Brown Wm. H. to Matthews Elizabeth K. 11 Jan 1843
Brown Zedekiah to Marsh Margaret Jane 12 Jan 1871
Bruce Granville to Jones Mary 5 Jul 1864
Bruff James to Horsey Sarah 10 Mar 1813
Bruff William T. to Riggin Nancy Elizabeth 17 Oct 1851
Brumbly William W. to Todd Adeline 7 Mar 1842
Buchanan John F. to Conner Mary E. 10 Jan 1865
Buck Elisha to Simpson Polly 16 Jan 1812
Bundick David to Mason Matilda 18 Jan 1870
Bundick William to Copes Levitha 28 May 1866
Bunting George to Cox Dolly 15 May 1807
Bunting George to Mitchell Betsy 17 Aug 1813
Bunting George to Lankford Sarah 21 Aug 1821
Bunting William to Parsons Esther 19 Dec 1848
Burgan William to Ritcher Eleanor Jun 1812
Burgiss James to Crockett Ailcey 13 Dec 1824
Burkett Abram to Leonard Mary 26 Aug 1867 C
Burnett Oliver P. to Cullen Nancy 21 Nov 1865
Burroughs Peterson to Pucket Mary 7 Jun 1853 C
Burroughs Rufus to Venables Arietta 4 Sep 1867 C
Burrows Ebben to Cottman Anna 9 Jan 1867 C
Burton Alexander to Webster Jane 3 Jul 1839
Burton Lsander to Beauchamp Mary E. F. 25 Nov 1863
Burton Philip to Windser Hester 17 Aug 1850
Burton William to Adams Zipporah 6 Jul 1825
Bush Joseph C. to Walter Sarah Anne 20 Nov 1838
Bush Joseph C. to Jackson Mary 29 Jun 1841
Bush Silas to Gale Augusta 8 Sep 1803
Bussells Isaac N. to Wallace Mary A. 16 Dec 1858
Bussels James H. to Davis Mary E. 8 Jun 1864
Bussels James H. to White Laura H. 2 Jul 1870
Bussils Milton to Bozman Eleanor 27 Apr 1847
Butler Lewis E. to Taylor Anna M. 8 Sep 1864
Butts Willis to Davy Mary 10 Dec 1867 C
Byrd Alexander S. to Lankford Amelia 12 Aug 1834
Byrd David to Blades Mary 29 Nov 1852
Byrd David to Sterling Elizabeth 11 Sep 1860
Byrd George to Cullen Marian A. 8 Jul 1856

Byrd George to Johnson Louisa 6 Jan 1857
Byrd George W. to Sterling Rowena 12 Oct 1869
Byrd James H. to Sterling Louisa 1 May 1866 C
Byrd John to Bell Maria L. 29 Jan 1833
Byrd John to Pollitt Elizabeth E. 17 Nov 1835
Byrd John to Somers Henrietta 3 Mar 1863
Byrd John H. to Cullin Sallie N. 13 May 1862
Byrd Littleton to Cottman Leah 1 Jul 1865 C
Byrd Lorenzo D. to Sterling Rachel M. 21 Jul 1870
Byrd Noah T. to Sterling Maria J. 16 Aug 1854
Byrd Reily F. to Toulsin Josephine 19 Jan 1864
Byrd Thomas to Hearn Elizabeth 7 Jan 1804
Byrd Thomas to Jones Lucretia 1 Feb 1822
Byrd Thomas to Parsons Esther 8 Nov 1847
Byrd Thomas to Wilson Kitty 7 Aug 1849
Byrd Thomas to Byrd Nancy S. 10 May 1853
Byrd Thomas to McBride Mary 18 Dec 1865 C
Byrd William to Tyler Phillis 31 Oct 1866 C
Byrd William R. to Pollitt Eleanor G. 19 May 1827
Byrd William R. to Hitch Sally 28 Jan 1845
Byrd William R. to Corbin Sally Jane 16 Mar 1852
Byrd William T. to Lawson Mary L. 23 Jun 1860
Cahoon John A. to Robertson Sally T. 15 Jan 1822
Calbert John to Schoolfield Amelia 4 Jan 1827
Callahan Samuel T. to Halsteind Margaret R. 9 Aug 1836
Callaway Henry R. to Ford Martha A. 15 Mar 1848
Callaway John to Rencher Sally 5 Feb 1811
Callaway William to Hasting Leah 19 Jul 1854
Calleny Edward P. to Miles Mary A. 24 Aug 1830
Calloway George to Riggin Nancy E. 12 Nov 1842
Calloway John to Ritchie Sally 11 Apr 1836
Campbell James A. to Wallace Aurelia F. 31 Jul 1869
Campbell John to Rowan Betsy 8 Nov 1800
Campbell John to Riggin Nancy 16 Jun 1821
Campbell John to Riggin Hetty 17 Jul 1827
Campbell John N. to Wilson Elizabeth T. 4 Jul 1832
Campbell Loudon to Gibbons Hetty 1 Jan 1828
Campbell Noah S. to Ward Elizabeth A. 14 Apr 1868
Campbell Thomas to Dorman Leah 8 Apr 1800
Campbell William to Wallace Rebecca 30 Nov 1802

Cana William to Holland Mary 21 Jul 1807
Canan Jenkins to Evans Anne 26 Dec 1842
Cane Zachariah to Horsey Peggy 5 Apr 1802
Cannon Boston to Costen Sally 12 Dec 1803
Cannon Burton to Harris Matilda C. 4 Jan 1827
Cannon Clement to Thomas Mahala 21 May 1844
Cannon Daniel B. to Johnson Sally A. 13 Nov 1866
Cannon John to Lankford Betsy 7 Jan 1823
Cannon John H. to Costen Anne 16 Feb 1813
Cannon Matthew to Adams Henrietta 1 Jan 1811
Cannon Thomas to Talbot Charlotte 2 Jan 1798
Cannon Thomas to Landsdale Dolly 7 Dec 1819
Cannon Valentine to Ruark Amelia Ann 3 Jun 1862
Cannon William W. to English Anne 23 Oct 1816
Canten John to Catlin Emeline 29 Mar 1836
Cantwell George W. to Jenkins Margarit A. 18 Dec 1856
Cantwell Hosea to Ellis Nancy 25 Feb 1824
Cantwell James to Lacay Frances 20 Dec 1796
Cantwell James to Jones Sarah 18 Feb 1839
Cantwell James to Palmer Mary 19 Apr 1843
Cantwell James to Jackson Elizabeth E. 8 Oct 1844
Cantwell John to Taylor Anne 10 Oct 1809
Cantwell Noah R. to Layfield Sallie Anne 15 Jan 1856
Cantwell Samuel to Furniss Delia 22 Sep 1858
Cantwell Thomas to Toadvine Jane 18 Dec 1822
Cantwell Thomas J. to Layfield Amanda J. 14 Mar 1853
Cantwell William B. to Holland Marietta 7 Jan 1852
Cantwell William E. to Maddux Mary E. 8 Jun 1870
Carew John to White Margaret 18 Oct 1827
Carew Thomas W. to Andrew Annie E. 13 Dec 1866
Carew William R. to White Mary A. 20 Dec 1853
Carey David to Brown Rhoda 1 Jan 1811
Carey George to Taylor Mary 26 May 1840
Carey Henry C. to Denson Emily I. 15 Dec 1868
Carey Henry H. to Turner Mary E. 30 Jan 1844
Carey John to Wallace Elizabeth 18 Jan 1841
Carey John to Cottman Priscilla 18 Jul 1850
Carey Michael to Jones Sally 26 Nov 1844
Carey Purnell B. to Garretson Priscilla 26 Feb 1828
Carey Richard to Daniel Rebecca 22 Jun 1835

Carey Thomas to Toadvine Nelly 7 Feb 1801
Carey William to Taylor Lydia 5 Jun 1832
Carey William to White Biddy 19 Jan 1836
Carman Gilbert to Ward Kitty Anne 24 Feb 1857
Carman Gilbert W. to Ward Jane 2 Mar 1861
Carnley Jerry to Waters Laura 14 Jan 1868 C
Carow William R. to Prlse Margaret 28 Sep 1859
Carroll Michael B. to King Mary Anne 15 Jan 1817
Carter Daniel J.G. to Crouch Margaret Ellen 23 Jan 1855
Carter Jethro to Catlin Nancy 27 Aug 1834
Carter John C. to Catlin Esther 12 Dec 1854
Carter Philip to Dashiell Ellen 11 Jan 1869 C
Carter Samuel to Dize Eleanor 12 Jun 1838
Carter Samuel to Johnson Elizabeth 21 Dec 1841
Carter Samuel J. to Catlin Mary E. 3 May 1865
Carter William to Bozman Sally 12 Jan 1830
Carter William to Lasby Margaret 8 Mar 1853
Carter William F. to Majors Sarah E. 11 Dec 1861
Carty Henry I. to Miller Sarah 25 Feb 1839
Carver Elijah W. to Stevens Sarah Elizabeth 9 Jan 1855
Carver George to Potter Harriet J. 7 Jun 1871
Carver James D. to Catlin Jane 14 May 1833
Carver John C. to Howard Leah J. 13 Feb 1866
Carver John W. to Shores Sally 29 Nov 1870
Carver Peter to Matthews Mary E. 18 May 1858
Carver Peter T. to Howard Sally 23 May 1837
Carver William J. to Dryden Sarah P. 29 Oct 1861
Carvey Peter to Coulbourn Mary 26 Apr 1820
Case Teagle to Bird Ann E. 11 Aug 1851
Cathel James E. to Harris Milcah A. V. 1 Jun 1858
Cathell James M. to Walker Eliza 3 Oct 1826
Catlin Alexander W. to Willing Mary W. 10 Dec 1855
Catlin Edward to Owens Sally 15 Sep 1866
Catlin Edward W. to Mezick Mary Ann 15 Nov 1847
Catlin Henry to Lankford Esther 8 Nov 1842
Catlin James H. to Lankford Elizabeth A. 10 Sep 1867
Catlin James T. to Carver Alvertir 27 Dec 1866
Catlin John to Dryden Harriet J. 14 Oct 1839
Catlin Luther A. to Lankford Margaret A. 1 Feb 1859
Catlin Nehemiah to Fitchett Betsy 20 Aug 1811

Catlin Sewel L. to Catlin Esther 11 Aug 1857
Catlin Thomas to Beauchamp Milly 27 Dec 1797
Catlin Thomas to Davis Nancy 24 Mar 1809
Catlin Thomas G. to Mitchell Jane 22 Feb 1831
Catlin William to Lankford Zipporah 21 Aug 1810
Catlin William to Moore Elizabeth A.G. 18 Mar 1848
Cattin John C. to Adkins Sally Anne 29 Apr 1851
Cattin Joseph to Sterling Ellen 25 Apr 1851
Cattin Wm. Henry to Townswell Esther 17 Feb 1852
Causey Franklin to Miller Nancy D. 6 Nov 1838
Causey Henry W. to Rencher Matilda 10 Sep 1860
Chaille Zachariah to Matthews Hessey 7 Jan 1801
Chamberlaine Jonathan to Holland Rachel 28 Sep 1812
Chapman John to Cottman Margaret B. 15 Jul 1818
Charnick William to Eva--(?) Elizabeth -- Jul 1850
Charnock George H. to Evans Maria 10 Mar 1870
Chase Samuel to Wright Rachel 7 Oct 1837
Chase William K. to Marshall Elizabeth 28 Feb 1865
Chatham John to Morris Cristi Ann 15 Jun 1859
Chattam James H. to Fields Kiziah 22 Dec 1847
Cheatham Elijah to Brooks Sarah Anne 25 Apr 1848
Cheatham Henry F. to Malone Elizabeth Anne 12 Dec 1855
Cheattam John P. to Cheattam Anne Maria 5 Mar 1850
Cheethan George to Fisher Betsy 7 Oct 1823
Chelten Fleet J. to Adams Leah A. 9 Mar 1844
Chelton Francis to Holland Emily C. 24 Nov 1860
Chelton John A. to Hines Jennie 22 Aug 1871
Chelton Stephen W. to Gibbons Amelia J. 5 Apr 1825
Cheney Ware to Colliar Elizabeth 18 Jul 1809
Chesam Charles H. to Corsey Virginia A. 6 Feb 1864
Chilton William to Davis Maria J. 9 Aug 1859
Chilton William H. to Taws Margaret J. 7 Apr 1863
Chittam John to Beard Sally 23 Apr 1802
Choley Richard H. to Webster Catherine B. 22 Feb 1854
Christian Levi H. to Ker Mary C. 2 Oct 1851
Christopher George H. to Hopkins Amelia 27 Aug 1835
Christopher William to Parks Annie 14 Jun 1831
Churn Edward to Moore Polly 22 Jun 1847
Clark Daniel P. to Humphries Mary E. 8 May 1871
Clark James to Scott Nancy 20 Mar 1826

Clark William to White Margaret 17 Apr 1822
Clark William to Holland Betsy 2 May 1826
Clarke Edward H. to Coston Mary E. 24 Nov 1868
Clarvoe John H. to Chelton Sarah A. 16 Feb 1825
Claver Bennet H. to Mitchell Jane 5 Feb 1816
Clayton Thomas to Taylor Hetty 18 Aug 1827
Clayvill Robert to Taylor Mary 7 Aug 1849
Cluff Edward to Walston Mary Anne 4 Dec 1829
Cluff Edward P. to Marshall Sally 21 Nov 1829
Cluff George J. to Coulbourn Margaret Elizabeth 28 Jun 1865
Cluff Jonathan to Sturges Sarah 6 Oct 1807
Cluff Michael to Polk Elizabeth 23 Jun 1807
Cluff Michael H. to Bell Margaret A. 1 Apr 1856
Cluff Robert W. to Broughton Anne 25 Nov 1857
Cluff Whittington P. to Walston Esther D. 17 Dec 1844
Cluff William T. to Adams Susan J.S. 17 May 1865
Coke Cotty to Bailey Eleanor 11 May 1825
Coke John J. to Sterling Sally L. 27 Aug 1846
Coke Thomas to Ingersoll Eliza C. 24 Aug 1852
Colbert Levin to Fitzgerald Mary 24 Nov 1835
Colbert Whittington to Dorsey Julia 31 Oct 1843
Colbert Whittington W. to Mitchell Elizabeth E. 3 Dec 1838
Colbert William to Howard Bridgett 6 Dec 1796
Coleman William to Holbrook Emily 10 Nov 1868 C
Colgan John W. to Anderson Sarah Ann 3 Jul 1850
Colgan Joseph I. to Adams Catherine Jane 27 Nov 1851
Colhoun John B. (Rev.) to Moore Elizabeth J. 4 Oct 1858
Collear Ebenezer to Winright Betsy 29 Jun 1802
Collear Robert to Nicholson Peggy 17 Jun 1811
Collier Chaney to Hickman Nancy 14 Jul 1818
Collier Charles to Street Mary E. 23 Feb 1864
Collier Esme to Hopkins Nelly 23 Nov 1811
Collier Esme to Horsey Eleanor 5 Nov 1819
Collier George to Christopher Gatty 10 Mar 1818
Collier George to Covington Prescilla 18 Oct 1825
Collier George to Hooper Sarah Jane --(?) 1837
Collier George E.R.J. to Jones Eleanor 27 Aug 1846
Collier George W. to Livingston Catharine J. 2 Mar 1858
Collier Henry W. to Caloway Hester 18 May 1854
Collier John F. to Leatherbury Miranda W. 8 Mar 1836

Collier Levin to Porter Betsy 12 Feb 1799
Collier Levin to Dashiell Ailsey 8 Feb 1817
Collier Levin to Bantain Eliza 20 Apr 1842
Collier Levin D. to Humphreys Laura A. 23 Mar 1858
Collier Levin M.B. to Kerwin Elizabeth J. 29 Dec 1864
Collier Nicholas E. to Collier Sarah E. 4 Dec 1855
Collier Nicholas E. to Collier Victoria S. 28 Jul 1859
Collier Perry to Allen Nicey 8 May 1866 C
Collier Robert to Ritchie Catty 24 Apr 1797
Collier Samuel to Ellensworth Margaret 10 Jul 1824
Collier William to Weatherly Arietta 19 Dec 1826
Collier William to Roberts Eleanor 8 Mar 1831
Collier William F. to Bayley Sarah J. 8 May 1848
Collins Alexander to Isham Polly 24 Dec 1799
Collins George to Francis Mary P. 21 Mar 1871 C
Collins Isaac(Jr) to Coulbourne Caroline 28 Dec 1870 C
Collins James A. to Parks Lucinda E. 22 Dec 1845
Collins James F. to Williams Mary J. 30 Mar 1869
Collins John H. to Harris Sarah Anne 20 Jan 1858 C
Collins John M. to Sudler Alice G. 3 Dec 1844
Collins Joseph to Fletcher Polly 4 Sep 1804
Collins Joseph to Rider Sarah 5 Mar 1811
Collins Joseph M. to Mills Martha W. 13 Nov 1865
Collins Lamartine to Hopkins Sarah E. 23 Feb 1869
Collins Littleton T. to Davis Elizabeth 5 Jan 1853
Collins Robert to Maddux Genilene 17 Jul 1867 C
Collins Samuel to Cannon Emily Francis 23 Mar 1868 C
Collins Stephen to Broughton Betsy 7 May 1825
Collins William to Malone Ellen 26 Jan 1847
Collins William H. to Tull Julianna Anne 24 Oct 1838
Collins William J. to Burton Isabella H. 20 Aug 1855
Collman Joseph to Bishop Sally 21 Jun 1814
Combs James to McDaniel Emily 24 Jul 1866
Conaway William to Donoho Betsy 4 May 1811
Condiff Henry to Harris Virginia 9 Sep 1847
Conley Charles H. to Marvel Mary E. 1 May 1863
Connally John H. to Disharoon Maria L. 25 Nov 1857
Connelly Isaac W. to Williams Caroline 23 Nov 1859
Connelly James E. to Humphreys Emily 23 Feb 1858
Connelly Matthew to Connelly Elizabeth 2 Mar 1842

Conner Benjamin to Coulbourn Grace 1 Apr 1797
Conner Benjamin to Lankford Nancy 15 Jul 1817
Conner Elijah to Otten Nancy 24 Mar 1797
Conner Elijah to Adams Zipporah 9 Jun 1812
Conner Elijah to Cox Nancy 22 Nov 1819
Conner Frederick to Ellegood Mary E. 20 May 1856
Conner Henry C. to Conner Mary A. T. 1 Mar 1838
Conner Isaac T. to Tull Anne O. 14 Nov 1865
Conner Isaac W. to Cahoon Mary 4 Mar 1817
Conner John to Swift Mary E. 19 Nov 1864
Conner John E. to Garrison Phebe A. 15 Feb 1871
Conner John W. to McCready Emeline 26 Jan 1860
Conner Levin to Adams Mary T. 5 Jun 1821
Conner Luther William to Taws Sophia 22 Mar 1845
Conner Nathan C. to Coulbourne Sally 19 Dec 1837
Conner Nathan P. to Whittington Eliza J. 24 Apr 1866
Conner Stephen to Sterling Euphemia 24 Aug 1810
Conner Stephen to Thomas Rosey 12 Jul 1826
Conner Stephen to Bozman Henrietta F. 15 Mar 1856
Conner Thomas to Cohoon Sarah Quinton 31 Jan 1810
Conner Thomas to Mason Betsy 11 Aug 1835
Conner William C. to Ford Mary E. 18 Jun 1867
Connerly Charles to Libby Leah 12 Feb 1810
Connerly William to Walker Betsy 5 Aug 1822
Conover William C. to Bowden Sarah J. 25 Dec 1869
Conoway James to Gates Mary J. 14 Feb 1865 C
Conway Bailey to Nicholas Charlotte 1 Jan 1867 C
Conway James to Mezick Martha 9 Oct 1833
Conway James R.W. to Smith Rebecca E. 22 Feb 1861
Conway Tubman R. to Donoho Mary H. 15 Apr 1851
Conway William to Crockett Nancy 13 Jan 1835
Conway William H. to Hopkins Harriet T. 16 Nov 1863
Cook Byard to Robertson Gatty 4 Mar 1853 C
Cook Francis R. to Bozman Anna 31 Oct 1866
Cook Henry C. to Dennis Rosalie E. 7 Dec 1871
Cook James B. to Wright Eliza 21 Aug 1843 C
Cooke Stephen to Wright Martha Jane 11 Oct 1847
Cookman George to Hull Delia 17 Mar 1868 C
Cooksey James to Malone Beddy 15 Sep 1832
Cooksey James M. to Houston Martha 20 Jan 1864

Cooksey James M. to Jones Amanda 16 Jan 1866
Cooksey Robert to Abbott Sally 31 Aug 1830
Cooksey Robert J. to Smith Anne E. 20 Feb 1855
Cooper George R. to Walter Anne W. 25 Sep 1854
Cooper Isaac J. to Anderson Mary R. 11 Dec 1844
Cooper Isaac J. to Byrd Louisa 25 Oct 1865
Cooper James A. to Leatherbury Matilda A. 4 Oct 1866 C
Cooper Joseph H. to Owens Elizabeth E. 11 Dec 1866
Cooper Lambert H. to Bradley Martha W. 4 Feb 1860
Cooper Levin to Walker Polly 6 May 1834
Cooper Severn B. to Weatherly Mary E. 21 Aug 1844
Cooper Thomas to Bosman Peggy 18 May 1818
Cooper William to Jackson Patience 27 Apr 1797
Copes William R. S. to Goslee Mary Anne 27 Aug 1846
Corbett Richard to Crockett Miranda 18 Jun 1861
Corbett William L. to Webster Julia Ann 19 Mar 1851
Corbin John to Porter Mariah 22 Jan 1839
Corbin John to Mills Maria 5 Jan 1863
Corbin Littleton to Broughton Rebecca 12 Nov 1838
Corbin Ralph to Milligan Mary 25 Jul 1820
Corbin Ralph to King Peggy 10 Jun 1834
Corbin Robert H. to Lankford Sally M. 17 Jan 1843
Corbin Robert J. to Matthews Mary W. 30 Oct 1857
Cordery John D. to Windsor Keziah 19 Oct 1859 C
Cordray Covington to Jones Nancy 28 Nov 1837
Cordray Doughty C. to Collier Elizabeth 13 Feb 1816
Cordray Elisha to Badley Priscilla 29 Apr 1833
Cordray George W. to Standford Mary E. 24 Mar 1840
Cordray James W. to Goslee Matilda E. 23 Apr 1867
Cordray John D. to Dashiell Eliza E. 28 Nov 1849
Cordry Asbury B. to Robertson Elizabeth J. 28 Nov 1854
Cordry James C. to Windsor Martha J. 7 Apr 1857
Cornish Albert F. to Wallace Sarah E. 25 Jul 1867
Cornish Horace to Dennis Matilda 17 Feb 1866
Cornish Joseph to White Charlotte 20 Dec 1854 C
Cornish Samuel to Roach Anne 1 Feb 1866 C
Cornish William to Covington Sarah M. 21 Dec 1870
Costen Henry to Sharp Anne 12 Dec 1803
Costen Henry R.K. to Nelson Priscilla 12 Jan 1815
Costen Isaac J. to Humphreys Rosina 18 Nov 1862

Costen Isaac T. (Dr.) to Adams Olivia 21 Feb 1866
Costen Julias to Collins Henrietta 21 Jun 1867 C
Costen Richard to Tilghman Sarah 22 Feb 1866 C
Costen Samuel S. to Miles Mary H. 1 Sep 1829
Costen Samuel S. to Lankford Josephine 12 Mar 1860
Costen William to Harris Mary M. 9 Jun 1807
Costen William to Taylor Rosey 22 Feb 1820
Costen William (Jr.) to Redden Mary H. 30 Apr 1839
Costen William A.B. to Dickinson Henrietta 15 Oct 1844
Costen William M. to Wilson Mary Ann 4 Mar 1851
Coston Isaac to Adams Sarah 19 Apr 1797
Coston James W. to Martin Mary A. 10 Aug 1852
Coston Samuel M. to Porter Sally A. 19 Apr 1870
Cottingham Edward to Croswell Susan 18 Feb 1868 C
Cottingham Jeffry to Potter Elizabeth 24 Jul 1848
Cottingham John T. to Whittington Esther A. 19 Dec 1843
Cottingham Thomas to Coulbourn Polly 9 Jun 1801
Cottingham Thomas to Horsey Caroline 26 May 1870 C
Cottingham Titus to Henry Nancy 3 Aug 1852 C
Cottingham William to Wilson Sally 4 Feb 1817
Cottman Aaron to Fields Eliza 16 Jan 1867 C
Cottman Arnold to Cottman Susan 22 Jan 1867 C
Cottman Benjamin to Callahan Polly 10 Oct 1807
Cottman Caleb to Fooks Hester J. 9 Feb 1869 C
Cottman Ebbin to Dennis Mary F. 13 Nov 1869 C
Cottman Henry to Gibbons Mary 3 Dec 1839
Cottman Henry to Milbourn Caroline 25 Aug 1846
Cottman Henry to Long Sarah 20 Nov 1860
Cottman Henry A. to Dennis Mary 17 Sep 1868 C
Cottman Isaac to Ballard Leah Jane 20 May 1858 C
Cottman Isaac to Wilson Fanny 28 Dec 1870 C
Cottman John to Kibble Bridgett 9 Nov 1815
Cottman Joseph to Hayward Rosetta 11 Sep 1867 C
Cottman Levin to Benson Martha 21 Feb 1867
Cottman Lewis to Cottman Jenny 3 Sep 1870 C
Cottman Louis to Burnett Nelly 4 Mar 1865 C
Cottman Peter to Jones Minty 4 Mar 1865 C
Cottman Robert to Johnson Mariah 4 Dec 1869 C
Cottman Sandy to Bell Fanny 15 Mar 1871 C
Cottman William to Ballard Elizabeth 13 Jun 1859

Coulbourn Benjamin to Johnson Mary 13 Feb 1816
Coulbourn Benjamin T. to Marshall Arianna 26 May 1863
Coulbourn Edward to Broughton Sally P. 24 Mar 1801
Coulbourn Elijah to Miles Elizabeth 28 Dec 1821
Coulbourn George to Cullin Lovey 7 Apr 1868
Coulbourn Isaac to Whittington Mary 23 Apr 1802
Coulbourn Isaac to Parker Leah 5 Apr 1809
Coulbourn James Curtis to Parker Zipporah 3 Jul 1819
Coulbourn James F. to Lankford Mary J. 29 Nov 1858
Coulbourn James H. to Tull Eliza A. 21 Jun 1842
Coulbourn John to Coulbourn Betsy 13 Dec 1814
Coulbourn John to Miles Sarah E. 15 Jan 1868
Coulbourn Joseph to Roach Mary E. 9 Jun 1851
Coulbourn Neal to Williss Ailse 10 Mar 1801
Coulbourn Noah to Johnson Anne 9 Jan 1810
Coulbourn Richard to Gibson Maria 3 Mar 1852
Coulbourn Robert to Stevenson Sally 28 Feb 1827
Coulbourn Robert H. to Horsey Mary E. 27 Dec 1827
Coulbourn Robert J. to Dize Virginia F. 13 Feb 1861
Coulbourn Samuel to Walston Leah 19 Sep 1838
Coulbourn Stephen to Cluff Elizabeth G. 9 May 1826
Coulbourn Stephen D. to Dashiell Emely C. 8 Sep 1841
Coulbourn Thomas L. to Adams Elizabeth M. 9 Feb 1847
Coulbourn William to Coulbourn Betsy 2 Mar 1799
Coulbourn William to Johnson Betsy 6 Jul 1803
Coulbourn William to Williams Peggy 10 Dec 1803
Coulbourn William to Wilson Sarah E. 11 Apr 1843
Coulbourn William to Stevenson Milcah A. 25 May 1852
Coulbourn William to Cluff Sally E. 9 Apr 1862
Coulbourne Henry J. to Moore Mary E. 31 Jan 1838
Coulter George T. to Bordley Elizabeth J. 14 Nov 1853
Covey Joshua K. to Jenkins Mary E. 17 Mar 1864
Covington _____ to Winright Anne 19 Dec 1797
Covington Abie to Byrd Polly 2 Jun 1812
Covington Aljah T. to Davis Margaret E. 19 Dec 1865
Covington George W. to Mills Lavinia 29 May 1833
Covington George W. to Dorman Leah R. 19 Nov 1839
Covington Isaac to Anderson Sarah 7 Jan 1819
Covington Isaac to Morris Mary Anne 4 Mar 1835
Covington Isaac to Leatherbury Eliza 9 Apr 1840

Covington Isaac J. to Riggin Mary F. 27 Jan 1858
Covington James to Green Polly A. 27 Apr 1811
Covington James to Larmore Sarah 17 May 1859
Covington John to Waters Elizabeth S.W. 21 Jan 1823
Covington John E. to Lankford Mary E. 4 Dec 1860
Covington John R. to Jackson Sarah E. 23 Oct 1848
Covington John T. to Walker Elizabeth W. 11 Jan 1843
Covington Levin A.T. to Marshall Sarah J. 28 Aug 1867
Covington Marcellus to Disharoon Susan J. 11 Sep 1838
Covington Nehemiah to Street Nancy B. 18 Nov 1856
Covington Philip to Evans Martha 31 Mar 1815
Covington Philip to Phillips Mary Jane 19 Feb 1861
Covington Phillip to Hopkins Peggy Nicholson 22 Nov 1803
Covington Phillip to Kelley Mary C. 1 Jan 1834
Covington Royston to Hargis Martha J. 4 Jun 1860
Covington William M. to Gibson Sarah Anne 8 Jan 1844
Cox Aaron W. to Moore Mary J. 13 Jun 1848
Cox Alfred to Anderson Emily 24 Feb 1859
Cox Benjamin to Hearn Anne 21 Dec 1830
Cox Benjamin T. to Dize Leah 10 Sep 1857
Cox Edward C. to Leach Sally W. 21 Aug 1862
Cox Eli to Ford Milcah 12 Mar 1863
Cox Elijah J. to Mure Caroline 22 Jul 1851
Cox George to Adams Louisa 26 Jan 1840
Cox George to Ford Margaret E. 10 Jan 1859
Cox James to Jackson Priscilla 9 Feb 1802
Cox James to Bradshaw Esther Anne 9 Jan 1857
Cox James E. to Purnell Margaret J. 14 Apr 1863
Cox John to Cadwin Sally 26 Jan 1808
Cox John to Goslee Sarah 19 Nov 1811
Cox John to Cullen Elizabeth 21 Dec 1816
Cox John to Parks Leah J. 23 Feb 1857
Cox Joseph to Williams Octavia A. 18 Dec 1865
Cox Josias to Milbourn Polly 26 Mar 1799
Cox Kendall to Holder Sarah 28 Aug 1828
Cox Peter to Jones Sally Anne 6 Jul 1852
Cox Samuel G. to Livingston Hester 18 Dec 1860
Cox Thomas to Dougherty Sally 17 Feb 1825
Cox William to Whittington Anne 18 Aug 1801
Cox William to Riggin Sally 6 Mar 1816

Cox William to Barkley Mary 17 Mar 1835
Cox William to Adams Henrietta 10 Jul 1855
Cox William to Russell Sarah 20 Jan 1858
Crawford Andrew to Moore Williamanna 16 Dec 1850
Crawford Andrew J. to Lowe Christiana J. 21 Sep 1858
Crawford H.N. to Phillips Lizzie A. 14 Jan 1862
Crawford Henry to Nelson Mary K. 24 Oct 1821
Crich William to Evans Roda 17 Jul 1849
Crisfield John W. to Johnston Ellen R. 1 Oct 1833
Crisfield John W. to Handy Mary W. 12 Apr 1843
Crisp John N. to Stewart Mary 23 Dec 1830
Critchett Joseph to Dashiell Zipporah 19 Oct 1864 C
Crockett Anamas R. to Riggen Sarah 12 Dec 1851
Crockett Charles V. to Bounds Amaryllis 25 May 1831
Crockett Daniel J. to McGrath Sarah 10 Sep 1846
Crockett Dempsey to Crockett Matilda 8 Apr 1861
Crockett Edward to Evans Margaret 2 Jul 1870
Crockett George to Barkley Jane 20 Apr 1811
Crockett George F. to Maddux Mary 14 Apr 1868 C
Crockett George R. to Karney Mary J. 18 May 1865
Crockett John to Parks Jemima 14 Mar 1827
Crockett John S. to Austin Emily M. 13 Jan 1835
Crockett Josephus H. to Bozman Priscilla 31 Jan 1862
Crockett Josephus H. to Parkinson Emily D. B. 7 Jan 1868
Crockett Josiah to Jenkins Elizabeth Sep 1830
Crockett Josiah to Jenkins Eliza 31 Dec 1838
Crockett Josiah S. to Lankford Caroline A.E. 7 Jul 1847
Crockett Josiah S. to Humphreys Sarah M. 17 Nov 1857
Crockett Lebrand to Evans Emily 21 Jul 1870
Crockett Levin to Venables Sarah Dashiell 22 Nov 1802
Crockett Levin to Anderson Betsy 13 Sep 1808
Crockett Nehemiah to Howard Eleanor 16 Nov 1802
Crockett Nehemiah to Weatherly Priscilla 7 Aug 1821
Crockett Nicholas to Hardy Mary 17 Sep 1816
Crockett Severn to Crockett Henny 4 Nov 1844
Crockett Shiles to Daltrien Elizabeth 3 Oct 1797
Crockett Shiles to Dashiell Anna 23 Dec 1800
Crockett William to Phillips Mary 30 Dec 1840
Crockett William B. to Wainright Anne F.D. 25 Feb 1835
Crosberry George to Mills Mary Anne 27 Sep 1859

Crosbury Samuel to Arvey Mary 23 Jun 1834
Crosbury Samuel to Dougherty Margaret 4 Sep 1855
Crosby George N. to Newton Julia L. 9 Feb 1857
Crosby William P. to Turner Mary P. 6 Aug 1856
Crosdale Edmund to Jones Julianna 6 Feb 1849
Crosdale Henry to Walton Mary E. 20 Apr 1843
Croswell Hance L. to Coulbourn Hetty W.A. 17 Aug 1824
Croswell Hans to Montgomery Mary 17 Nov 1798
Croswell Hans (Sr) to Evans Rachel 8 Apr 1823
Croswell Harman S. to Adams Elizabeth J. 11 Aug 1847
Croswell Henry S. to Chilton Anne S. 20 Mar 1837
Croswell Hiram S. to Johnson Mary A. 19 Dec 1849
Croswell John W. to Potter Caroline A. 4 Jan 1858
Croswell Robert H. to Coulbourn Leah Clara 23 Apr 1867
Croswell Severn to Ward Priscilla 4 Jun 1811
Croswell Severn F. to Muir Mary F. 28 Nov 1854
Croswell Washington S. to Potter Dolly E. 1 Aug 1848
Croswell Washington S. to Potter Julia Anne 1 Dec 1853
Croswell William to Tiler Zeborah 25 May 1812
Croswell William F. to Pearson Martha E. 25 Sep 1866
Crouch Anthony B. to Surman Anne M. 28 Jan 1845
Crouch Charles to Moore Sally 2 Jan 1849
Crouch George T. to Fisher Elizabeth 9 Jun 1853
Crouch Isaac to Turner Polly 25 Jan 1812
Crouch Isaac to Brewington Frances 22 Oct 1845
Crouch Isaac to Smulling Harriet A. 27 Dec 1861
Crouch John to Smith Sally 13 Apr 1812
Crouch Joshua to Sanders Sarah E. 4 Jun 1850
Crouch Joshua to Denson Esther 2 Feb 1864
Crouch Joshua (Jr.) to Hearn Anne 6 Aug 1846
Crough Joshua to Mills Maria 2 Sep 1828
Cullen Isaac S. to Wilson Jemima 4 Dec 1860
Cullen Isaac W. to Byrd Nancy 31 May 1834
Cullen Jacob to Riggin Grace 15 Nov 1797
Cullen Jacob to Milligan Sarah 28 Dec 1831
Cullen Jacob H. to Bell Auriathia J. 7 Dec 1870
Cullen Jacob J. to Lawson Mary A. 1 Dec 1854
Cullen John to Ward Betsy 15 Nov 1816
Cullen John to Foxwell Leah 28 Feb 1865
Cullen John T. to Sterling Lavina C. 20 Dec 1864

Cullen Josiah to Moore Kitty Anne 24 Feb 1834
Cullen Michael to Smulling Mary 28 Nov 1807
Cullen Severn T. to Lankford Sarah A. 13 Sep 1854
Cullen Travers to Moore Ann 3 Sep 1824
Cullen Travers to Bird Jemima 14 Jan 1847
Cullen William to Maddux Hetty 16 Jan 1798
Cullen William to Douglas Ibby 1 Oct 1799
Cullin Job M. to Somers Cornelia F. 28 Dec 1866
Cullin Josiah L. to Somers Elizabeth E. 4 Apr 1867
Cullin Simon to Broughton Louisa 6 Jan 1866 C
Cullin William A. to Sterling Mary A. 14 Jun 1864
Cullough John W. to Bradley Virginia C. 2 Jan 1866
Culver Elijah to Ricketts Polly 15 Sep 1812
Culver Elijah to Bounds Anna 4 Dec 1849
Culver George A. to Miller Lydia A. 6 Dec 1869
Culver Jeptha J. to Langsdale Matilda 28 Jan 1833
Culver Joshua J.S. to Long Adaline 7 Feb 1871
Culver Levin to Nicholls Elizabeth 25 Sep 1804
Culver Prettyman to Kersey Anne Eliza 17 Aug 1857
Culver William to Larmore Elizabeth 21 Jul 1852
Curren Thomas to Records Sarah 8 Sep 1810
Curtis Cyrus to Gibson Adeline 14 Sep 1869
Curtis Isaac H. to Waters Priscilla 18 Feb 1868 C
Curtis John to Ballard Sarah 25 Nov 1833
Curtis John B. to Curren Lydia 6 Feb 1817
Curtis John W. to Hayward Peggy 12 Oct 1797
Curtis Rodney to Hopkins Anne 17 Dec 1830
Curtis Thomas to Bloodsworth Peggy 30 Nov 1797
Curtis Thomas to Elzey Sally 22 Jan 1801
Curtis Thomas to Stuart Susan H. 20 Sep 1807
Curtis William H. to Adams Mary W. T. 28 Oct 1828
Dailey James M. to Jones Mary L. 17 Jan 1871
Dailey James Washington to Fletcher Maria Ellen 7 Sep 1859
Dailey Samuel J. to Fooks Leah J. 11 Aug 1866
Daily John to Olliphen Sarah 28 Apr 1819
Daily Samuel to Banks Molly 18 Jan 1803
Dakes Daniel to Dryden Sarah 23 Aug 1825
Dakes George to Lankford Elizabeth 6 Jul 1808
Dakes George to Adams Sally 17 Jan 1831
Dalby Stephen W. to Simpkins Henrietta J.T.C. 11 Feb 1856

Dale Charles G. to Fleming Anna 26 Jan 1871
Dale William A. to Parks Harriet E. 20 Jun 1864
Daley Samuel to Carpenter Esther 18 Apr 1826
Daley William to Umstead Betsy Dashiell 6 Feb 1816
Damarill William to Windsor Sarah D. 19 May 1865
Damerel William to Price Charlotte E. 6 Jul 1871
Daniel James T. to Rowe Louisa E. 6 Jan 1855
Daniel Pointdexter to Travers Margaret 19 May 1824
Daniel Traverse to Wallace Mary 11 Jan 1808
Danson William to Howarth Jane 27 Feb 1856
Darby Benjamin T. to Harris Martha J. 17 Dec 1839
Darby Benjamin W. to Taylor Amanda 1 Nov 1854
Darby Benjamin W. to Lankford Nancy 23 Feb 1857
Darby John T. to Harris Mary Elizabeth 5 Apr 1836
Darby Samuel to Petit Sarah 9 Feb 1809
Darby Samuel to Chesser Ann Maria 9 Jan 1838
Darby Samuel to Adams Leah J. 25 Dec 1855
Darby William to Wills Henny 25 Feb 1823
Darby William to Dougherty Hetty E. 5 Feb 1851
Darby William T. to Campbell Anne 18 Jan 1853
Dartens Samuel to Wilson Harriet 5 May 1835
Darter Samuel to Lingo Lotty 5 Jan 1818
Dasharoon Winder to Furbush Sally 6 Jun 1820
Dashiell Alfred to Nutter Elizabeth Anne 12 Aug 1856 C
Dashiell Alginon S. to Jones Sarah Elizabeth J. 5 Nov 1833
Dashiell Arthur to Horsey Sarah Ann 19 Aug 1822
Dashiell Arthur to Covington Mary Elizabeth 16 Jul 1827
Dashiell Arthur (Sr) to Philips Betsy 13 Nov 1798
Dashiell Babel to Pollitt Emily 16 Dec 1868 C
Dashiell Benjamin to Robertson Elizabeth 24 Mar 1798
Dashiell Benjamin to Stuart Matty 12 Feb 1811
Dashiell Benjamin to Dashiell Charlotte 29 Jun 1822
Dashiell Benjamin J. to Ker Esther 16 Oct 1821
Dashiell Benjamin J. to Thorne Sarah Owens 27 May 1822
Dashiell Benjamin J. to Stewart Leah M. 16 Jun 1847
Dashiell Benjamin W. to Purnell Malvania 31 May 1866 C
Dashiell Chapman to Donono Nancy 10 Oct 1816
Dashiell Chapman to Dashiell Delilah 26 Mar 1823
Dashiell Charles to Chandler Kitty 28 Jun 1817
Dashiell Charles to Kennerly Anne 21 Sep 1825

Dashiell Ebenezer H. to Hull Maria 12 Jan 1830
Dashiell Edward to Hurley Milcah E. 5 Dec 1860
Dashiell Edward to Sudler Charlotte A. 12 Jan 1867 C
Dashiell Edwin to Dashiell Harriet 22 Jan 1828
Dashiell Edwin to Robertson Elizabeth E. 8 Jan 1850
Dashiell Edwin (Jr.) to Gordon Ellen 25 Mar 1851
Dashiell Frank to Jones Martha 11 Feb 1868 C
Dashiell George to Wilson Sarah 1 Sep 1798
Dashiell George to Jones Eleanor 13 Oct 1801
Dashiell George to Cottman Sarah 15 Dec 1824
Dashiell George to Collier Elizabeth 28 Jan 1825
Dashiell George to Winright Leah 23 Nov 1865 C
Dashiell George to Jackson Mary 10 Sep 1867 C
Dashiell George (of Jno.) to Beauchamp Harriett L. 14 Dec 1831
Dashiell George (of Wm.) to Hopkins Eliza. 28 Jan 1818
Dashiell George A. to Lowes Elizabeth 20 Jan 1820
Dashiell George S. to Ross Mary E. 29 Jan 1863
Dashiell George W. to Dashiell Virginia R.E. 31 Mar 1841
Dashiell Hamilton H. to Kennerly Mary Ellen 13 Jul 1847
Dashiell Hampden H. to Kennerly Aurelia 3 May 1855
Dashiell Hampden H. to Polk Elizabeth W. 13 Jun 1861
Dashiell Haste W. to Dashiell Elizabeth 21 Dec 1819
Dashiell Henry to Cottingem Sanne 21 Feb 1797
Dashiell Henry to Crockett Priscilla 25 Jan 1836
Dashiell Henry James to Willing Hannah B. 6 Mar 1835
Dashiell Ichabod to Dashiell Priscilla 25 Nov 1799
Dashiell Isaac to Rider Matilda 31 May 1866 C
Dashiell Isaac to Robertson Margaret 6 Feb 1867 C
Dashiell J.M. to Leonard Lydia A. 1 Feb 1856
Dashiell Jacob to Wilson Esther --(?) 1838 C
Dashiell James A. to Dashiell Charlotte E.S.P. 19 Dec 1843
Dashiell James F. to Jones Jane W. 1 Jun 1858
Dashiell James Henry to Wright Tenneface 15 Jan 1868 C
Dashiell John to Nutter Sarah 10 Oct 1826
Dashiell John to McGrath Peggy 9 Mar 1831
Dashiell John to Walston Nancy 8 Oct 1834
Dashiell John to King Susan 19 Dec 1838
Dashiell John H. to Irving Emily W. 21 Dec 1841
Dashiell John J. to Wailes Mary A. 31 Aug 1839
Dashiell John R. to Dashiell Susanna J. 26 Jun 1838

Dashiell John W. to Polk Eliza 14 Apr 1852
Dashiell Joseph to Libby Delila Richie 5 May 1812
Dashiell Lambert H. to Hughes Eliza Jane N. 2 Sep 1834
Dashiell Lambert H. to Humphreys Martha W. 5 Oct 1858
Dashiell Levin to Follin Polly 3 Mar 1801
Dashiell Levin to Dashiell Mary Anne 16 Jan 1826
Dashiell Levin to Rider Martha 2 May 1866 C
Dashiell Levin J. to White Martha W. 9 Dec 1862
Dashiell Levin M. to Powell Ellin 22 Oct 1866
Dashiell Marcellus to White Elizabeth 30 Dec 1851 C
Dashiell Marcellus to Dashiell Susan J. 1 Apr 1865 C
Dashiell Matchell to Adams Sally 30 Mar 1816
Dashiell Mathias to Hull Mary 19 Dec 1826
Dashiell Matthias to Whitelock Rebecca 21 Jan 1813
Dashiell Mesheck to Nutter Mary W. 11 Oct 1865 C
Dashiell Nathan to Chase Margaret 12 Feb 1868 C
Dashiell Nathaniel P. to Robertson Maria H.E. 21 May 1867
Dashiell Nathaniel Potter to Kennerly Clarissa 26 Apr 1852
Dashiell Nicholas to Dashiell Mary 2 Oct 1813
Dashiell Peter to Hayman Julia Ann 29 Jun 1836
Dashiell Peter to Simpkins Elizabeth 14 Jan 1862
Dashiell Pitt to Willin Biddy 11 Aug 1847
Dashiell Robert to Leatherbury Eleanor 10 Mar 1813
Dashiell Robert to Rider Mary 5 Oct 1819
Dashiell Robert to Waller Sallie E.M. 27 Apr 1864
Dashiell Robert to Beauchamp Jane 27 Jan 1865 C
Dashiell Robert A. T. to Bonnawell Mary T. 6 Nov 1855
Dashiell Robert H. to Jones Rosey 7 Jun 1870 C
Dashiell Robert H. to Wilson Josephine 31 Jan 1871 C
Dashiell Samuel to Simms Mary E. 30 Dec 1840
Dashiell Samuel to Purnell Alice 7 May 1866
Dashiell Seth to Harris Elenor C. 17 Jan 1824
Dashiell Seth B. to Dashiell Aurelia J. 21 Jan 1850
Dashiell Seth H. to Blake Martha 29 Jun 1867 C
Dashiell Stephen to White Rachel 4 Jan 1866 C
Dashiell Theodore to Ford Georgiana 8 Aug 1867
Dashiell Theodore C. to Ward Matilda T. 7 Jan 1823
Dashiell Theodore G. to Gullett Elizabeth M. 17 Sep 1846
Dashiell Thomas to Porter Anne 28 Oct 1800
Dashiell Thomas (Jr) to Wailes Elizabeth 22 Jan 1798

Dashiell Thomas W. to Allen Margaret P. 8 Mar 1849
Dashiell Tobias to Nutter Priscilla 10 Feb 1840
Dashiell Wesley to Horner Virginia 4 Apr 1859
Dashiell William to Nichols Mary 3 Jul 1804
Dashiell William to White Margaret 11 Nov 1817
Dashiell William to Magraw Amada 3 Mar 1843
Dashiell William F. to Disharoon Mary 7 Dec 1825
Dashiell William F. to White Anne P. 7 Nov 1860
Dashiell William S. to Graham Charlotte A.H. 29 Mar 1819
Daugerty Severn to Riggin Nancy 11 Feb 1819
Daugherty Benjamin to Miles Priscilla 24 Sep 1828
Daugherty Eli to Kellum Mary W. 16 Aug 1830
Daugherty Elijah to Ward Nancy 24 Dec 1812
Daugherty Elijah to Matthews Mary 13 Sep 1815
Daugherty Henry to Johnson Patty 4 Sep 1827
Daugherty Isaac to Taws Mary 9 Nov 1802
Daugherty Isaac to Green Leah 19 Oct 1819
Daugherty Isaac to Tull Maria 22 Sep 1820
Daugherty John to Crumble Mary Weatherly 1 May 1804
Daugherty John to Lard Charity 9 Jul 1811
Daugherty John to Daugherty Rachel 4 Jul 1815
Daugherty John to Winright Hetty 27 Sep 1816
Daugherty John to Brown Mary 1 Dec 1819
Daugherty John to Thomas Jane 8 Apr 1831
Daugherty Joshua to Johnson Esther 14 Jan 1826
Daugherty Josiah to Brittingham Mary 25 May 1819
Daugherty Levi to Miles Esther W. 27 Feb 1816
Daugherty Nathaniel to Daugherty Martha 2 Aug 1808
Daugherty Nathaniel to Miles Valaria 10 Jan 1826
Daugherty Obed to Daugherty Anne 4 Sep 1827
Daugherty Peter to Lankford Ailse 8 Mar 1816
Daugherty Stephen to Twilley Sarah 1 Jan 1805
Daugherty Teague to Walter Betsy 28 Apr 1801
Daugherty Thomas to Daugherty Catherine 18 Jan 1837
Daugherty Thomas H. to Graham Amy 26 Jun 1832
Davey George E. to Dodson Arabella F. 18 Jan 1871
Davey Henry P. to Waters Mary Elizabeth H.W. 11 Dec 1838
Davey John U. to Ballard Priscilla W. 22 Oct 1866
Davey Titus to Lankford Frances 1 Aug 1865
Davey William to Davey Maria W. 1 May 1843

Davis Aden to Miles Emma F. 18 May 1858
Davis Arthur to Dorman Betsy 10 Jan 1814
Davis Azariah W. to Rider Martha W. 8 Feb 1842
Davis Benjamin to Matthews Sarah 3 Jan 1798
Davis Benjamin to Dorman Nancy 28 Jun 1814
Davis Benjamin to Price Margaret 9 Feb 1828
Davis Benjamin to Evans Milcah Anne 24 May 1834
Davis Benjamin to Adams Elizabeth T. 25 Sep 1849
Davis Charles to Elliss Polly 19 Nov 1811
Davis Daniel to Bell Nelly 16 May 1800
Davis Elijah to Taylor Sarah Anne 5 Feb 1836
Davis Elzy to Knight Mary 27 Feb 1798
Davis Francis A. to Long Sally P. 11 Mar 1867
Davis George to Ballard Ann M. 31 May 1843
Davis Henry to Linton Eleanor 15 May 1855
Davis Isaac to Evans Anne Maria 19 Jul 1821
Davis James to Nelson Sally 27 Jun 1809
Davis James to Riggin Milcah A. 21 May 1835
Davis James to Robertson Emaline (Miss) 15 May 1849
Davis James to Handy Elizabeth 24 Feb 1852
Davis Jeremiah to Fooks Julia A. 24 Sep 1867 C
Davis John to Jones Mary 6 Nov 1799
Davis John to Bozman Tabitha 15 Dec 1869
Davis John B. to Nelson Lucinda 1 Feb 1847
Davis John D. to Bennett Esther 4 Apr 1848
Davis John H. to Evans Mary M.D. 12 Jun 1855
Davis John J. to Roach Mary 3 Aug 1815
Davis John W. to Miles Charlotte A. 23 Nov 1858
Davis Josiah to Wallace Mary Anne 7 Nov 1840
Davis Josiah to Serman Margaret T. 29 Jan 1866
Davis Josiah to Hayden Catharine M. 16 May 1866
Davis Noah to Adams Elizabeth 31 May 1797
Davis Peter B. to Harriss Jane 23 Jan 1828
Davis Risden to Kelly Mary E.B. 11 Aug 1847
Davis Risdon to Kelly Sarah Ann 26 Aug 1841
Davis Robert to Fitzgerald Mary E. 4 Jun 1863
Davis Robert H. to Adams Catherine 5 Dec 1860
Davis Robert M. to Todd Eliza Anne --(?) 1838
Davis Robert M. to Bell Sally C. 30 Aug 1841
Davis Samuel to Windsor Anne 14 Dec 1854

Davis Samuel T. to Sheppard Elizabeth Anne 9 Feb 1837
Davis Samuel Taylor to Records Amelia 13 Oct 1807
Davis Thomas to Lankford Sally 9 Feb 1802
Davis Thomas J. to Smith Elizabeth 16 Dec 1854
Davis Wilbur F. to White Margaret E. 29 May 1866
Davis William T. to Henderson Mary E. 12 Mar 1862
Davy George to Sudler Martha A. 19 Jul 1826
Davy Henry to Maddux Drucilla 18 Feb 1850
Davy Robert to Sterling Alsa 1 Sep 1821
Davy William to Sterling Margaret 15 Nov 1856
Dawson John W. to Dorsey Mary E. 14 Jun 1852
Dawson Richard to Mealy Mary Jane 8 Jan 1866
Dawson Thomas McK. to Duer Sarah A.W. 12 Feb 1861
Dawsy Josiah to Cullen Nelly 10 May 1803
De Bonne Anthony to Lang Sally 18 Nov 1796
De Bonne Anthony to Dorsey Sally 30 Dec 1820
De Bonne Tubman to Walston Sally 10 Sep 1825
Deal James to Evans Margaret 25 Jul 1836
Dean Daniel to Acworth Betsy 8 Dec 1807
Dean James to Green Eleanor 27 Dec 1808
Dean John to Powell Rebecca 20 Sep 1804
Dean Joseph to Boston Elizabeth 2 Mar 1813
Dean Joshua to Huffington Polly 31 Aug 1814
Dean Joshua to Gilliss Rachel 31 Dec 1818
Dear Kendal O. to Puzey Nancy 12 Jan 1814
Dear Levi to Winsor Anne 15 Jul 1820
Demby John to Quinton Mary Ann Maria 18 Aug 1852 C
Dennis Charles W. to Williams Amanda E. 20 Dec 1853
Dennis Elijah to Wilson Elizabeth 5 May 1840
Dennis Elijah to McCollister Nancy 18 Mar 1840
Dennis George R. (Dr.) to Johnston Ellen R. 16 Apr 1856
Dennis James to Dashiell Serena 12 Jul 1866 C
Dennis John to Jones Sally E. 5 Dec 1833
Dennis John H. to Pollitt Lucy 31 Aug 1868 C
Dennis John K. (Junr.) to Long Henrietta A. 22 Feb 1843
Dennis John U. to Dashiell Elizabeth 14 Jul 1813
Dennis Joshua to Robertson Maria E. 26 Jun 1821
Dennis Littleton to Wilson Sally 7 Aug 1867
Dennis Littleton U. to Robertson Sarah A. 27 Jun 1826
Dennis Nelson to Miles Fassett 22 Jan 1839

Dennis Robert S. to Mason Indianna 8 Feb 1865
Dennis Samuel to Handy Eliza 29 Jun 1870 C
Dennis Samuel K. to Crisfield Sallie H. 20 Apr 1865
Dennis William B. to Fletcher Mary 27 Mar 1860
Dennis William J. to Waters Jane 7 Sep 1865 C
Dennis Zadock to Lawes Nancy 12 Nov 1804
Denson Ephraim A. to Banks Eleanor R. 11 Mar 1837
Denson Henry J.W. to Culver Hester E. 13 Jan 1863
Denson Isaac to Dashiell Sarah 19 Nov 1822
Denson Isaac J. to Bloodsworth Mary J. 22 Dec 1840
Denson James to Bloodsworth Nancy 13 Jan 1836
Denson James E. to McGrath Mary E. 11 Oct 1870
Denson William to Morris Eliza A. 19 Jan 1843
Denson William I. to Parks Rebecca C. 18 Apr 1826
Denston Ephraim to Layfield Sally 3 Oct 1798
Denston James to Willing Mary 1 Jul 1802
Denton William E. to Insley Rosa J. 26 Jan 1864
Denwood Arthur to Cannon Luiza 11 Apr 1804
Dickerson Charles to Horsey Emma 30 Oct 1866 C
Dickerson Emory to White Polly 30 Nov 1803
Dickerson Francis M. to Insley Catherine 6 Dec 1853
Dickerson Henry F. to Heath Mary C. 6 Dec 1853
Dickerson Isaac to Dreaden Ann 30 Aug 1814
Dickerson Isaac to Long Nelly 26 Jan 1818
Dickerson Mitchell to Porter Biddy 16 Feb 1825
Dickerson Mitchell A. to Mezick Martha W.H. 23 Oct 1838
Dickerson Samuel to Insley Eliza 4 Apr 1820
Dickerson Sydney to Gale Julia 14 Sep 1867 C
Dickerson William to Redden Rebecca 18 Sep 1799
Dickerson William to Robertson Tabitha E. 1 Feb 1848
Dickerson William P. to Larmore Mary 6 Dec 1853
Dickey T. Lyle to Hirst Beulah C. 18 Aug 1870
Dickinson Henry J.P. (Dr.) to Waller Mary E.A. 8 Apr 1851
Dickinson James T. to Porter Mary Anne 8 May 1843
Dies Richardson to Landon Rachel 17 Dec 1813
Digner Charles to Clark Polly 25 Dec 1798
Dikes Benjamin to Leonard Elizabeth 13 Jul 1856
Dikes John H. to Ward Matilda C. 16 May 1867
Dise Annanias to Laird Nancy --(?) 1838
Dise Ephraim to Somers Elizabeth 19 Jan 1833

Dise George to Ford Charlotte 11 Mar 1848
DIse Henry to Bradshaw Julia A. 1 Sep 1857
Dise Lewis to Ward Sally 8 Feb 1847
Dise Severn to Thomas Ritta 15 Aug 1848
DIse Smith to Wilson Jane 7 Apr 1848
Dise Stephen to Lankford Polly 23 Jul 1817
Disharoon A.C. Calvin to Price Hester A. 8 Nov 1864
Disharoon Alexander to Moore Matilda 16 Jan 1866
Disharoon Azariah P. to Dove Sarah E. 19 Mar 1867
Disharoon Caleb to Lankford Elizabeth 4 Feb 1823
Disharoon Ebenezer to Cullen Charlotte 19 Jul 1825
Disharoon Edward A. to Hearn Olivia F. 19 Jan 1864
Disharoon Francis to Vincent Henrietta 8 Jan 1820
Disharoon Freelinghuysin to Larmore Margaret E.B. 1 Jan 1867
Disharoon Henry to Pollitt Charlotte 1 Apr 1828
Disharoon James to Jenkins Sarah 22 Jul 1818
Disharoon James to Cullen Hetty 30 May 1826
Disharoon James to Hitch Mary 17 Feb 1829
Disharoon James to Smith Priscilla 5 Jan 1841
Disharoon James to Malone Amelia 12 Oct 1841
Disharoon John to Banks Sarah 29 Nov 1836
Disharoon John W. to Malone Mary E. 20 Dec 1866
Disharoon Joseph to Dashiell Sally E. 22 Mar 1853
Disharoon Levin W. to Davis Elizabeth 11 Feb 1823
Disharoon Matthias H. to Morris Nancy 21 Jan 1828
Disharoon Robert to Disharoon Sallie Ann 15 Aug 1855
Disharoon Samuel I. to Isham Mary E. 17 Dec 1856
Disharoon Samuel T. to Williams Mary E. 8 Jan 1861
Disharoon Thomas to Adams Sarah Ann 1 Mar 1831
Disharoon Thomas to Hayman Matilda 7 Feb 1861
Disharoon Thomas to Dove Betsey 16 Sep 1868
Disharoon Thomas A. to Hearn Hester A.M. 15 Aug 1853
Disharoon William to Stewart Amanda 18 Nov 1862
Disharoon William S. to Jones Elizabeth D.W. 1 Jul 1817
Disharoon William W. to Bounds Cinderilla E.W. 12 May 1846
Dix John to Daniel Margaret 3 Jun 1834
Dix Thomas to Bendicks Margaret 29 Nov 1849
Dix William S. to Fitzgerald Elizabeth 11 May 1841
Dixe William to Wallace Samuel 7 Feb 1809
Dixon Ambrose to Croswell Mary 7 Jun 1836

Dixon Benjamin to Hayman Catherine Anne 19 Jan 1858
Dixon Charles to Wallace Anne 23 May 1871 C
Dixon George C. to White Virginia 25 Oct 1848
Dixon George S. to Miles Alvie 20 Nov 1869
Dixon Handy to Taylor Mary J. 2 Jul 1868 C
Dixon Isaac to Holland Louisa 19 Nov 1816
Dixon Isaac to Robertson Louisa 18 Sep 1821
Dixon James Thomas to Gullett Elizabeth Ellen 20 Sep 1853
Dixon Nathaniel to Corbin Anne 1 Sep 1808
Dixon Nathaniel to Shockley Mary E. 20 Sep 1849
Dixon Richard to Hallise Mary 26 Jul 1869
Dize Augustus to Mister Elizabeth 30 Sep 1862
Dize Charles W. to Evans Julia Anne 14 Aug 1866
Dize Edward to Tyler Famy A. 25 Jun 1851
Dize Ephraim to Shores Helen 1 Aug 1860
Dize Fielder to Somers Grace 6 Dec 1853
Dize Gilbert to Evans Pothanna M. 3 Jan 1868
Dize Henry to Riggin Alexina 21 Aug 1866
Dize Hiram to Ford Mary 26 Apr 1850
Dize John to Evans Chloe 2 Dec 1800
Dize John to Dougherty Matilda 1 Jun 1844
Dize John W. to Marshall Margaret H. 24 Jan 1860
Dize Joshua to Charlick Maranda 9 Mar 1870
Dize Mordecai to Johnson Jane 8 May 1833
Dize Noah to Dougherty Sarah J. 2 Feb 1858
Dize Samuel to Webster Matty 27 Jun 1850
Dize Stephen to Beauchamp Peggy 27 Dec 1811
Dize Thomas to Ward Jane 3 Aug 1841
Dize Thomas E. to Miles Martha I. 8 Dec 1869
Dize Travers to Dougherty Mary H. 9 Nov 1863
Dize Wesley to Evans Annie A. 8 Mar 1864
Dize William to Bozman Elizabeth 21 Oct 1833
Dize William to Dize Sally A. 6 Jan 1863
Dize William to Coulbourn Mary E. 8 Apr 1865
Dize William to Stewart Rebecca 3 Apr 1867
Dobson Benjamin to Lankford Elizabeth S. 24 Apr 1856
Done John to Bowland Martha 12 Mar 1868 C
Donn Moses to Messick Mary 20 Dec 1796
Donnell James H. to Jones Ritta J. 23 Feb 1863
Dono William to Haynie Charlotte 10 Nov 1814

Donoho Azariah to Evans Jane 2 Nov 1839
Donoho James to Webster Biddy 9 Jun 1818
Donoho James to Webster Nancy 1 May 1821
Donoho Joshua to Cox Molly 9 Jul 1811
Donoho Joshua to Goddard Mary 9 Feb 1819
Donoho Philip to Stanford Priscilla 1 Dec 1818
Donoho William to Graham Elizabeth 12 Feb 1821
Donoho William to Donoho Juliann 24 May 1842
Donoho William D. to Wilson Sarah P. 11 Sep 1849
Donoho William F.M. to Austin Sarah E. 29 Jan 1866
Dority Elijah to Lord Catherine 26 Jun 1821
Dorman Alexander C.H. to Milligan Eliza R. 30 Jan 1850
Dorman Enick to Young Polly 14 Dec 1802
Dorman George to Rhodes Rachel 5 Oct 1802
Dorman George to Kelly Priscilla 22 Oct 1821
Dorman Henry to Horner Betsy 13 Jun 1832
Dorman Hezekiah to Hayman Amelia 20 Jan 1801
Dorman James to Walker Jane D. 10 Jan 1827
Dorman James to Hopkins Virginia 15 Feb 1854
Dorman James to Bradshaw Magdeline 30 Apr 1870
Dorman Jesse to Gale Leah Anne 6 Dec 1808
Dorman John to Smulling Prissy 25 Mar 1801
Dorman John to Whit Betsy 25 Jul 1809
Dorman John to Langsdale Laura E. 28 Jan 1867
Dorman Levin to Cornish Elizabeth 27 Dec 1870
Dorman Levin (Jr) to Dashiell Anne Jones 20 Nov 1810
Dorman Levin (Jr) to Dashiell Elizabeth 9 Nov 1813
Dorman Levin (Jr) to Johnson Hetty 19 Feb 1829
Dorman Levin K. to Waller Rachel 17 Jun 1845
Dorman Matthias to Holt Emeline 24 Mar 1829
Dorman Matthias to Nelson Esther Anne 19 Jun 1833
Dorman Matthias to Goslee Elizabeth 13 Jan 1835
Dorman Mitchell to Austin Leah 30 Sep 1824
Dorman Peter to Farrington Martha 2 Jan 1866 C
Dorman Robert to Mezick Kitturah D. 14 Jan 1840
Dorman Samuel J. to Smith Josephine 26 Jul 1859
Dorman Solomon to Morris Mary 10 Oct 1809
Dorman Thomas to Cantwell Polly 30 May 1811
Dorman Thomas C. to Windzor Sophia 8 Nov 1808
Dorman Tubman to Carew Matilda 8 Oct 1833

Dorman Uriah to Nelson Eleanor 26 Dec 1820
Dorman William to Dorman Rachel 29 May 1809
Dorman William to White Eleanor 12 Jun 1827
Dorothy John to Dise Mary 3 Oct 1798
Dorothy Joshua to Stevenson Polly 28 May 1818
Doroty Jonathan to Fletcher Martha 21 Mar 1809
Dorrity Robert to Weatherly Hetty 15 Dec 1810
Dorsey Caleb to Merrill Asenah 19 Dec 1801
Dorsey Caleb to Millican Nancy 3 Apr 1804
Dorsey Daniel to Small Amelia 29 Dec 1871 C
Dorsey Francis to Fitzgerald Juliet 12 Mar 1833
Dorsey Francis H. to Bozman Margaret A. 24 Oct 1859
Dorsey George M. to Chilton Virginia A. 31 Jan 1866
Dorsey George M. to Bell Sarah E. 23 Jan 1869
Dorsey Henry L. to Hall Anne B. 26 Feb 1833
Dorsey Isaac H. to King Mary 29 Dec 1846
Dorsey James T. to Parks Sarah F. 15 Sep 1863
Dorsey Jeremiah to Wallace Jane 28 Oct 1857
Dorsey Robert H. to McLane Margaret 13 Apr 1841
Dorsey Samuel L. to Chelten Emily A. 26 Dec 1871
Dorsey Thomas to Wilkins Harriet B. 13 Jan 1830
Dorsey Thomas C. to Stewart Eleanor E.W. 26 Jan 1841
Dorsey William to Maddux Milcah 20 Dec 1836
Dorsey William to Maddux Elizabeth M. 2 Dec 1845
Dougherty Azariah D. to Howarth Julia Ann 11 Jun 1850
Dougherty Benjamin F. to Dougherty Julia F. 1 Jul 1865
Dougherty Charles to Green Sarah E. 16 Oct 1857
Dougherty David to Miles Mary 14 Nov 1853
Dougherty David A. to Dougherty Rachael 24 Mar 1847
Dougherty George L. to Dougherty Olivia M. 15 Aug 1862
Dougherty Henry C. to Thomas Elizabeth Anne 11 Aug 1847
Dougherty Isaac to Thomas Mary 11 Aug 1831
Dougherty Isaac to Taylor Elizabeth 7 Jun 1845
Dougherty Isaac H. to Dougherty Elizabeth 26 Jan 1863
Dougherty Isaac T. to McCoy Henrietta 23 Jan 1856
Dougherty James W. to Brattan Mariah T. 6 Jan 1841
Dougherty John to Walter Margaret E.D. 29 Apr 1839
Dougherty John to Bowland Mary D.H. 8 Feb 1843
Dougherty John S. to Newman Nancy N. 11 Aug 1847
Dougherty John W. to Riall Louisa Ann 9 Jan 1861

Dougherty Luther to Milligan Harriet 14 Dec 1853
Dougherty McKenny to Johnson Sally 7 Mar 1848
Dougherty Robert to Adams Mary E. 12 Jun 1860
Dougherty Robert W. to Bowland Sallie 2 Aug 1853
Dougherty Severn to Ward Emily S. 27 Oct 1847
Dougherty Stephen to Wright Hetty 18 Dec 1802
Dougherty Thomas H. to Arvey Margaret (Mrs.) 2 Jun 1847
Dougherty Thomas S. to Johnson Susannah 5 Jun 1846
Dougherty William to Leon Rhoda 29 Apr 1834
Dougherty William C. to Bennett Mary 22 Oct 1852
Dougherty William H. to Bradshaw Mary E. 13 Feb 1857
Douglass James to White Rebecca 17 Oct 1848
Douglass James to White Mary 18 Jan 1859
Douglass Jesse A. to Willing Mary Washington 19 Feb 1849
Douglass Nathaniel to Horner Maria 9 Feb 1858
Douglass Nehemiah to White Margaret 16 Jun 1845
Douglass Ward to Elzy Lucretia 12 Mar 1850
Douglass William to Evans Betsy 3 Jan 1816
Douglass William John to Willing Anne Maria 30 Jun 1846
Dove Benjamin to Prior Anne P. 28 Aug 1838
Dove Benjamin to Christopher Anjeline 19 Jan 1842
Dove James to Smith Anne M. 24 Feb 1854
Dove James to Shores Elizabeth 30 Nov 1859
Dove John to Dorman Jane 8 Feb 1837
Dove John to Porter Rebecca 2 Dec 1845
Dove Lorenzo W. to Denson Sarah J. 21 Jan 1861
Downing George A. to Collins Martha C. 5 Oct 1857
Downing Sampson P. to Tilghman Marianna 30 Mar 1863
Downing William T. to Wainright Delia C. 6 Dec 1862
Downs Wilson to Brinkley Nancy 21 Jun 1869 C
Dreaden Littleton to Powell Polly 18 Sep 1810
Dreadon Mills to Murry Betsy Winder 14 Nov 1798
Druely Noah to Anderson Polly 1 Dec 1801
Druer John to Miles Eliza Jane 12 Nov 1863
Drummond John R. to Ayres Sarah R. 2 Oct 1854
Drura George to Benson Harriet 13 Jul 1816
Drura George to Long Margaret 18 Feb 1839
Drura Stephen to Heath Leah 31 Dec 1818
Drura Stephen to Fields Lurenna 22 Jul 1829
Drura Stephen to Mezzick Mary 19 Feb 1850

Dryden Albert F. to Corbin Mary E. 27 Mar 1866
Dryden David to Wilson Sarah A. 24 May 1842
Dryden Edward to Long Mary 14 Jan 1857
Dryden Edward L. to Gibbons Mary M. 25 Feb 1868
Dryden George J. to Jones Catherine E. 3 Jan 1855
Dryden George W. to Gibbon Margaret P. 11 Sep 1865
Dryden Hiram to Carver Margaret A. 1 Oct 1862
Dryden Isaac to Duer Esther Anne 25 Jun 1844
Dryden Isaac H. to Dykes Eliza Jane 18 Dec 1827
Dryden Isaac H. to King Mary 30 Jun 1841
Dryden Isaac H. to Stevens Henrietta J. 27 Sep 1870
Dryden James to Williams Henny 27 Jul 1830
Dryden James to Miles Harriet 13 Nov 1833
Dryden James to Dorsey Sally 22 Dec 1840
Dryden James to Marriner Priscilla 25 Dec 1865
Dryden John S. to Riggin Mary E. 26 Jan 1847
Dryden Joseph H. to Warwick Ellen A. 17 Mar 1863
Dryden Joseph H. to Warwick Elizabeth 25 Apr 1865
Dryden Kendal to Barnewell Margaret C. 6 Jan 1846
Dryden Lemuel to Riggin Sarah 12 Jan 1847
Dryden Levin to Adams Elizabeth 14 Dec 1829
Dryden Littleton to Levingston Peggy 15 May 1797
Dryden Littleton to Ward Jane 20 Oct 1835
Dryden Littleton to Ford Charlotte E. 24 Feb 1864
Dryden Littleton to Wallace Rena 26 Dec 1865
Dryden Purnell H. to Long Elizabeth 25 Nov 1834
Dryden Purnell H. to Dryden Matilda 14 Feb 1866
Dryden Samuel M. to Disharoon Eleanor 12 Mar 1829
Dryden Sovern to Reddin Nancy 5 Jun 1807
Dryden Thomas to Bell Susan Ann 10 Mar 1819
Dryden Thomas to Landen Ailce 3 Jan 1829
Dryden Thomas A. to Willis Grace 14 Sep 1824
Dryden Thomas James to Harris Mary 21 Feb 1860
Dryden Tubman to Riggin Sarah 12 Jun 1828
Dryden Uriah to Layfield Matilda 10 Sep 1851
Dryden William to Collins Nancy 10 Aug 1813
Dryden William to Adams Harriet 14 Dec 1829
Dryden William to Adams Maria 7 Feb 1838
Dryden William to Hudson Elizabeth 3 Apr 1847
Dryden William to Adams Sarah E. 29 Jan 1855

Dryden William H. to Ballard Elenorah N. 27 Jan 1865 C
Dryden William H. to Johnson Mary I. 12 Oct 1867
Dryden William T. to Melvin Hester J____ 4 Feb 1851
Dryden William T. to Cannon Lydia A. 14 Jan 1862
Duer Edward to Sturgess Anne 8 Jan 1829
Duer Edward F. to Dixon Virginia W. 27 Jan 1864
Duer William to Dryden Mary A. 2 Apr 1856
Duett Whittington to Davy Lovey 17 May 1799
Duffee John to Cantwell Elizabeth 27 Oct 1818
Duffy John to Taylor Priscilla 23 Jun 1810
Dulaney Dennis to Anderson Maria 18 Feb 1823
Dulaney Henry to Tunis Sophia 28 Jan 1825
Dulaney Isaac H.A. to White Anne M. 2 Dec 1851
Dulany Hany to Goddard Rhoda 6 May 1800
Dun James to Bloodsworth Margaret 24 Dec 1851
Duncan Elisha J. to Parks Sarah J. 1 May 1860
Duncan George to Bozman Isabella 10 Oct 1854
Duncan Lewis to Bradshaw Harriet 4 Feb 1840
Duncan William to L(?) Mary 4 Jan 1849
Dunn Benjamin to Horner Margaret 17 Jul 1834
Dunn George Byard to Jackson Hesther 20 Jan 1838
Dunn George H. to Wilson Mary E. 6 May 1858
Dunn James to Jones Matty 22 Jul 1820
Dunn John to Hopkins Susan 18 Jan 1826
Dunn John to Bloodsworth Mary 20 May 1828
Dunn John S. to Hughes Leah 10 Jan 1810
Dunn Joseph to Mezick Kitturah 14 Feb 1823
Dunn Joseph to Horsman Susan 17 Oct 1838
Dunn Joseph to Dunn Eliza Anne 4 Jun 1858
Dunn Matthias to McGrath Elizabeth 6 Jun 1854
Dunn Moses to Jones Sukey 7 Aug 1798
Dunn Moses to Walter Priscilla E. 24 May 1826
Dunn Perry to Wilson Zipporah 2 Dec 1862
Dunn Richard to Larrimore Mary 8 May 1798
Dunn Richard to Taylor Priscilla 17 Jan 1805
Dunn Richard to Dunn Priscilla 7 Nov 1820
Dunn Thomas to Larmore Margaret 17 Mar 1829
Dunn Thomas E. to Moore E. Cody 2 Jan 1861
Dunn Thomas J. to Long Sarah Jane 9 Mar 1842
Dunn William to Insley Catherine 9 Jan 1829

Dunn William to Larimore Priscilla J. 15 Mar 1853
Dunn William to Gibson Catharine A. 27 Jul 1869
Dunn William H. to Culver Sarah E. 21 May 1867
Dunnock Samuel R. to Weatherly Sarah E. 12 Dec 1849
Durham John to Dorman Anne 18 Feb 1815
Durham John H. to Holland Sarah 20 Sep 1821
Durham Thomas to McGrath Sally 25 Jul 1825
Durham Thomas to Herrington Eliza 20 Sep 1838
Durham William to Evans Margaret 2 Jul 1851
Durham William S. to Smith Elizabeth E. 3 Sep 1839
Dutton Esme to Hayman Louisa 30 Jun 1846 C
Dutton George to Hill Kitty 8 Sep 1847 C
Dutton Gilly to Turner Sarah Ellen 5 Feb 1867 C
Dutton John L. to Black Miranda 14 Mar 1843
Dutton Levin G. to Saulsbury Sally J. 25 Aug 1857 C
Dutton Roger to Wright Shela 31 Oct 1800
Dykes John to Turner Elizabeth 2 Jan 1855
Dymock Edward to Smith Anne --(?) 1837
Dymock George W. to Mumford Virginia E. 5 Jan 1865
Dyse Fielding to Sterling Keziah 13 Sep 1864
Dyze Stephen T. to Evans Melissa 12 Dec 1865
Eashom James to Malone Nancy 19 Jul 1836
Ellegood Robert to Kennerly Betsy 1 Dec 1807
Ellet William to Nichols Jane 1 Mar 1823
Elligood Robert H. to Ruark Martha Ann 24 Dec 1855
Elligood William to Sowen Nancy 9 Feb 1861 C
Ellingsworth Josiah to Brewington Maria 20 Feb 1832
Elliott Elijah M. to Trader Sarah J. 14 Apr 1865
Elliott Hudson to Phillips Eleanor 27 Sep 1831
Elliott James to Dorman Maria 10 Feb 1834
Elliott James B. to McGrath Mary C. 8 Jan 1862
Elliott James H. to Brown Margaret E. 15 May 1863
Elliott James Wilson to Vance Mary Owens 4 Apr 1815
Elliott John to Daugherty Elizabeth 1 Dec 1819
Elliott John to Pepper Huldy 11 Sep 1832
Elliott John to Wright Mary E.H. 23 Dec 1851
Elliott Levin to Abbott Louisa 26 Nov 1861
Elliott Levin to James Windsor Elizabeth J. 1 Mar 1858
Elliott Robert to Dunn Henrietta 2- Jan 1851
Elliott Samuel R. to Pollitt Margaret 19 Jun 1866

Elliott Thomas to Abbott Mary Jane 23 Jun 1857
Elliott William to Gravenor Mary 26 Dec 1827
Elliott William to Adams Emeline 24 Nov 1838
Elliott William to Long Margaret E. 30 Nov 1847
Elliott William to Holden Alery Anne 16 Feb 1852
Elliott William to Stewart Mary J. 17 Jul 1860
Elliott William F. to Beauchamp Charlotte A. 11 Jan 1870
Elliotte Jesse to Jones Elizabeth 10 Nov 1801
Ellis George to Jenkins Charlotte E. 27 Apr 1857
Ellis John to Parker Leah W. 1 Sep 1841
Ellis Wilmer to Venables Anne 26 Jul 1842
Ellis _____ to Marshall Eliza 2- Aug 1851
Elliss Thomas to Moore Rebecca 3 Dec 1844
Ellmore Frederick to Tull Emily F. 9 Jul 1861
Elsey Gabriel to Jones Ritty 6 Nov 1850
Elzey Alfred Poke to Stewart Elizabeth 4 Oct 1870 C
Elzey Arnold to Wilson Anne 1 Mar 1803
Elzey Charles to Gale Ellen 24 Dec 1855 C
Elzey Daniel to Coulbourn Caroline 7 Oct 1865 C
Elzey Edward K. to Davy Louisa 7 Apr 1857 C
Elzey Ephraim to Brown Polly 15 Mar 1802
Elzey George to Coulbourn Adeline 28 Dec 1843
Elzey George to Wilson Sarah E. 27 Oct 1870
Elzey Harry to Thompson Mary 28 Dec 1858 C
Elzey James to Elzey Anne 9 Nov 1867 C
Elzey James E. to Fountain Henrietta 3 Aug 1814
Elzey Jesse to Williams Caroline 19 Oct 1867 C
Elzey John to Bailey Nancy 6 Jan 1846
Elzey John to Nutter Susan 2 Mar 1852
Elzey John A. to White Eliza E. 11 Apr 1867
Elzey Robert M. to Robertson Sarah Ann 6 Jan 1851
Elzey Samuel to Dashiell Matilda 7 Dec 1852
Elzey Shiles Crockett to Layfield Mary E. 13 May 1834
Elzey Thomas to Green Mary 31 Oct 1809
Elzey Washington to Smith Mary Anne 15 Mar 1853 C
Elzey William K. to Graham Sally Elizabeth 19 Jan 1849
Elzey William S. to Parks Gatty 7 Apr 1853 C
Emenirzer John to Lankford Nancy 1 Oct 1844
Eminizer Thomas to Layfield Mary 30 Apr 1867
Emory James to Shores Amanda 6 May 1851

English Alfred to Bennett Isabella 1 Jan 1851
English Cornelius W. to Wright Louisa H. 23 Jan 1866
English John to Bennett Rhoda 22 Dec 1823
English Levin to Taylor Elizabeth 26 Jan 1830
English Robert C. to Bennett Mary L. 23 Feb 1867
English Samuel S. to Dashiell Anne M. 5 Feb 1866
English Thomas to Giles Mary 30 Dec 1828
English William to Nelson Hetty 11 May 1824
English William T. to Hasty Sarah E. 30 Nov 1859
Ennis Arthur W. to Dashiell Maria C. 18 Jan 1848
Ennis Elijah H. to Johnson Elizabeth Jane 20 May 1846
Ennis Gilbert J. to Davis Mary C. 2 Jun 1847
Ennis Henry C. to Matthews Ellin M. 14 Jan 1868
Ennis Jesse to Simms Anne Maria 24 May 1866
Ennis John to Jones Mary 13 Apr 1865
Ennis Rufus M. to Jones Martha J. 21 Jan 1840
Ennis William to Parsons Margaret 1 Dec 1852
Enson Jesse D. to Insley Louisa 26 Jan 1842
Entrup Bernard H. to Benson Annie H. 23 Aug 1862
Eskridge Oakley T. to Griffith Mary 27 Nov 1837
Evans Abihu to Bratcher Anne 15 Jan 1821
Evans Abraham to Revell Esther 4 Jul 1807
Evans Alexander S. to Crockett Leah Elizabeth (I) 24 Apr 1823
Evans Alexander S.D. to Nicols Margaret 16 Jan 1834
Evans Alexander W. to Broadshaw Sardelia 27 May 1867
Evans Alonzo to Turner Shady 30 May 1871
Evans Arthur to Johnson Hetty 24 Jan 1834
Evans Charles N. to Brewington Sarah Ann 8 Dec 1838
Evans Christopher W. to Lewis Mary D. 12 Dec 1871
Evans Denwood to Evans Hannah 27 Dec 1808
Evans Edward to Insley Anne Maria 29 Oct 1831
Evans Edward to Roberts Henrietta 10 Dec 1838
Evans Edward to Evans Triffa 23 May 1870
Evans Elijah T. to Dize Sally E. 24 May 1870
Evans Elzey to Evans Rachel 12 Jan 1813
Evans Elzey to Webster Elizabeth 13 Aug 1839
Evans Elzey to Hall Susan U. 27 Aug 1844
Evans Francis to Evans Polly 26 Aug 1809
Evans George to Wilson Susan 12 May 1846
Evans George to Turner Anne 30 Jun 1851

Evans George to Jones Elizabeth 24 Dec 1861 C
Evans George E. to Prewitt Ann E. 24 May 1864
Evans Henry to Walston Peggy 3 Aug 1803
Evans Henry to Mackey Susan 29 Jun 1808
Evans Henry to Barkley Adeline 4 May 1858 C
Evans Henry to Gibson Julia 20 Dec 1869
Evans Hezekiah to Evans Sally 19 May 1812
Evans James (Jr) to Dashiell Susan J. E. 16 Jul 1819
Evans Jesse to Taylor Harriet 28 Nov 1821
Evans Jesse to Bradshaw Levina 9 Aug 1861
Evans John to Dorothy Esther 16 Jun 1818
Evans John to Wainwright Eleanor 29 Sep 1840
Evans John to Mezick Sarah 2 Feb 1855
Evans John to Kaylor Catharine 9 Dec 1856
Evans John to Rowe Fanny 25 Apr 1859
Evans John to Hoofman Malinda 17 Oct 1865
Evans John to Pruitt Triffa 9 Mar 1870
Evans John S. to Crist Mary P. 21 Jan 1851
Evans John T. to Dougherty Emily S. 27 Apr 1866
Evans John Welsey to Dix Mary Catherine 11 Aug 1855
Evans Laban to Tyler Betsy 26 Dec 1812
Evans Laban to Jones Mary Anne 27 Aug 1838
Evans Laben to Parks Sally 16 Jul 1819
Evans Levin to Nicols Elizabeth 23 Aug 1831
Evans Levin(?) to Mezick Elizabeth 24 Jan 1810
Evans Marcellus to Covington Margaret 25 Jan 1841
Evans Marcellus R. to Jones Elizabeth H. 7 Mar 1861
Evans Markaduke to Simpkins Levinia 23 Jun 1823
Evans Mitchell to Dougherty Rebecca 21 Mar 1838
Evans Mitchell to Evans Sardelia 18 Jan 1841
Evans Nathan to Bratcher Rhoda 11 Jun 1824
Evans Noah to Minter Patience 25 Jul 1832
Evans Peter to Evans Zipporah 16 Jun 1808
Evans Peter to Handy Maria 22 Dec 1835
Evans Purnell to Dennis Lavinia 26 Dec 1865 C
Evans Richard to Marshall Grace 14 Jan 1817
Evans Robert to Parks Jemima 6 Jan 1834
Evans Robert to Evans Lucy 23 May 1843
Evans Solomon to Bratcher Polly 24 Dec 1799
Evans Solomon to Marshall Priscilla 5 Jul 1819

Evans Solomon to Price Nancy 19 Jun 1846
Evans Solomon to Bratcher Arabella 3 Oct 1854
Evans Thomas to Nichols Mary 5 May 1812
Evans Thomas D. to Hughes Mary 24 Nov 1830
Evans Thomas D. to Hayward Charlotte E. S. 11 Mar 1837
Evans W.H. to Marsh Rhoda C. 9 Feb 1864
Evans William to Walston Polly 13 Jun 1797
Evans William to Roe Jean 10 Aug 1802
Evans William to Evans Nancy 16 Jun 1808
Evans William to Garrettson Nelly 22 Jan 1816
Evans William to Kelly Sally 15 Feb 1825
Evans William to Collier Matilda 9 Feb 1836
Evans William to Evans Polly 13 Jan 1838
Evans William to Hughes Caroline R.A. 19 Oct 1841
Evans William to Roberts Sarah A. 15 Nov 1859
Evans William to Thomas Margaret 6 Sep 1869
Evans William B. to Gie Virginia 20 May 1862
Evans William M. to Bailey Amanda J. 8 Dec 1843
Evans William S. to Garner Mary C. 31 Jul 1856
Evans William T. to Mister Kiziah 9 Feb 1850
Evans William Wallace to Evans Susan L. 12 Feb 1840
Evans Zacharia to Evans Delilah 25 Jul 1816
Eversham James to Lloyd Eliza A. 23 Jan 1865
Eversham John to Denson Elizabeth 1 Nov 1838
Ewell Francis W. to Hasting Charlotte 25 Jul 1859
Ewell Henry to Smith Rosey 9 Dec 1823
Fallen David to Purkins Esther 29 May 1798
Faller Greenbury to Cannon Eunice 30 Oct 1840
Fapitt George W. to Holloway Sally A. E. 18 Aug 1856
Farlow Jesse to Dikes Eliza 6 Dec 1866
Farrington Theodore to Roach Betsy Ann 12 Nov 1822
Farrington William H. to Kennerly Zenophene 16 Feb 1848
Farris Edwin C. to Hearn Mary M. 13 Dec 1865
Farrow Charles to Johnson Nancy 9 Apr 1803
Faulkner William to Goslee Maria 2 May 1842
Feals John to Hitch Matilda 30 Jun 1842
Feals Rufus to Dutton Elizabeth 5 Jan 1857 C
Feals William to Toadvine Elizabeth 30 Jan 1836
Feddeman Emmerson F. to Broughton Emily 26 Jun 1865
Feddeman James to Dashiell Henrietta 25 Dec 1827

Fields Christopher to Daley Kaziah 19 Aug 1845
Fields Emory to Durham Vandelia A. 18 Aug 1858
Fields George to Jenkins Eliza Anne 15 Jan 1818
Fields George to Currie Patty 3 May 1831
Fields George to Rook Nancy 24 Dec 1833
Fields George Edward to Jones Emily 27 Dec 1869 C
Fields George H. to Kibble Mary Anne 14 Apr 1857
Fields George W. to Jenkins Charlotte A. 24 Aug 1858
Fields Jno. to Taylor Nelly 9 Apr 1834
Fields John to Turner Letitia E. 26 May 1863
Fields John W. to McGrath Mary E. 28 Jan 1857
Fields Joseph to Carroll Emily C. 26 Jan 1870 C
Fields Lewis to Adams Polly 5 Mar 1836
Fields Perry Frances to Cooksey Mary R. 25 Jan 1859
Fields Rufus to Dalton Jane 18 Apr 1837
Fields Stephen B. to Owens Clanetta E. 14 Jan 1845
Fields Thomas to Surman Sally 30 Jan 1816
Fields Thomas to Ruke Mary 25 Dec 1849
Fields John to Jenkins Hetty 30 Dec 1835
Fippin Belitha to Booth Margaret 6 Apr 1829
Fisher Henry to Brewington Nancy 12 Mar 1828
Fisher Henry L. to Webster Eliza J. 5 May 1868
Fisher John D. to Taylor Delilah P. 8 Apr 1854
Fisher Thomas to Dennis Ann E. 14 May 1816
Fisher Thomas Oliver to Shores Frances 9 Nov 1868
Fisher William to Simms Williamanna 18 Oct 1870
Fisher William H. to Miller Priscilla Anne 9 Jan 1839
Fisher William H. to Bell Margaret A. 14 Aug 1854
Fitsgerald Elisha to Croswell Mary 2 Jan 1816
Fitzgerald Anthony to Ingersoll Maria J. 15 Mar 1853
Fitzgerald Elijah to Lister Sarah 12 Apr 1799
Fitzgerald Elijah to Walston Sarah 29 Jul 1800
Fitzgerald Jesse B. to Hall Sarah 29 Jan 1811
Fitzgerald Robert to Brooks Polly --(?) 1838
Fleming Alfred to Mandry Elizabeth Anne 1 Jan 1856
Fleming Henry to Sturgis Anne 14 Sep 1813
Fleming James A. T. to Mills Mary E. 23 Mar 1869
Fleming John to Harris Eliza 12 Feb 1828
Fleming John to Harris Elizabeth 13 Jan 1840
Fleming John T. to Disharoon Martha Jane 12 Jul 1865

Fleming William to Woods Sarah 7 Aug 1801
Fleming William to Tull Elizabeth 5 Apr 1803
Fleming William to Tull Sally 7 Dec 1813
Fletcher Clement B. to Byrd Margaret S. 11 Mar 1817
Fletcher Cottman to Green Nancy 27 May 1823
Fletcher George W. to Dorman Catherine 31 May 1858
Fletcher James to Bedsworth Sarah 11 Aug 1819
Fletcher James to Jones Betsy 28 Feb 1826
Fletcher John to Carey Margaret 18 Jan 1844
Fletcher John W. to Davis Martha 16 Oct 1854
Fletcher Leonard to James Eleanor 30 Jul 1823
Fletcher Levin J. to Brereton Eleanor J. 30 Jan 1844
Fletcher Thomas W. to Goslee Sarah P.W. 3 Sep 1833
Fletcher William to Surman Prisce 23 Aug 1831
Fletcher William to Fields Temperance 26 Aug 1834
Fletcher William C. to Washbire Louisiana F. 3 May 1860
Flowers Jeremiah to Mills Betsy 24 Dec 1804
Flowers John to Howard Charlotte 30 Aug 1810
Floyd Huett to Clark Polly 23 Apr 1810
Fluhart William to Evans Emaline 26 Dec 1861
Follin Henry to Miles Polly 23 Feb 1799
Follin John H. to Collins Zipporah 18 Feb 1871 C
Follin William J. to Windsor Eliza 30 Jan 1869
Fontaine Charles to Fontaine Susan 19 Jan 1836
Fontaine Frederick to Wilson Hester 15 Nov 1870 C
Fontaine James Mc. L. to Taylor Virginia 15 Mar 1854
Fontaine James McC. to Riddell Anne M. 21 Oct 1828
Fontaine John to Ballard Anne 2 Aug 1815
Fontaine John Elzey to Miles Caroline A. 19 Apr 1843
Fontaine Levin I. to Mezick Eleanor 24 Dec 1821
Fontaine Marcey F. to Rider Gertrude 1 Feb 1869
Fontaine Peter to Fontaine Annie 24 Feb 1868 C
Fontaine Whitty to Cullen Hessy 18 Jan 1842
Fontaine William C. to Polk Imogene G. 3 Oct 1867
Fontaine William H. to Elzey Sally A. 15 Dec 1830
Fookes Thomas to Bayly Leah 22 Jun 1802
Fooks Charles B. to Fitsgerald Rosa 25 Jan 1855
Fooks Ebben to Bailey Polly 28 Aug 1833
Fooks Henry to Bevans Hester 22 Feb 1871 C
Fooks James to Pollitt Mattie 8 May 1815

Fooks John T. to Owens Mary 17 Apr 1860
Fooks John T. to Goslee Matilda C. 1 Jan 1868
Fooks Severn to Disharoon Betsy 23 Jan 1827
Fooks Thomas to Disharoon Mariah 11 Oct 1831
Ford Absolom to Budd Nancy 23 Mar 1824
Ford Charles to Somers Peggy 27 Aug 1828
Ford Charles T. to Landing Mary A. 16 Feb 1840
Ford Charles W. to Ford Mary E. 16 Aug 1853
Ford Daniel to Summers Mary 15 Apr 1811
Ford Daniel to Somers Hessy 12 Jan 1842
Ford Daniel to Ford Mary A. 18 May 1847
Ford Daniel J. to Green Mary R. 5 Jan 1859
Ford Daniel P. to Parks Sarah H. 18 Jul 1867
Ford Edward to Scott Virginia M. 9 May 1849
Ford Edward to White Eliza 26 Oct 1867
Ford Elzey to Bonnewell Maria 4 Jan 1819
Ford George E. to Rura Martha P. 15 Feb 1864
Ford George W. to Warwick Priscilla 16 Feb 1870
Ford Gilbert to Adams Esther 22 Dec 1796
Ford Henry to Miles Mary 9 May 1827
Ford Henry C. to Patterson Elizabeth J. 29 Nov 1853
Ford Hugh to Parks Nancy 11 Mar 1834
Ford Hugh to Walston Mary Ellen 27 Dec 1847
Ford James to Conner Lewey 18 Sep 1820
Ford James to Lord Aurelia 18 Sep 1857
Ford James to Windslow Francis 26 Sep 1871
Ford James L. to Croswell Mary A. 8 Jun 1863
Ford John to Parks Margaret 15 Jul 1828
Ford John H. to Ford Sarah E. 30 Jun 1858
Ford John Henry to Ford Elizabeth 22 Jun 1852
Ford John S. to Ford Elizabeth J. 6 May 1871
Ford Samuel to White Harris 1 Jan 1805
Ford Samuel to Walston Milcah Anne 8 Feb 1837
Ford Samuel to Chelton Sarah E. 22 Mar 1861
Ford Samuel L. to Beauchamp Harriet A. 20 Jun 1862
Ford Silas to Bozman Mary 29 Jan 1833
Ford Silas to Simpkins Sally 2 Sep 1869
Ford Thomas to Howarth Mary 21 Jun 1825
Ford Thomas E. to Croswell Elizabeth 29 Dec 1858
Ford Thomas E. to McDaniel Margaret 5 Jan 1860

Ford William to Campbell Hannah 3 Jan 1832
Ford William to Durham Rebecca 20 Dec 1838
Ford William A. to Mears Mary 30 May 1862
Ford William E. to Muir Milcah E. 28 Nov 1855
Ford William S. to Howard Susan 7 Dec 1852
Ford William S. to Ford Sarah M. 21 Jul 1868
Ford William T. to Mure Harriet E. 17 Jul 1860
Ford William T. to Tyler Margaret A. 27 Jul 1870
Foreman Isaac to Kirwan Mary 20 Jan 1835
Foreman James to Harrington Maria 14 May 1833
Foreman James to Moore Ceeney 1 May 1837
Foreman Reuben to Paden Elizabeth 26 Jan 1841
Forge (Ford) Daniel to Somers Priscilla 5 Jan 1830
Foster C.F. to Marshall Ella R. 7 May 1860
Foster George to Stevens Anne 21 Aug 1849
Foster James T. to Johnson Sarah E. 28 Jun 1870
Foster William to Jones Sally 27 Jan 1817
Fountain William H. to Fountain Mary M. 25 Sep 1838
Fountane John E. to Pollitt Margaret 17 Jan 1849
Fourbush Joseph to Parr Nancy 11 Oct 1808
Fowler Edward to Roberts Eleanor 11 May 1799
Fowler Edward to Harris Ellen E. 17 Apr 1861
Fowler Handy I. to Toadvine Aurelia H. 25 Jul 1854
Fowler John E. to Cathill Mary Jane 26 Mar 1850
Fowler Robert to Fowler Sarah 29 Nov 1796
Fowler William to Jones Sarah 2 Aug 1808
Fowler William to Walter Sally 9 Apr 1833
Foxwell Aaron G. to Sturgiss Betsy 15 Jan 1810
Foxwell Benjamin to Furniss Elizabeth 6 Jan 1852
Foxwell Benjamin H. to Dashiell Cortly (?) 6 Nov 1841
Foxwell Gabriel to Alpha Grace 30 Oct 1816
Foxwell Henry to Walston Leah 14 May 1810
Foxwell Henry to Paden Susan 25 Aug 1830
Foxwell Henry (Jr)(Burton) to Benton Lizzy 19 Jul 1825
Foxwell John H. to Austin Eliza Anne 3 Jan 1854
Foxwell Noah to Nelson Harriet 18 Oct 1830
Foxwell Robert S. to Bloodsworth Elizabeth 8 Aug 1839
France James to Cowley Catharine B. 26 Jun 1858
Francis Augustus Theodore to Malcomb Sarah Emily 21 Jan 1844
Freed Albert H. to Windsor Jane 29 Apr 1862

Freeney John to Jones Esther 11 Sep 1866 C
Freeney William to Morris Anna Maria 13 Jun 1836
French Samuel to Blake Mary S. 25 Jun 1861
Fromentin Eligius to Polk Betsy 28 May 1800
Furbush George to Nutter Nancy 31 Dec 1814
Furbush George to Furbush Polly 10 Dec 1823
Furbush George W. to Russell Mary 4 Jun 1833
Furbush James to Horner Maria 12 Oct 1867
Furbush James H. to Douglass Maria E. 15 Oct 1867 .
Furnis Littleton to Foxwell Elizabeth 5 Jan 1846
Furniss Alexander W. to Phoebus Maria H. 5 Dec 1861
Furniss Davis to Wright Sally 16 Nov 1867 C
Furniss Ephraim to Adams Mary Jane 22 Sep 1829
Furniss Ephraim to Jones Mary Amanda 8 Feb 1833
Furniss Isaac J. to Powell Mary W. 10 Jun 1856
Furniss Joseph S.C. to Phoebus E. Emily 14 Feb 1867
Furniss Josiah to Purkins Nancy 23 Feb 1808
Furniss Littleton to Hughes Sarah A. 4 Aug 1826
Furniss Littleton to McIntrye Eleanor 24 Nov 1829
Furniss Orlando to Vetra Orzella 28 Nov 1854
Furniss Stephen to Barkley Lydia W. 28 Feb 1865 C
Furniss William to Moore Milly 29 Mar 1801
Furniss William to Harris Leah 23 Dec 1834
Furniss William to Powell Mary E. 19 Dec 1854
Gage William L. to Fitzgerald Harriet 18 Apr 1848
Gale David to Jones Ellen 19 Jan 1865 C
Gale Edward to Fletcher Mary 5 Mar 1868 C
Gale George to Snelling Jane 17 May 1808
Gale George H.W. to Lowse Hester 19 Apr 1869 C
Gale Henry to Weatherly Anne 26 May 1807
Gale Henry to Goslee Ottilda E.S. 8 Feb 1831
Gale John to Windsor Rachel A. 17 Nov 1866 C
Gale John to Waters Anna 2 Sep 1869 C
Gale John H. to Nelson Leah J. 7 Apr 1863
Gale John Henry to Cornish Caroline 22 Mar 1853 C
Gale John P. to Jones Caroline A. 9 Sep 1819
Gale Levin J. to Rider A.L.V. 16 Dec 1863
Gale Robert to Kennerly Esther 22 Apr 1865 C
Game Charles to Sanders Rebecca 15 Sep 1812
Game George to Noble Leah 6 Dec 1799

Game Perry to King Lucy 28 Feb 1866 C
Game William to Wright Ann Maria 1 Feb 1820
Gardner Benjamin F. to Parks Matilda F. 24 Dec 1868
Gardner Clarke Graham to Brown Henrietta 28 Nov 1833
Gardner Grenville G. to Dashiell Sallie W. 5 Dec 1867
Gardner William to Bedsworth Margaret 27 Nov 1849
Garner Griffin to Parks Lucretia 4 Sep 1823
Garner Griffin to Evans Emily R. 21 Aug 1850
Garretson Freeborn to Waters Elizabeth H. 23 Sep 1823
Garretson John to Collins Sarah 15 Jan 1833
Garretson John Wesley to Nutter Margaret 9 Jul 1862
Garretson Jonathan to Beauchamp Leah 20 Dec 1803
Garretson Thomas to Evans Priscilla Ann 5 Feb 1821
Garretson Thomas to Conwav Margaret 6 Aug 1863 C
Garrison James H. to Green Sarah J. 17 Oct 1863
Garrison John T .K. to Mason Virginia 5 Jan 1869
Garrison Levin H. to Williams Margaret E. 30 Sep 1863
Gates Charles to Newman Leah 20 Jul 1813
Gates Charles to Beauchamp Betsy 7 Sep 1816
Gates William to Fisher Molly 23 Apr 1813
George Elmodom to Tankersley Mary E. 24 Oct 1867
Gerald Edward to Bush Henrietta C. 22 May 1866
Gibbon John Wesley to Benton Melvina 31 Dec 1863
Gibbons Burton C. to Parsons Elizabeth P. 24 Dec 1839
Gibbons Eli to Tilghman Milly 12 Jan 1799
Gibbons Elijah T.P. to Dryden Adeline F. 12 Sep 1865
Gibbons Ezekiel to Lankford Eleanor Anne 9 Mar 1819
Gibbons Ezekiel to Gibbons Priscilla 9 Dec 1829
Gibbons Ezekiel to Bloyd Mary 2 Jan 1838
Gibbons Ezekiel to Parker Susan 15 Jun 1858
Gibbons Henry to Webb Leah 5 Jan 1808
Gibbons Isaac to Smith Hetty 12 Jan 1802
Gibbons Isaac to Curtis Anne 29 Mar 1825
Gibbons Isaac to Parsons Sarah P. 2 Dec 1862
Gibbons James to Owens Pallace 25 Jun 1801
Gibbons James to Robertson Mary C. 2 Oct 1827
Gibbons James F. to Bunting Sarah 3 Feb 1840
Gibbons John to King Priscilla 7 Dec 1852
Gibbons John to Parsons Roza Anne 10 Nov 1857
Gibbons John E. to Parker Esther Anne 12 Aug 1858

Gibbons Joseph to Bozman Cenia Anne 10 Sep 1856
Gibbons Levin to Handy Betsy 14 Mar 1815
Gibbons Noah J. to Miller Mary J. 24 Aug 1871
Gibbons Peter to Powell Orpha 28 Feb 1804
Gibbons Peter to Landon Margaret 24 Mar 1812
Gibbons Peter to Gibbons Esther 4 Nov 1829
Gibbons Reubin to Scott Mary 2 Jan 1817
Gibbons Robert to Maddux Mary 19 Feb 1833
Gibbons Samuel to McGredy Catherine 3 Dec 1808
Gibbons Samuel to Cullen Mary T. 23 Jan 1871
Gibbons Theodore T. to Milbourn Julia Ann 1 Jul 1834
Gibbons Thomas to Watson Nancy 16 Sep 1854
Gibbons William to Floyd Sally 7 Jun 1825
Gibbons William to Long Matilda 13 Oct 1858
Gibbons Zadock to Lankford Milly 22 Nov 1804
Gibbons Zadock to Long Sarah 9 Jan 1829
Gibson Elijah to Webster Ellen 15 Apr 1841
Gibson George to Wilson Elizabeth 13 Aug 1851
Gibson Henry to Webster Maria 5 Jan 1830
Gibson Henry to Johnson Nancy 10 Sep 1844
Gibson Henry S. to Tankersley Elizabeth J. 16 Nov 1861
Gibson John to Acworth Sally 7 Apr 1808
Gibson John to Parks Jemimah 24 Dec 1810
Gibson Nathaniel to Johnson Maria 20 Jun 1838
Gibson Samuel to Byrd Minia 1 May 1829
Gibson Samuel H.W. to Riggin Susan F. 19 Dec 1859
Gibson William to Webster Kitty 9 Aug 1809
Gibson William to Smith Sarah 15 Jul 1839
Gie Henry to Evans Martha E. 11 Mar 1862
Giles John to Philips Kiturah 23 Oct 1821
Giles John H. to White Margaret M. 25 Feb 1863
Giles Sidney to Griffith Anne 17 Jan 1843
Giles Thomas to Leatherbury Betsy 18 Dec 1798
Giles Thomas to Leatherbury Betsy 21 Dec 1798
Giles Thomas to Giles Clara 10 May 1865
Giles William to Dorman Catherine 17 Dec 1816
Gilless Thomas to Langsdale Sally 18 Mar 1822
Gillet John to Betsworth Sally 13 Apr 1808
Gillis Levin to Morris Elizabeth 14 Apr 1832
Gillis Thomas C.C. to Twilley Elizabeth E. 3 Feb 1852

Gilliss Beacham L. to Anderson Martha 29 May 1849
Gilliss Clement to Bailey Bridget Anne 11 Mar 1840
Gilliss Clement to Bennett Sally Ann 13 Jan 1847
Gilliss Ezekiel McClemmy to Holbrook Sally Dennis 23 Feb 1802
Gilliss Joseph to Dashiell Esther 6 May 1800
Gilliss Joseph to Taylor Elizabeth Anne 5 Jan 1852
Gilliss Josiah to Gray Betsy 19 Jan 1813
Gilliss Josiah to Gray Nancy 4 Feb 1817
Gilliss Peter to Nelson Elizabeth 27 Nov 1827
Gipson James to Merreday Nancy 8 Oct 1798
Gist James H. to Cottingham Mary 15 Dec 1812
Givans Peter to Layfield Polly 10 Mar 1819
Gladden George W. to Shores Elizabeth L. 7 Oct 1852
Gladden George W. to Rowe Mary Jane 10 Jan 1852
Glasgow John to Milbourn Mary 16 Aug 1825
Glasgow John to Reeder Elizabeth 13 Aug 1844
Glasgow William J. to Wheelan Leah Jane 10 Feb 1852
Goddard George to Elliott Elizabeth 1 Feb 1836
Goddard Thomas to Reddish Charlotte 18 Mar 1812
Goldsborough M. Worthington to Jones Henrietta M. 8 Nov 1858
Goodman James to Farrington Betsy 18 Mar 1800
Gordon James to Insley Keturah 10 Feb 1825
Gordon Samuel to Bozman Betsy 2 May 1811
Gordy Benjamin to Dorman Anne 26 Nov 1833
Gordy Benjamin H. to Vincent Elizabeth S. 5 Oct 1841
Gordy Daniel to Ballard Elizabeth 13 Jan 1870 C
Gordy Elijah to Black Frances 30 Dec 1828
Gordy Levin S. to Holliday Dolly 26 Jan 1857
Gordy Levin S. to Hearn Maria 28 Jun 1861
Gordy Samuel to Humphreys Leah M. 4 Dec 1843
Gordy William P. to Holland Leah A. 8 Oct 1867
Goslee Alpheus to McIntyre Susan 28 Jan 1868
Goslee Clement to Walter Olivia E. 12 Apr 1836
Goslee Edmond to Weatherly Mary Anne 8 Aug 1826
Goslee Edmund to Dove Caroline 11 Jan 1848
Goslee Edwin to Price Olivia 7 Feb 1871
Goslee Elijah to Venables Eliza 12 Nov 1833
Goslee James to Weatherly Sally 26 Feb 1805
Goslee James M. to Adams Susan 8 Feb 1836
Goslee John to Huffington Nancy 23 Jun 1818

Goslee John to Goslee Ruth 2 Nov 1853
Goslee John S. to Betham Anne Maria 14 Oct 1845
Goslee John T. to Ruark Mary 25 Jan 1848
Goslee John Thomas to Dashiell Elizabeth J. --(?) 1838
Goslee Josiah to Goslee Leah 4 Apr 1804
Goslee Levin to Jones Nelly 8 Jul 1800
Goslee Levin to Moore Elizabeth 31 Jul 1800
Goslee Levin to Hopkins Ann M. 29 Oct 1856
Goslee Levin to Hubbard Leah 1 Jan 1866 C
Goslee Samuel to Phillips Ardilla P. 22 May 1833
Goslee Samul to Culver Martha 7 Feb 1867
Goslee Thomas to Denwood Nancy 15 May 1798
Goslee Thomas to Austin Amelia 1 May 1802
Goslee Thomas to Covington Elizabeth 28 Feb 1809
Goslee Valentine O. to Jenkins Elizabeth J. 4 Aug 1860
Goslee William to Newcomb Sarah 12 Sep 1797
Goslee William J. to Leatherbury Sarah E. 25 Apr 1865
Goswelling David to McCain Anne 11 Feb 1818
Goswelling David to Reese Nelly 19 May 1818
Gouldy Charles to Smith Eliza Anne 8 Feb 1831
Graham Henry R. to Winder Charlotte A.H. 13 Jun 1809
Graham James to Bennett Priscilla 2 Mar 1826
Graham James to Walker Eliza 21 Dec 1830
Graham James to Bennett Nancy 31 Aug 1833
Graham James to Mills Lovey 22 Nov 1843
Graham John to Collier Sally 21 Jan 1800
Graham John to Mitchell Leah 8 Jan 1850
Graham John H. to Webster Nancy L. 1 Nov 1866
Graham Levin to Elliott Ellen 14 Dec 1859
Graham Peter to English Amey 18 Feb 1817
Graham Philip to Stewart Nancy 23 Mar 1813
Graham Philip to Bedsworth Zipporah 28 Jan 1823
Graham Samuel A. to Collier Louisa A. 31 Aug 1852
Grant William to Floyd Leah 15 Mar 1810
Gravener Clement J. to Wright Brittania 31 Mar 1857
Gravenor Benjamin to Graham Polly 5 Jul 1817
Gravenor Benjamin T. to Russell Elizabeth L. 7 Mar 1864
Gravenor Thomas to Walker Margaret 18 Jul 1825
Gravner Benjamin P. to Bennett Eleanor 6 Dec 1847
Gravner Urias T. to Masey Elizabeth 11 Apr 1840

Gray Benjamin to Lowes Esther 14 Nov 1816
Gray John to Adams Margaret 7 Dec 1841
Gray Joshua to Long Mary Anne 1 Jun 1854
Gray Levin to Wright Elizabeth 4 Jan 1803
Gray Peter to Moore Betsy 4 Oct 1813
Gray William to Ross Mary E. 1 May 1854
Gray William P. to Ross Hester S. 14 Nov 1855
Grayham James to Bennett Sally 6 Apr 1847
Grayham Lewis to Wilson Mary 29 Oct 1811
Green Abednego to Lankford Mary 8 Nov 1808
Green Abednego to Daugherty Priscilla 1 Jan 1817
Green Abednego to Johnston Sarah L. 19 Jul 1864
Green Alexander H. to Bailey Mary E.W. 12 Jan 1864
Green Anthony B. to Dashiell Mary E.J. 3 Aug 1837
Green Asa to Green Elizabeth 5 Jan 1805
Green Asa to Christopher Eliza Jane 8 Feb 1848
Green Benjamin F. to Parkinson Anne E. 14 Aug 1865
Green Benjamin K. to Wallace Elizabeth 16 Jul 1834
Green Benjamin K. to Mure Eliza 5 Oct 1857
Green Benjamin K. to Revill Caroline E. 29 Mar 1859
Green Charles C. to Hughes Alice H. 14 Apr 1857
Green Frederick to Whitney Drusilla 27 Dec 1821
Green Henry J. to Dunn Biddy J. 10 Jan 1854
Green James to Holder Louie 18 Aug 1823
Green James to Johnson Eliza 8 Jun 1858 C
Green James S. to Bailey Sallie A. 25 Jun 1863
Green John to Johnson Polly 2 Apr 1811
Green John Wesley to Roach Susan Rosanna 21 May 1868 C
Green Joseph to Lankford Anna 5 Aug 1868 C
Green Joshua to Webster Sally 5 Dec 1798
Green Josiah to Gale Margaret 18 Aug 1866
Green Robert H. to Phillips Mary C. 12 May 1863
Green Samuel to Lankford Mary 26 Dec 1826
Green Theodore B.L. to Lankford Mary J. 10 Feb 1871
Green William to Russell Mary 29 Feb 1820
Green William S. to Leach Anne R. 31 Jul 1855
Green Zadock to Holder Eleanor 17 Sep 1798
Green Zebedee to Majors Mary Ann 15 Jan 1850
Greene Charles C. to Beauchamp Amelia H. 16 Dec 1834
Greene Isaac K. to Lankford Dolly B. 27 Jan 1834

Griffin Azariah to Moore Sarah Catherine 27 Apr 1866
Griffin Azariah to Black Mary E. 2 Jan 1871 C
Griffin John H. to Hayman Sarah M.M. 18 Dec 1839
Griffith Daniel to Jones Betsy 11 Aug 1829
Griffith Henry P. to Pool Ella B. 13 Sep 1871
Griffith John J. to Robertson Elizabeth E. 16 Feb 1864
Griffith Salathiel to Rickets Phillis 23 Jul 1814
Griffith Salathiel to Harris Hetty 20 Feb 1828
Grimes John to Kennerly Patty 14 Dec 1813
Grimes Major to Jackson Sally 20 Dec 1838
Grimes Major to Jones Lizzie 9 Dec 1868 C
Grinnolds Henry C. to Fletcher Sally S. 29 Oct 1846
Grooms William to Abbott Polly 9 Aug 1826
Grove Augustus G. to Morgan Mary E. 11 Jun 1853
Grumble James to Wright Elizabeth 29 Jan 1811
Guillet Gilbert to Fontaine Elizabeth 11 Mar 1834
Gullett William to Miller Lovey 9 Jun 1807
Gullette Peter to Porter Jane 11 Nov 1818
Gunby David to Evans Grace 14 Dec 1802
Gunby David to Sloans Mary 15 Jul 1812
Gunby Elisha to Coulbourn Milcah 1 Aug 1826
Gunby Elisha J. to Costen Anne Eliza 16 May 1848
Gunby George to Robinson Sarah 25 Apr 1867 C
Gunby Hiram H. (Dr.) to Riggin Emily F. 18 Jan 1856
Gunby James to Ballard Priscilla 25 Aug 1868 C
Gunby John to Somers Charlotte 18 Dec 1838
Gunby William to Somers Jane 16 Jun 1829
Gupton Peter to Cantwell Betsy 28 Nov 1815
Gurley Joseph to Wright Polly 25 Jul 1800
Gurney John to Earnest Eleanor 2 Jan 1817
Hack James D. to Ballard Caroline E. 11 Jan 1859
Hack James D. to Dashiell Clara G. 22 Jun 1868
Hagerson William to Dixon Mary 9 Nov 1808
Hales Francis to Ford Martha P. 21 Jun 1864
Hales Jacob to Langsdale Sarah 22 Feb 1825
Hales John H. to Revill Mary J. 29 Dec 1869
Haley James H. to Covington Henrietta 15 Apr 1851
Haley John S. to Hemingway Mary A. 6 Sep 1864
Hall Asa to Brodwater Cordelia 6 Dec 1848
Hall Charles to Tawes Peggy 14 Jul 1809

Hall Daniel to Ballard Maria 10 Feb 1817
Hall Daniel to Ballard Gatty 21 Jan 1868 C
Hall Edward L. to Riggin Martha 4 Sep 1824
Hall Edward L. to Gibbons Elizabeth 21 Feb 1827
Hall Elijah T. to Tull Maria A. 10 Oct 1848
Hall Elijah T. to Tull Sarah J. 13 Nov 1860
Hall George to Waters Margaret 2 Jan 1868 C
Hall George A. to Lawrence Elizabeth A. 26 Apr 1866
Hall George W. to Kellum Mary Caroline 29 Oct 1856
Hall George W. to Gale Maria 10 Apr 1866 C
Hall Henry to Robinson Mary C. 21 Mar 1871 C
Hall Henry W. to Whittington Sarah E. 12 May 1856
Hall James to Addams Sarah 16 Nov 1801
Hall James to Mungar Peggy 23 May 1820
Hall James to Sudler Eleanor 16 Apr 1836
Hall Jesse to McCready Mary 2 Jun 1807
Hall Jesse to Chamberlin Rachel 3 Aug 1822
Hall John to Puss Lucresa 14 Jun 1803
Hall John to Miles Atalanta 24 Jan 1815
Hall John to Stevenson Harriet 21 Jan 1825
Hall John to Hall Martha 22 Nov 1864
Hall John M. to Adams Emiline R. 30 Apr 1832
Hall John M. to Williams Mary Jane 26 Oct 1833
Hall John W. to Waters Susan S. 17 Apr 1819
Hall Lazarus M. to Disharoon Elizabeth E. 18 Dec 1838
Hall Lazarus M. to Shores Mary 4 Jan 1865
Hall Levin to Adams Zipporah 31 Jan 1820
Hall Levin to Sudler Eleanor G. 5 Dec 1837
Hall Littleton J.H. to Hall Julia A.K. 9 Feb 1863
Hall Noah to Layfield Betsy 24 Jan 1797
Hall Philip to Price Leah 16 Jun 1799
Hall Philip to Mezick Nancy 5 Apr 1824
Hall Richard to Moore Sally 20 Mar 1804
Hall Richard to Lankford Patty 4 Jan 1815
Hall Robert to Conner Elizabeth 26 Feb 1799
Hall Robert H. to Holland Harriet 14 Jan 1845
Hall Robert L. to Landon Phebe E. 30 Oct 1866
Hall Samuel to Hall Matilda 7 Jul 1809
Hall Samuel L. to Miles Mary C. 1 Mar 1862
Hall Thomas to Chambers Polly 25 Dec 1797

Hall Thomas to Scott Molly 8 Sep 1801
Hall Thomas to Cox Sally 14 Jul 1829
Hall Thomas E. to Dorsey Elizabeth 1 Jun 1864
Hall Thomas E. to Dorsey Susan 12 Oct 1869
Hall Tubman to Mure Mary E. 2 Jan 1855
Hall Tubman L. to Maddux Sarah H. 17 Nov 1829
Hall Walter J. to Sparrow Mary E. 18 Feb 1867
Hall Wesley to Davis Alice 9 Jun 1871 C
Hall William to Long Rose 31 Dec 1808
Hall William C. to Maddux Mary Anne 9 Feb 1836
Hall William H. to Sterling Laney C. 30 Dec 1862
Hall William J. to Kimble Carrie E. 8 Aug 1871
Hall William Samuel to Briddle Martha 22 Jan 1856
Halsey Martin to Carter Polly 19 Jun 1827
Hambury Jesse to Travers Eleanor 30 Dec 1844
Hambury John to Covington Priscilla 22 Nov 1838
Hambury Thomas to Evans Jane 8 Feb 1848
Hammond Charles to Davis Mary 19 Nov 1822
Hammond John T. (Dr.) to Toadvine Esther P. 16 Nov 1858
Hanbury John to Barkley Jane 2 Sep 1856
Hancock William T.(?) to Fields Darky 29 Oct 1816
Handy Albert F. to White Nancy 22 Sep 1868
Handy Alexander H. to Stuart Susan N. 14 Jan 1835
Handy Alfred to Handy Adelia 24 Dec 1867 C
Handy Arthur to Davy Milcah 3 Nov 1865 C
Handy Erastus to Adams Virginia 31 May 1855
Handy George to Wilson Sally 20 Dec 1815
Handy George to Wilson Mary Ellen 4 Jul 1844
Handy George to Whittington Anne 28 Jul 1857
Handy George to Gibbons Margaret 23 Dec 1867 C
Handy Henry to Campbell Nancy 28 Jan 1797
Handy Henry to Marshall Mary I. 18 May 1813
Handy Henry to Waters Sarah J. 3 Nov 1871
Handy Henry S. to Parks Eliza J. 31 Jan 1852
Handy Isaac to Marshall Hetty 25 Dec 1815
Handy Isaac to Gale Adeline 4 Oct 1866 C
Handy Isaac to Milbourn Mary F. 25 Dec 1871 C
Handy James to Reddish Tarsey 5 Jan 1802
Handy James to Milbourn Harriet 24 Jun 1828
Handy James to Jones Martha 3 Feb 1836

Handy James to Davey Margaret 26 Dec 1865 C
Handy James C. to Cluff Sarah 22 Jan 1816
Handy James H. to Gilliss Maria A.P. 19 Jun 1812
Handy John S. to Hughes Elizabeth T. 10 Sep 1834
Handy John T. to Holland Caroline J. 4 Dec 1837
Handy Joseph to Waller Mary 19 Mar 1798
Handy Joseph to Jenkins Mary 19 Mar 1810
Handy Joseph to Turpin Anne 24 Mar 1812
Handy Levin to Cluff Susan 15 Aug 1815
Handy Littleton D. to Jones Sophia E. 13 Apr 1837
Handy Noah to Goslee Rachell 4 Jan 1827
Handy Richard H. to Gordon Betsy 16 Jun 1798
Handy Samuel K. to Wilson Henrietta M. 7 May 1832
Handy Samuel S. to Powell Virginia A. 28 Jun 1858
Handy Severn to Miller Sarah A. 19 Dec 1854
Handy Stephen to Collins Martha Jane 20 Jan 1859 C
Handy Thomas H. to Wilson Ritta M. 15 Dec 1846
Handy Thomas H. to Dougherty Mary 16 Mar 1869
Handy Thomas J. to Miles Marian O. 6 Jan 1868
Handy Thomas W. to Henry Matilda 7 Jan 1801
Handy Thomas W. to Roberts Sarah 3 Oct 1814
Handy Thomas W. to Lowe Mary C. 1 Oct 1866 C
Handy William to Cox Martha 13 Feb 1816
Handy William to Lankford Julia Anne 17 Sep 1856
Handy William to Miles Milly 27 Dec 1864 C
Handy William H. to Lankford Sarah E. 7 Mar 1871
Haney Henry S. to Bell Jane W. 13 Sep 1831
Hanson James to Dashiell Adaline 20 Dec 1871 C
Harcum Elisha B. to Hitch Mary 8 Dec 1829
Harcum Henry L. to Allen Elizabeth A. 20 Nov 1844
Harcum John to Polk Nancy 22 Feb 1803
Harcum Lee to Polk Elizabeth 17 Feb 1801
Harcum Lee P. to Jones Mary 15 Nov 1823
Hardesty Henry S.C. to Lowe Elizabeth A. 22 Apr 1867
Harding Charles W. to King Elizabeth 4 Apr 1821
Hargis George to Collins Betsy 23 Feb 1829
Hargis John P. to Toadvine Caroline C. 8 Dec 1856
Hargis William T. to Costen Sarah E.N. 3 Nov 1846
Harman John Wesley to Dutton Mary 4 Jan 1870 C
Harmon Levin Thomas to Black Nelly Jane 19 Mar 1855

Harper William to Polk Nelly 24 Jul 1798
Harper William to Polk Rebecca 23 Oct 1811
Harrington Alfred to Denson Julia 22 Jan 1850
Harrington James to Street Nelly 6 Jul 1833
Harrington John to Summers Harriet 12 Oct 1819
Harrington John to Paden Elizabeth 12 Nov 1846
Harrington John to Moore Sally J. 7 Aug 1866
Harrington John P. to McNeal Sarah A.M. 18 Apr 1854
Harrington John W. to Croswell Mary Ann 10 Nov 1863
Harrington Joseph to Bailey Leah 17 Dec 1834
Harrington Samuel to McNeal Louisa I. 10 Mar 1854
Harrington Shepherd to Horner Patty 21 Jun 1810
Harrington William to Durham Anne 7 Jan 1800
Harrington William to Mezick Christianna 22 Apr 1863
Harris Epraim to Cox Betsy 20 Mar 1804
Harris George S. to Cannon Elizabeth A. 16 Jan 1834
Harris Henry to White Louisa 1812
Harris Howard to Harris Leah 3 Jan 1867 C
Harris Isaac to Taylor Marget 24 Jan 1797
Harris Isaac to Davis Sarah 25 Sep 1827
Harris Isaac to Bounds Sarah Ann 24 Jun 1851
Harris Isaac to Simms Rosina 5 Nov 1866
Harris Isaac to Cornish Esther 3 Mar 1869 C
Harris Isaac (of John) to Adams Mary 14 Apr 1819
Harris James to Hobbs Mary R. 17 Jul 1798
Harris James to Worten Polly 1 Sep 1810
Harris James to Wilson Eleanor 22 Jun 1819
Harris John to Webster Betsey 12 Nov 1811
Harris John to Harris Anne 3 Oct 1814
Harris John to Lord Caroline 14 Dec 1843
Harris John W. to Watson Catherine 2 Apr 1870
Harris Levin M. to Dryden Matilda A. 31 Dec 1861
Harris Littleton to Campbell Mary 10 May 1810
Harris Littleton to Disharoon Amelia 29 Jun 1813
Harris Littleton to Abbott Polly 6 Aug 1816
Harris Littleton to Harris Mary R. 27 Jun 1822
Harris Littleton to Moore Elizabeth 22 Jan 1851
Harris Littleton T. to Coulbourn Joanna G. 29 Jun 1848
Harris Perry to Cheser Nancy 5 Jun 1834
Harris Samuel J. to Sims Francis A. 9 Mar 1863

Harris Samuel J. to Shores Mary A. 19 Sep 1867
Harris Sl(???) to Mezick Nancy 28 May 1844
Harris Solomon to Roberts Elizabeth 14 Dec 1841
Harris Solomon to Williams Milcah 25 Jan 1866
Harris Stephen to Owens Sally 15 Jan 1799
Harris Stephen to Hopkins Lucresa 21 Aug 1804
Harris Thomas to Harris Louisa 19 Dec 1822
Harris Thomas H. to Harris Frances 13 Jan 1869
Harris William to Evans Jane 25 Jul 1815
Harris William to Mezick Mary 25 Feb 1834
Harris William to Miles Catharine 1 Jun 1841
Harris William to Webster Polly 4 Mar 1845
Harris William to Furbush Getturah 7 Dec 1852
Harris William to Renshaw Jane 17 Mar 1869
Harris William J. to Phillips Sally E. 12 May 1840
Harris William J. to Gibson Margaret E. 5 Jan 1860
Harris William P. to Moore Ann 27 Sep 1825
Harrison James to Dashiell Alliphair 2 Jun 1802
Harriss Joseph C. to Palmer Elizabeth 30 Jan 1838
Harriss Robert H. to Horsey Emily C. 18 Apr 1870 C
Hart George B. (Lieut.) to Parsons Mary W. 4 Feb 1862
Harvey Daniel James to Waters Sarah Elizabeth 1 Nov 1865 C
Harwood William B. to Waters Rebecca B. 3 Jul 1833
Hasting Stephen to Henderson Elizabeth 21 Mar 1854
Hastings Alexander to Malone Dolly R. 29 Jun 1844
Hastings Alexander C. to Beauchamp Matilda E. 4 Jan 1842
Hastings Elzey to Ellis Phillis 9 Oct 1847
Hastings Jehu P. to Mason Sarah 1 Feb 1869
Hastings Joshua to Callaway Elizabeth 20 Nov 1838
Hastings Thomas D. to Parks Ann Maria 16 Jan 1850
Hattan Charles W. to Molir Martha E. 4 May 1867
Hattan Elijah T. to Humphreys Mary M. 20 Jan 1865
Hatton Francis to _____ Mary Anne 1 Nov 1836
Hatton John C. to Green Esther 24 Dec 1808
Hawes Charles to Martin Betsey 14 Apr 1801
Hawes James to Owens Hetty 5 Jul 1815
Hawes James to Bromley Polly 15 Sep 1818
Hawes James to Malone Sally 6 May 1833
Hawes Samuel to Gray Polly 9 Mar 1821
Hawkins Henry. to Ward Milcah 7 Nov 1868

Hawkins Walter to Duncan Caroline 31 Aug 1847
Haws Samuel J.M. to Majors Isabella J. 28 Jun 1859
Haydon Henry L. to White Hester 17 May 1859
Hayman Alexander to Jones Elizabeth 6 Nov 1871 C
Hayman Alfred I. to Vincent Annie A. 19 Dec 1867
Hayman Cornelius Riggin to Smith Anne 17 Dec 1799
Hayman David J. to Toadvine Ellena 11 Jan 1837
Haynab George to Tilghman Sarah 11 Dec 1823
Hayman George to Underhill Eliza 14 Oct 1841 C
Hayman George W. to Marriner Mary 23 Mar 1871
Hayman Gilliss W. to Brown Mary 2 Feb 1841
Hayman Handy to Brown Polly 2 Feb 1808
Hayman Harrison to Jones Julia 9 Apr 1867 C
Hayman Henry to Covington Eunice 11 Jan 1814
Hayman Henry J. to Moore Margaret C. 2 Sep 1862
Hayman Henry M. to Saucer Sarah Anne 16 Oct 1834
Hayman Hezekiah to Riggin Hetty 18 Mar 1800
Hayman Hezekiah to Costen Esther E. 28 Apr 1842
Hayman James to Pollitt Eleanor 22 Aug 1815
Hayman James to Crouch Elizabeth F. 5 Feb 1867
Hayman James H. to Tull Henrietta 7 Mar 1870
Hayman James R. to Hitch Eleanor 27 Sep 1826
Hayman Jeptha to Fooks Mahala 30 Jan 1838
Hayman Jeptha to Benson Sally W. 27 Jan 1847
Hayman John to Tilghman Nancy 16 Kay 1809
Hayman John to Marshall Betsy 7 Dec 1833
Hayman John to Bailey Eliza J. 22 Jun 1864
Hayman John S. to White Matilda 30 Dec 1867 C
Hayman John T. to Hayman Mary M. 28 Fe8 1854
Hayman John W. to Puzey Louisa 31 Mar 1858
Hayman Joseph H. to Adams Mary 2 Sep 1835
Hayman Levin P. to Brown Rebecca Ann 26 Jun 1838
Hayman Littleton to Christopher Sarah 7 Mar 1831
Hayman Randall to Pollitt Mary 25 Feb 1862
Hayman Revill to Moore Elizabeth 17 Mar 1829
Hayman Revill to Huffington Martha Jane 19 Jan 1853
Hayman Stephen to McGrath Betsey 6 Jun 1804
Hayman Thomas to Covington Polly 28 Mar 1815
Hayman Thomas W. to Washburn Sally E. 6 Feb 1866
Hayman Uriah W. to Brown Susan R. 26 Mar 1845

Hayman William to Lankford Cassey 31 Oct 1817
Haymond Levin H. to Gordy Lavinia E. 28 Aug 1866
Haynie Gamaliel C. to Leech Emily J. 13 May 1870
Haynie John H. to Zeen Cornelia E. 29 Oct 1866
Hayward George to Crosdale Anne 14 Oct 1863
Hayward Lewis to Costen Laura 23 Jun 1870 C
Hayward Robert J. to Dixon Anna M. 13 Nov 1850 C
Hearn Benjamin to Vincent Elizabeth 23 Apr 1825
Hearn Daniel to Miller Aurelia 24 May 1842
Hearn Harvey to Hearn Mary Ellen 30 Nov 1863
Hearn Hiram to Lowe Jane 19 Mar 1828
Hearn Ichabod to Harris Lucretia 17 Sep 1833
Hearn Jacob to Hyland Elizabeth A. 2 Jun 1863
Hearn James to Knipshilt Betsy 31 Jul 1810
Hearn John to Graham Hester 14 Dec 1853
Hearn John A.S. to Catlin Alice C. 12 Nov 1866
Hearn John William to Dashiell Adeline O.31 Oct 1855
Hearn Jonathan to Sirmon Sarah 15 Oct 1851
Hearn Nathaniel to Purnell Leah 16 Feb 1857
Hearn Spencer to Wilson Eliza 15 Apr 1797
Hearn William to Hearn Sarah 7 Jan 1804
Hearn William to Wilson Julietta 20 Feb 1832
Hearn William W. to Jenkins Eliza J. 11 Dec 1860
Heath James to Walston Jane 4 Jul 1827
Heath John M. to Pollitt Mary 7 May 1829
Heath John M. to Willing Mary Anne 21 Jul 1835
Heath John T.W. to White Susan P. 7 Jan 1854
Heath Josiah to Lokey Henrietta 22 Nov 1859
Heath Josiah W. to Hall Leah 25 Feb 1818
Heath Samuel to Turpin Peggy 29 May 1799
Heath Thomas to Mure Mary Ellen 19 Dec 1850
Heath Tubman to Phoebus Sally 28 Jul 1863
Heath Tubman to Hopkins Sarah 29 Dec 1868
Heath William to White Mary 12 Aug 1822
Heath William S. to White Elizabeth E. 30 Jan 1849
Heaton Austin C. to Jones Arianna F. 2 Oct 1861
Helfenstein Edward to Long Julia A. 25 Jun 1855
Hemmingway Thomas L. to Tull Ann M. 23 Jul 1851
Hemmons John to Jackson Sarah 19 May 1829
Henderson David to Stevenson Sally A. 11 Nov 1862

Henderson Henry J. T. to Merrill Amanda M. 12 Sep 1867
Henderson Henry S. to Lankford Mary S. 3 Mar 1841
Henderson Jacob to Taylor Hetty 11 Dec 1821
Henderson James to Milbourn Elizabeth A. 17 Jul 1848
Henderson Rouse to Paden Sarah 30 Oct 1832
Henderson Thomas to Adams Hester Jane 7 Jan 1851
Henderson William to Taylor Anne Scarborough 21 Dec 1848
Henderson William to Nelson Cassy 12 Feb 1856
Henry Charles C. to Briding Leda 18 Feb 1837
Henry Hugh M. to Gale Harriett 26 Jan 1802
Henry John H. to Spence Eva 12 Apr 1853
Henry John H. to Furniss Sally R. 16 Oct 1854
Henry Josiah to Outten Milly 6 Sep 1853 C
Henry Robert to Waters Lovey Ann 8 Dec 1856
Heron Thomas to Abbitt Mary 31 Jan 1797
Herron Edward to Parks Martha 6 Nov 1829
Hewett James to Nelson Naomi 20 Feb 1804
Hewett James to Blake Hester Anne 18 Jul 1843
Hewett William J. to Merideth Sarah E. 8 Jun 1870
Hickey Dennis to Burdick Melinda 24 Jul 1868
Hickman Edward W. to Anderson Minerva C. 25 Oct 1870
Hickman George R. to Price Letitia A. 27 Sep 1860
Hickman Isaac to Tyler Eleanor 21 Dec 1835
Hickman John W. to Miles Hester A. 24 Jan 1871
Hickman Robert to Jones Clementine 31 Jan 1861
Hickman Theodore F.J. to Cottingham Mary E.F. 3 Apr 1866
Hickman William to White Nelly 11 Mar 1800
Hickman William to Shores Margaret 14 Feb 1868
Hickman William to White Mary E. 14 Sep 1870
Hickman William R. to Dixon Olivia A. 29 Nov 1870
Hicks Levi to Gale Leah 4 Aug 1869 C
Higgins Francis to Riggin Priscilla 5 Mar 1845
Higgins James to Walter Elizabeth 20 Jan 1840
Hill Aaron to Taylor Margaret A. 5 Feb 1861
Hill Augustus to Hopkins Elizabeth 9 Oct 1822
Hill Charles to Linton Rosa Anne 25 May 1847
Hill James to Ford Elizabeth 24 May 1859
Hill James (Jr) to Williss Nancy 9 Oct 1797
Hill John S. to Rider Anne 21 Jul 1812
Hill Joshua to Moore Hetty 25 Jul 1814

Hill Reuben to Collins Nancy 28 Feb 1815
Hill Reuben Henry to Jones Polly 4 Mar 1800
Hill Severn James to Culver Amy 12 Jan 1847
Hill William to Wilkison Sarah 2 Jul 1832
Hillman George to Richardson Lecay 5 Dec 1820
Hillman James Winder to Polk Martha Ellen 2 Oct 1857
Hilman James W. to Cary Jane 1 Oct 1844
Hilman Thomas C. to Polk Sally 2 May 1855
Hitch Adam to Malone Eveline 13 Feb 1828
Hitch Adams to Fookes Polly 25 Jul 1809
Hitch Benjamin to Taylor Leah 28 May 1803
Hitch Benjamin to Lankford Mary 8 Jun 1830
Hitch Ezekiel to Crockett Lerepta 16 Dec 1843
Hitch George W. to Seward Esther Anne 13 Mar 1838
Hitch Isaac to Gale Martha E. 6 Jun 1871 C
Hitch John to Polk Jane 23 Jan 1797
Hitch John to Disharoon Milly 21 Feb 1797
Hitch Joseph to Muir Sarah 24 Sep 1799
Hitch Joshua L. to Cathell Martha E. 29 Jan 1867
Hitch Levin to West Alice 1 Mar 1808
Hitch Levin to McBryde Sally 2 Jan 1832
Hitch Littleton to Graham Jane 18 Dec 1832
Hitch Robert to Sutton Leah 20 Dec 1803
Hitch Robert to Brewington Martha 15 Dec 1824
Hitch Robert to Hearn Nancy 23 Jan 1854
Hitch Robert J. to Phoebus Sarah A. 11 Jan 1865
Hitch Thomas to Leatherbury Mary 31 Dec 1822
Hitch Thomas to Hitch Elizabeth 7 Apr 1825
Hitch Thomas to Phillips Elizabeth 23 Nov 1836
Hitch Thomas to Mills Maria J. 27 Jan 1840
Hitch Thomas to Pollitt Eliza E. 17 Feb 1840
Hitch Thomas J. to Mezick Elizabeth J. 9 Jan 1856
Hitch Tubman to Malone Mary 6 Feb 1833
Hitch William to Morris Nancy 23 Oct 1827
Hitch William A. to Bassett Rosanna 28 Jul 1829
Hitchens William to Horner Nancy 2 Jan 1838
Hitchens William to Horner Nisey E. 17 Apr 1845
Hitchings George W. to Walters Teresa 9 Mar 1860
Hitchins George W. to Webster Mary C. 3 Dec 1870
Hobbs Gabriel to Hayman Elizabeth H. 16 Jan 1838

Hobbs James to Palmer Nancy 18 Jan 1820
Hobbs John to Kemp Rebecca 5 Jun 1804
Hobbs John to Wilson Nancy 17 Jul 1832
Hobbs John to Wilson Mary Ann 5 Oct 1838
Hobbs John L. to Blunt Anne 16 Jan 1812
Hobbs Levin to Simpkins Mary 17 Jan 1833
Hobbs Littleton to Ingersoll Sarah 11 Aug 1824
Hobbs Matthias to Whitney Esther 11 Feb 1800
Hobbs Matthias to Cullen Sarah 2 Oct 1802
Hobbs William to Walter Charlotte 9 May 1832
Hoffman Daniel to Gibson Ellen 24 May 1854
Hoffman John to Howard Katharine 6 Dec 1803
Hogskin James (aka Miller) to Hobbs Mary 25 Jul 1815
Hogskin James (alias Miller) to Hobbs Mary 25 Jul 1815
Hogue William V. to Hyland Virginia L. 18 Jun 1866
Holbrook Hampleton to Pollitt Sally 27 Jun 1867 C
Holbrook Samuel to Gilliss Nelly D. 23 Oct 1798
Holerook Samuel to Dashiell Jane Lucas 26 Jul 1803
Holbrook Samuel G. to Leatherbury Priscilla A. 18 Apr 1822
Holbrook Samuel G. to Woolford Maria 7 Aug 1844
Holbrook Thomas to Irving Ann 7 Sep 1825
Holbrook Thomas to Morris Sarah 21 Jan 1833
Holbrook Thomas (Jr) to Elzey Mary 3 Jun 1816
Holbrook Thomas W. to Dashiell Araminta M. 17 Jun 1857
Holder William to Seabreeze Eleanor 15 Feb 1825
Holder Zebedee to Durham Betsy 17 Feb 1827
Holder Zebedee to Hopkins Martha Anne 30 Dec 1843
Holladay William H. to Langsdale Jane 9 Nov 1831
Hollady Joshua W. to Layfield Mary E. 4 Jan 1864
Holland Daniel to Miles Rachel 1812
Holland George to Lankford Mary Ann 24 Feb 1824
Holland George to Howard Sarah E. 4 Jan 1868
Holland George S. to Ward Elizabeth 21 Feb 1849
Holland Isaac to Ford Mary 2 Jul 1816
Holland James to Dryden Nancy 22 Feb 1817
Holland James E. to Ford Mary M. 6 Mar 1866
Holland Jeremiah to Price Damarias 7 Sep 1861
Holland Jesse to Wilkins Nancy 18 Feb 1799
Holland John to Miles Nancy 27 Jul 1824
Holland John to Lankford Emeline 5 Jul 1825

Holland John H. to Russell Catharine 25 Jun 1842
Holland John H. to Langford Julia F. 10 Nov 1846
Holland John H. to Stevenson Sarah A. 8 Feb 1859
Holland Josiah to Boston Bridget 19 May 1809
Holland Norah to Marshall Hetty 27 Oct 1829
Holland Samuel to Adams Mary 17 Jan 1831
Holland Smith to Cox Mary A. 6 Jul 1848
Holland Smith H. to Lankford Aurelia 8 Feb 1837
Holland Smith H. to Hudson Harriet 14 Aug 1845
Holland Stokely to Ford Charlotte T. 28 Aug 1849
Holland Thomas to Benson Pollyy 4 Jun 1816
Holland Thomas to Lankford Betsy 4 Dec 1821
Holland Thomas H. to Hasting Mary E. 4 May 1865
Holland Thomas J. to Bailey Amanda J. 23 Nov 1847
Holland William to Spence Sophia 12 Jan 1819
Holland William to Lankford Leah A. 27 Jan 1824
Holland William to Ford Nelly W. 12 Jul 1825
Holland William to Disharoon Louisianna 8 Mar 1859
Holland William to Williams Mary E. 29 Jan 1862
Holland William J. to Nelson Hattie 9 May 1870
Holland William T. to Croswell Mary W. 6 Jan 1858
Holleren Bartholomew to Caldwell Ann 22 Jan 1798
Holliday George to Grant Sophia N. 16 Oct 1834
Holliday John to Floyd Sarah 10 Sep 1834
Holliday John to Collier Sarah Anne 12 Mar 1839
Holloway Daniel I. to Adkins Gertrude 23 Jan 1867
Holloway Ephraim to Cordray Mary 19 Dec 1848
Holloway John to Turner Mary 15 Nov 1864
Holoway John W. to Hearn Mary E. 4 Sep 1855
Holt Greenbury to Crockett Eleanor 23 Jul 1833
Holt Robert to Bramble Belilah 6 Mar 1810
Homer James M. to Kelly Keziah E. 2 May 1849
Hopper James to McCree Eleanor 11 May 1829
Hooper Thomas to Sturgis Sally 24 Nov 1803
Hooper William T. to Freeney Leah 7 Jan 1845
Hooston John to Hicks Anna 19 Mar 1866
Hooton George to Lokey Sarah 27 Apr 1870
Hopewell Jesse to Johnson Amely 8 Nov 1871
Hopkins Elijah to Parks Polly 12 Mar 1814
Hopkins George to Nicholson Elizabeth 9 Feb 1808

Hopkins George to Holder Molly 8 Jul 1817
Hopkins George to Cannon Nicy 24 Mar 1819
Hopkins George to Phobus Mary Anne 1 Nov 1836
Hopkins George to Windsor Sarah Anne 30 Jun 1847
Hopkins George (of Matt) to Winright Jane E.B. 15 Jan 1822
Hopkins George A.J. to Larmore Hester A. 20 Nov 1855
Hopkins George W. to Nelson Elizabeth E. -- Jun 1837
Hopkins Henry to Foxwell Mahala 1 Jul 1824
Hopkins Henry to Moore Molly 11 Jan 1839
Hopkins Henry to Shores Martha 19 Apr 1870
Hopkins Henry F. to Haws Mary C. 13 Sep 1853
Hopkins Isaac to Harris Martha 16 Jan 1798
Hopkins Isaac to Graham Leah 6 Dec 1833
Hopkins Isaac S. to Webster Melissa 25 Nov 1863
Hopkins James to Walston Peggy 8 Oct 1808
Hopkins James to Walston Polly 21 Aug 1811
Hopkins James to Larmore Margaritta 22 Feb 1854
Hopkins James A. to Harrington Molly 10 May 1834
Hopkins Jesse K. to Dorsey Elizabeth S. 20 Sep 1827
Hopkins John to Dickerson Leah 7 Nov 1797
Hopkins John to Foxwell Nancy 21 Jan 1800
Hopkins John to Ackworth Mary Ann 11 Sep 1821
Hopkins John J. to Mills Amanda 8 Nov 1853
Hopkins John M. to Phillips Margaret E. 25 Jul 1865
Hopkins Joseph to Parks Martha 18 Oct 1855
Hopkins Joshua to Mills Sarah 10 Aug 1865
Hopkins Matthias D. to Dashiell Nelly 16 Mar 1799
Hopkins Mitchell to Drain Mary W. 3 Sep 1834
Hopkins Onesimus to Insley Elizabeth A. 21 Aug 1866
Hopkins Richard to Twilly Elizabeth 13 Dec 1796
Hopkins Richard to Airse Sally 23 Apr 1799
Hopkins Richard to Taylor Mary E. 15 Sep 1835
Hopkins Samuel to Moore Jemima 24 Oct 1799
Hopkins Samuel to Kennard Polly 13 Sep 1804
Hopkins Stephen to Wilson Elizabeth 30 Aug 1808
Hopkins Stephen to Handy Priscilla 13 Jan 1817
Hopkins Stephen to Dashiell Margaret 2 Jan 1821
Hopkins Stephen to Jones Sarah J. 17 Mar 1841
Hopkins Stephen A. to Linton Sarah 10 Feb 1852
Hopkins Stephen A. to Jackson Esther 25 Oct 1865

Hopkins Thomas to Reddish Hetty 3 Aug 1797
Hopkins Thomas to Collins Emma 30 Oct 1815
Hopkins Washington to Brown Emeline 4 Jan 1855
Hopkins William to Collier Leah 13 Jan 1801
Hopkins William to Linton Sally 27 Mar 1838
Hopkins William (Jr) to Wailes Margaret 24 Oct 1825
Hopkins William (of Levi) to Collier Elizabeth 11 Oct 1814
Hopkins William W. to Taylor Henrietta 24 Feb 1863
Hopkins Zacheous to Standford Sally 7 Jan 1817
Horner Benjamin to Webster Sarah Ellen 5 Mar 1844
Horner David to Webster Melissa J. 30 May 1854
Horner Francis to Horner Emily 10 Apr 1866
Horner George to Horner Charlotte 14 Jun 1848
Horner George W. to Bramble Susan 16 Jun 1864
Horner James to Horner Sarah 2 Jan 1816
Horner James to Kirwin Betsy 29 Dec 1827
Horner Jakes to Riche Mary 10 Apr 1863
Horner Jesse H. to Patent Mary E. 27 Aug 1860
Horner John to Marsh Elizabeth 12 Jan 1836
Horner John T. to Shores Mary Jane 2 Aug 1849
Horner John W. to Jackson Maria J. 3 Jul 1860
Horner Levi to Dunn Dolly 5 Dec 1820
Horner Levi W. to Messick Elizabeth 28 Aug 1849
Horner Levin to Lecompte Mary 12 Mar 1834
Horner Louder T. to Webster Amanda J. 11 Jun 1849
Horner Loudy to Lewis Lucinda 17 Jan 1834
Horner Moses to Williams Susan 15 Oct 1828
Horner Moses to Bloodsworth Kitty 14 Jan 1833
Horner Traverse to Webster Rebecca 2 Jan 1805
Horner William to Jones Anne 3 Feb 1826
Horner William to Wallace Mary 3 Jan 1834
Horner William to Willy Harriet 22 Jan 1834
Horner Willim to Calloway Nancy 26 Sep 1862
Horner William B. to Webster Mary A. 29 Aug 1865
Horseman Alexander to Covington Anne 20 Mar 1848
Horseman Arnold to Bozman Betsy 18 Jan 1817
Horseman Henry to Dunn Priscilla 14 Aug 1818
Horseman Hugh to Dix Anne 10 Apr 1861
Horseman Jesse to Willey Nancy 10 Dec 1850
Horseman John to Timmons Mary 17 Nov 1801

Horseman John to Brown Sally A. 12 Feb 1861
Horseman Severn to Larmore Mary 24 Nov 1824
Horseman William J. to Livingston Mary A. 17 Feb 1852
Horsey Albert R. to Somers Leah 12 Jan 1847
Horsey Charles to Selby Hessey 25 Apr 1815
Horsey Charles to Phillips Milcah 11 Aug 1830
Horsey Custis W. to Handy Sarah E. 27 Apr 1869
Horsey Daniel J. to Waters Mary W. 8 Jun 1867 C
Horsey Edgar W. to Hickman Mary E. 3 Apr 1860
Horsey Edmund C. to Kennerly Eglentine 17 Feb 1840
Horsey Edward to Lankford Lovey 14 May 1816
Horsey Edward to Johnson Leah I. 4 Mar 1868 C
Horsey Frank to Waters Anne 1 May 1869 C
Horsey Isaac to Sterling Hetty 12 Jan 1819
Horsey Isaac to Evans Catherine 11 Aug 1852 C
Horsey Isaac to Wilson Candace 8 Aug 1868 C
Horsey James L. to Wilkins Henrietta C. 21 Dec 1847
Horsey James S. to Miles Mary E. 14 Oct 1862
Horsey John to Skinner Molly 25 Dec 1804
Horsey John to Rencher Susan 12 Sep 1808
Horsey John to Curtis Sally 22 May 1860 C
Horsey John C. to Newman Eleanor 22 Sep 1842
Horsey John C. to Costen Mary M. 4 Aug 1848
Horsey John Coleman to Schoolfield Nancy 3 Oct 1810
Horsey John S. to Selby Eliza A. 10 Apr 1861
Horsey John T. to McCready Mary J. 12 Mar 1863
Horsey Joshua T. to Mills Henrietta L. 3 Apr 1835
Horsey Littleton J. to Harman Mahaly J. 9 Jan 1868 C
Horsey Oliver S. to Cox Elvira H. 19 Apr 1856
Horsey Revell to Dixon Betsy 21 Feb 1804
Horsey Robert to Done Margaret 8 Jan 1868 C
Horsey Samuel to Miles Juana 19 Jun 1860 C
Horsey Smith to Sterling Milcah 13 Apr 1869 C
Horsey Stephen to Marshall Peggy 13 May 1817
Horsey Thomas to Lankford Mary 18 Sep 1839 C
Horsey Wesley to Jewitt Gustena 19 Dec 1865
Horsey William to Hayman Emily 22 Jun 1868 C
Horsman Bosley to Phillips Drusilla 18 Jan 1842
Horsman Constant to Dunn Leah 19 Jun 1818
Horsman John to Jarrett Julia Ann 2 May 1849

Horsman John F. to Boswell Francis C. 24 May 1853
Horsman Perry to Covington Susan 19 Aug 1845
Horsman Perry to Covington Adaline 17 Oct 1848
Horsman Robert to Street Elizabeth 11 Sep 1849
Horsman Severn to Insley Mary Ellen 19 Aug 1845
Hortman Jonas to Smith Sally 9 Mar 1825
Houston Isaac H. to Rider Mary E. 22 May 1866
Houston Joseph to Revell Anne 21 Feb 1797
Houston William C. to Parsons Elizabeth Anne 12 May 1860
Howard Alexander to Adams Anne A. 4 Dec 1860
Howard Ashbury C. to Todd Sally 12 Mar 1829
Howard Beacham to Howard Mahala 18 Mar 1830
Howard Benjamin to Windsor Rebecca 22 Dec 1803
Howard Ebenezer D. to Kelly Elizabeth 4 Nov 1823
Howard Edward to Lankford Elizabeth 27 May 1817
Howard Edward to Matthews Rebecca 9 May 1840
Howard Edward H. to Green Julia F. 20 Dec 1854
Howard Ellsa to Cottman Leah 14 Oct 1840 C
Howard Francis to Marshall Julia 7 May 1859
Howard George to Kersey Leah 21 Nov 1799
Howard George to Dryden Nancy 24 May 1840
Howard George to Bennett Eliza A. 15 Jan 1855
Howard Henry Thomas to Windsor Margaret 5 Sep 1866
Howard Hiram H. to Taylor Mary H. 6 May 1861
Howard James to Denson Eleanor 6 Apr 1841
Howard James to Smith Sallie 2 May 1854
Howard James to Sterling Harriet 29 Nov 1859
Howard James to Tull Elizabeth 17 Jan 1860
Howard John to Dykes Betsey 10 Mar 1801
Howard John to Dykes Mary A. 4 Dec 1824
Howard John to Taylor Emerillus 9 Apr 1856
Howard John (Sr) to Broughton Sally 15 Jun 1824
Howard John G. to Carew Elizabeth 23 Sep 1851
Howard Joseph to Howard Sally 11 Nov 1815
Howard Noah to Goslee Hetty 5 May 1824
Howard Samuel E. to Conner Sally A. 20 Nov 1867
Howard Severn J. to Tull Mary E. 14 Nov 1865
Howard Thomas to Fitzgiles Sally 29 Aug 1865
Howard William to Lankford Sally C. 2 Jul 1816
Howard William to Lankford Eleanor 22 Nov 1842

Howard William to Holland Marianne 20 Nov 1850
Howard William to Bailey Sally Elizabeth 4 Mar 1857
Howard William to Ford Hetty 19 Apr 1859
Howarth Charles to Croswell Amelia 3 Sep 1812
Howarth Elias E. to Mure Harriet 21 Aug 1860
Howarth George W. to Miles Indiana S. 20 Oct 1863
Howarth John to Shores Mary 23 Nov 1835
Howarth John T. to Parks Harriet 3 Jun 1867
Howarth Lambert to Russell Margaret 16 Jul 1842
Howarth Levi to Ward Nancy 23 Aug 1830
Howarth Severn T. to Milbourn Mary Jane 31 Jul 1860
Howarth William to Croswell Zippy 31 May 1827
Howarth William D. to Howarth Margaret W. 17 Sep 1856
Howeth Charles to Ford Annie 14 Jun 1869
Hoyt Samuel H. to Denson Nancy 30 Apr 1839
Hubbard Isaac to Quinton Sinah Jane 18 Aug 1847 C
Hubbard James (Rev.) to Weatherly Elizabeth 12 Oct 1858
Hubbard Richard to Webster Caroline 5 Jan 1830
Hubbell Josiah to Dashiell Leah 24 Feb 1818
Hudson George to Phoebus Margaret Elvia 13 Dec 1865
Hudson John to West Leah 14 Aug 1810
Hudson Peter to McCready Mary 13 Mar 1851
Hudson Peter J. to Landon Mary G. 13 Jul 1858
Hudson Teagle to Hall Mary J. 15 Jan 1855
Hudson William A. to Bell Matilda J. 29 Jul 1862
Huffington James to Weatherly Ellender 21 Apr 1802
Huffington James to Goslee Reeta 24 May 1837
Huffington James to Pollitt Eliza 13 Mar 1849
Huffington Jonathan to Adams Hetty 21 Jan 1815
Huffington Jonathan to Benson Sarah 6 Jan 1841
Hughes Caleb to Nelson Mary 12 Oct 1812
Hughes Caleb to Nelson Charlotte 25 Jan 1825
Hughes Caleb R. to Benson Emily A. 3 Dec 1850
Hughes Isaac to Wainright Ibby 18 May 1865
Hughes James to Insley Ritty 26 May 1817
Hughes James to Smith Sarah Anne 15 Dec 1852
Hughes Jesse to Waters Sarah Harmonson 3 Jun 1801
Hughes John to Shores Tabitha 11 Jan 1853
Hughes to John S.C. to Dashiell Mary J. 17 Jan 1860
Hughes Joseph R. to Bradshaw Alice E. 24 Oct 1871

Hughes Josiah to Smith Peggy 13 Oct 1807
Hughes Josiah to Harris Louisa L. 7 Jan 1840
Hughes Levi T. to Harris Alice 11 Jan 1842
Hughes Thomas B.F. to Jones Mary E. 20 Feb 1850
Hughes Thomas B.F. to White Elizabeth J. 16 Mar 1857
Hughes William to Powell Peggy 7 Aug 1838
Hughes William to Hughes Esther 19 Jul 1869 C
Hull Beacham G. to Goslee Clarissa R. 11 May 1841
Hull Brittingham to Sterling Sally McClester 6 Jun 1799
Hull Edward T. to Maddux Sarah S. 24 May 1836
Hull Joshua to Miles Elizabeth 25 Jul 1798
Hull Napoleon W. to Graham Mary E. 4 Jul 1843
Hull Samuel G. W. to Jones Leah A. 30 Oct 1869 C
Humphreys Archelaus to Humphreys Margaret 1 Dec 1829
Humphreys Charles W. to Mitchell Amelia A. 2 Sep 1834
Humphreys Fontaine to Mayfield Sarah 9 Feb 1831
Humphreys George W. to Miles Matilda 19 Dec 1833
Humphreys James to North Mary 3 Dec 1835
Humphreys John to Humphreys Peggy 10 Aug 1827
Humphreys Joseph to Green Priscilla 18 Dec 1821
Humphreys Joseph to White Mary 12 Mar 1840
Humphreys Josephus to Johnson Anne N. 7 Apr 1835
Humphreys Joshua N. to Darby Henny Anne 11 May 1859
Humphreys Josiah to Griffith Susan E. 15 Jan 1851
Humphreys Robert G. to Humphreys Mary A. 5 Jan 1858
Humphreys Thomas to McCree Frances 14 Mar 1815
Humphreys Washington to Russell Anne 27 Jun 1833
Humphreys William Alexander to Weatherly Elizabeth J. 13 Feb 1866
Humphreys William E. to Dashiell Jane Adaline 17 Feb 1851
Humphreys William E. to Mezick Sarah E.J. 27 Apr 1854
Humphreys William J. to Goslee Nancy 30 May 1854
Humphries John to Vance Matty 14 Jan 1800
Humphries Joseph to Jackson Dolly 28 Jan 1800
Humphries Thomas to Bowles Nancy 16 Oct 1807
Humphries Thomas J. to Smith Elizabeth E. 10 Aug 1867
Humphris Joseph to Layfield Elizabeth 27 Jul 1813
Humphris Zachariah to Reddish Nelly 13 Jun 1810
Humphriss Cathell to Walker Leah 18 Apr 1821
Hunt George W. to Wallace Julia 29 Nov 1864
Hunt Wilson to Denson Leah 28 Oct 1801

Huntington John W. to Morris Mary E.J.W. 20 May 1845
Hurley Alexander to Lloyd Elizabeth Anne 19 Mar 1844
Hurley John to Weatherly Elizabeth 22 Feb 1809
Hurley Lorenzo E. to Mandus Mary E. 14 Apr 1860
Hurley Mister to White Anna 30 Oct 1862
Hurley Samuel to Dean Rachel 15 Apr 1828
Hurley William to Walton Rhoda 20 Aug 1799
Hurly Henry D. to Shrives Ann M. 16 Jan 1856
Hurly John to Blake Ellen A.W. 20 May 1848
Hurst Edward to Venables Sally 19 Aug 1817
Hurst John to Mister Mary C. 25 Dec 1845
Hurst Joseph to Green Mary 3 Sep 1824
Hurt Ebenezer to Marine Amelia 29 Oct 1833
Hurt Henry (Rev.) to Sudler Leah 2 Dec 1856 C
Hurt William T. to Hawkins Caroline 10 May 1864
Husk William to Mazick Patty 23 May 1827
Huston Alfred to Huston Rosetta 22 Aug 1863 C
Huston John to Dashiell Sarah 2 Dec 1800
Hyland George to Parker Charlotte 20 Feb 1866 C
Hyland Henry to Aires Harriet E. 6 Apr 1819
Hyland James Charles to Dashiell Matilda Lucas 7 Feb 1804
Hyland Lambert to Ennis Mary G. 8 Nov 1864
Hyland Wesley to Johnson Margaret 7 Jun 1871
Ingersoll George to Acworth Margaret 28 Jul 1852
Ingersoll Thomas to Hobbs Ann 18 Sep 1823
Insley Denwood to Jackson Margaret 22 Nov 1845
Insley Elijah H. to Larmore Margaret E. 18 Dec 1865
Insley Esau S.D. to Dunn Caroline F. 27 Sep 1859
Insley Isaac to Insley Dorothy 13 Jan 1857
Insley James P. to Mezick Biddy A. 8 Nov 1865
Insley Jesse to Dayly Eliza 11 Nov 1830
Insley John to Jones Amelia 10 Oct 1797
Insley John to Dunn Susan 1 Feb 1820
Insley John to Simpkins Elizabeth 23 Sep 1825
Insley Oliver P. to Hemons Emily C. 17 Dec 1861
Insley Robert to Dorman Ann 22 Aug 1829
Insley Valentine to Larmore Mary 12 Aug 1830
Insley Washington to White Sarah E. 2 Feb 1859
Insley William to Jarrett Rhoda 9 Aug 1814
Insley William to Larmore Elizabeth 3 Jul 1838

Insley William M. to Willing Mary A. 7 Mar 1854
Ironmonger Charles B. to Miles Sarah 13 May 1851
Irving Handy H. to Handy Peggy K. 8 Jun 1810
Irving James to Fountain Sally 29 Nov 1796
Irving John to Shiles Nelly 26 Jan 1798
Irving John to Jones Anne 21 Aug 1817
Irving William to Landen Nancy 22 Mar 1803
Jackson Andrew W.L. to Twilly Mary Anne 1 Jun 1847
Jackson Charles to Dear Anne 25 Aug 1830
Jackson Elihu to Rhodes Peggy 20 Apr 1802
Jackson George to Greene Polly 31 Jan 1827
Jackson George Decatur to Larmore Matilda 12 Jul 1853
Jackson Henry to Huston Allifair 20 May 1831
Jackson Henry to Huston Allifair 20 May 1831
Jackson Hugh to Humphriss Sarah M. 29 Sep 1835
Jackson James to Floyd Betsy Aug 1798
Jackson James to Mezick Sarah 16 Jun 1812
Jackson James to Barnes Sally 24 Apr 1827
Jackson John T. to Taylor Elizabeth A. 24 Jan 1860
Jackson Jonathan to Webster Polly 6 Mar 1804
Jackson Jonathan H. to Mitchell Mary Ann L.B. 15 Jun 1844
Jackson Joshua to Mezick Louisa 20 Nov 1824
Jackson Joshua to Larmore Jane 7 Jul 1856
Jackson Noah to Covington Matilda E. 26 May 1835
Jackson Peter W. to Furbush Elizabeth R. 26 Sep 1865
Jackson Samuel to Mezick Maria 30 Jan 1821
Jackson Samuel to Badley Delilah Anne 20 Oct 1857
Jackson Samuel to Mills Mary Ann 14 Jan 1862
Jackson Samuel R. to Dickerson Sarah A. 20 Feb 1849
Jackson Thomas L. to Taylor Amanda J. 5 Jan 1854
Jackson Tubman to Sterling Susan 25 Nov 1845
Jackson William to Bell Ellen S. 15 Mar 1845
Jackson William to Collier Margaret 22 Sep 1846
Jackson William to Handy Louisa 18 Jun 1868 C
Jackson William G. to Brown Elizabeth 28 Mar 1864
Jackson William H. to Humphreys Arabella 7 Nov 1863
James Jacob to Austin Nelly 15 Sep 1812
James John to Done Sally P. 1 Oct 1818
James John R. to Ashby Margaret S. 27 Apr 1869
James Samuel to Farrington Emma 2 Dec 1815

Jarman George W. to Brittingham Sarah A. 29 Nov 1858
Jarrett Abel to Dunn Susan J. 6 Jan 1857
Jarrett Abraham to Insley Molly 18 May 1813
Jarrett Hazzard to Dayton Sarah Anne 4 Dec 1845
Jarrett William to Insley Milly 12 May 1846
Jarritt Mitchell to Hopkins Charlotte 2 Dec 1841
Jenkins Addison to _____ Mary 26 Nov 1850
Jenkins Alexander to Bounds Henrietta 6 Feb 1855
Jenkins Archibald to Malone Eliz 11 Jan 1825
Jenkins Curtis to Riggin Betsy 13 Nov 1809
Jenkins David to Shermon Rebecca 26 Jun 1798
Jenkins David to Humphries Rebecca 30 Jan 1804
Jenkins David to Williams Henrietta 26 May 1840
Jenkins Fielder D. to Adams Nancy 14 Feb 1839
Jenkins George to Abbott Elizabeth E. 27 Feb 1834
Jenkins George to Malone Leah 23 Aug 1836
Jenkins George C. to Jenkins Anne 24 Aug 1837
Jenkins Jarvis to Gray Ardilla 23 Feb 1854
Jenkins Levi to Jenkins Sarah 31 Jul 1810
Jenkins Levi to Hitch Patty 12 May 1835
Jenkins Levin A. to Nelson Mary S. 12 Sep 1866
Jenkins Littleton to Hitch Jane 29 Aug 1835
Jenkins Littleton to Taylor Jane 30 Dec 1840
Jenkins Mitchell to Conner Mary 23 Jan 1838
Jenkins Richard to Sutton Suckey 18 Jan 1814
Jenkins Richard to Parker Gatty H. 9 Apr 1845
Jenkins Samuel S. to Cannon Drucilla 14 Jul 1863
Jenkins Sewell T. to Roach Ann W. 16 Sep 1829
Jenkins Thomas to Carey Rodah 27 Oct 1840
Jenkins Wesley to Turner Hester 9 Feb 1840
Jenkins Wesley to Russell Susan 1 Oct 1866
Jerrald Elisha to Crowell Betsy 19 Mar 1811
Jester John to Willey Elizabeth 24 Feb 1863
Jester John to Willing Anne 11 Aug 1865
Johnson Algernon to Kennerly Priscilla 14 Nov 1843
Johnson Algernon to Robertson Elizabeth 22 Jan 1855
Johnson Ambrose to Johnson Sophia 21 Dec 1865 C
Johnson Augustus J. to Sturgis Elizabeth 18 Jan 1848 .
Johnson Benjamin to Hearn Juliana 15 Jul 1828
Johnson Charles J. to Ward Harriet E. 22 Jun 1855

Johnson Charles N. to Moore Maria S. 18 Nov 1835
Johnson Charles N. to Croswell Elizabeth A. 10 Feb 1857
Johnson Charles N. to Moore Amelia 3 Oct 1859
Johnson Charles W. to Dryden Elizabeth 23 May 1865
Johnson Christopher C. to Moore Mary O. 7 Mar 1866
Johnson Christopher C. to Moore Alice A. 24 Sep 1867
Johnson Clemuel to Bayly Rebecca 11 May 1803
Johnson Dennis to Jones Susan 9 Mar 1871 C
Johnson Elijah to Disharoon Sally 14 Apr 1818
Johnson Elijah to Dashiell Clara 5 Aug 1851
Johnson Elijah T. to Mason Annie L. 25 Apr 1868
Johnson George to Pinkett Mary 18 Mar 1867 C
Johnson George to Lankford Mary 8 Dec 1868
Johnson Hamilton to Hudson Eliza 4 Feb 1823
Johnson Harvey F. to Cullen Mary S. 27 Jul 1847
Johnson Henry to Prior Sarah 6 Mar 1810
Johnson Henry to Lawson Ritty Ann 8 Feb 1821
Johnson Henry to Gibbons Mary 4 Dec 1838
Johnson Henry to Wallace Angie 20 May 1871 C
Johnson Henry J. to Taylor Zipporah 3 May 1859
Johnson Henry J. to Boston Mary A. 12 Mar 1863
Johnson Isaac to McCready Gertrude 23 Sep 1812
Johnson Isaac to Ward Lovey 11 Nov 1833
Johnson Isaac H. to Ward Maria H. 4 Jan 1837
Johnson Isaac H. to Dougherty Eliza 3 Aug 1855
Johnson James to Johnson Nancy 20 May 1803
Johnson James to Gl(ascow) Anna Maria 19 Jan 1813
Johnston James to Conner Elizabeth C. 30 Nov 1817
Johnson James to Wilson Ann Mary 30 Jun 1829
Johnson James to McDaniel Hester Anne 2 Jul 1842
Johnson James to Milbourn Araminta 1 Aug 1848 C
Johnson James to Jones Maria Anne 25 Jul 1856 C
Johnson James to Whittington Mary 16 May 1865 C
Johnson James to Thomas Amanda 2 Feb 1869 C
Johnson James H. to Johnson Sally Sep 1830
Johnson Jesse to Johnson Betsy Feb 1799
Johnon John to Sterling Sally 5 Apr 1803
Johnson John to Somers Exemon 28 Jul 1832
Johnson John E. to Dorsey Susan Ann 25 Feb 1868
Johnson John H. to Gibson Elizabeth P. 1 Sep 1871

Johnson John Henry to Rounds Harriet A. 30 May 1860 C
Johnson John S. to Cottingham Priscilla 29 Dec 1868 C
Johnson John T. to Wingate Rosanna 11 Jun 1862
Johnson John W.D. to Parker Sally Ann 16 Jun 1856
Johnson John Wesley to Howard Anne Eliza 4 Dec 1860
Johnson Joseph H. to Abbott Virginia A. 16 Nov 1871
Johnson Joshua to Rider Emeline 1 Nov 1828
Johnson Joshua D. to Long Charlotte M.K. 23 Jan 1839
Johnson Joshua H. to Thomas Sally A. 13 Mar 1861
Johnson Josiah to Roach Eleanor 4 May 1802
Johnson Josiah to Humphreys Martha Ann 23 Jan 1849
Johnson Littleton to Evans Sarah Ann 4 Jul 1823
Johnson Littleton to Ward Sally 22 Apr 1828
Johnson Luther to Roach Elizabeth 25 Jan 1870 C
Johnson Purnell to Humphreys Sarah E. 23 Jan 1860
Johnson Richard M. to Serman Dodie J. 1 Jul 1865
Johnson Robert H. to Moore Maria Esther 4 Apr 1865
Johnson Samuel to Cottman Sally 13 Apr 1865 C
Johnson Samuel H. to Hughes Emily F. 16 Aug 1871 C
Johnson Samuel M. to Waters Henrietta M. 15 Jun 1848
Johnson Selby to Floyd Nancy 28 Dec 1819
Johnson Smith to Williams Sarah 15 Jul 1862 C
Johnson Thomas to Smith Margaret 26 Apr 1866 C
Johnson Thomas to Pollitt Matilda 26 Apr 1871 C
Johnson Whittington to Ward Elizabeth 10 Mar 1823
Johnson William to Johnson Ann 5 Apr 1798
Johnson William to Holland Juliann 2 Nov 1841
Johnson William E. to Gibson Mary W. 28 Feb 1860
Johnson William S. to Hitchens Esther Ann 22 Nov 1854
Johnson William W. to Tilghman Elizabeth W. 29 Oct 1829
Johnson William W. to Marsh Elizabeth A. 6 Jun 1848
Johnson William W. to Disharoon Mary Caroline 13 Jan 1852
Johnson William W. to Slemons Mary A. 27 Jan 1857
Johnston John W. to Thomas Elizabeth S. 15 Oct 1857
Jolley William to Quinton Harriet E. 30 Oct 1856 C
Jones Alexander to Carew Betsy 22 Jun 1813
Jones Alfred H. to Done Henrietta H. --(?) 1838
Jones Alfred H. to Stewart Elizabeth K. 16 Dec 1847
Jones Arnold E. to Jackson Anne W. 2 Nov 1808
Jones Benjamin to Wallace Sarah 27 Jan 1800

Jones Benjamin to Wallace Nelly 6 Mar 1815
Jones Benjamin J. to Wainright Biddy Jane 2 Jan 1840
Jones Benjamin J.M. to Scott Arianna Olivia 26 Apr 1853
Jones Charles to Fleming Hetty 27 Nov 1798
Jones Charles to Wood Elizabeth 24 Jul. 1810
Jones Charles to Waters Mary 10 Dec 1867 C
Jones Charles A. to Jones Mary 28 Jun 1870 C
Jones Cleophus to Tignor Mary T. 17 Nov 1871
Jones Cottman to Taylor Nancy 21 Dec 1830
Jones Cyrus L. to Venables Harriet H. 10 Aug 1837
Jones Cyrus L. to Jones Adeline 20 Apr 1842
Jones Daniel W. to Scott Julia A. 9 Nov 1858
Jones David to White Emeline 9 Sep 1828
Jones Edward to Smith Sally 29 May 1810
Jones Edward to Meredith Susan 25 Nov 1837
Jones Edward to Walls Mary Jane 25 Dec 1854
Jones Elijah M. to Vetra Mary F.A. 12 Jan 1858
Jones Enos to Waters Francis 2 Feb 1869 C
Jones Francis to Sermon Sally 11 Feb 1835
Jones Francis to Jones Delia 1 Nov 1870 C
Jones Gabriel H. to Duncan Margaret A. 15 Jun 1865
Jones Gabriel H. to White Priscilla H. 24 Jan 1868
Jones George to Bounds Elizabeth 9 Mar 1814
Jones George to Simms Rebecca 22 Apr 1828
Jones George to Parks Lovey 7 May 1844
Jones George to Brinkley Clarisa 19 Dec 1860
Jones George to Conway Mary 26 Nov 1861 C
Jones George to Dashiell Betsy 15 Jan 1862 C
Jones George to Windsor Matilda 30 Dec 1862
Jones George to Crockett Rachel 23 Dec 1867
Jones George (of Robt.) to Fleming Sally 24 Sep 1829
Jones George F. to Lewis Ella 16 Dec 1871
Jones George H. to Jones Arianna E. 4 Jun 1863
Jones George H. to Waters Mary 4 Jan 1866 C
Jones George I. to Jones Eleanor D. 8 Oct 1822
Jones George L. to Haily Emily J. 23 Aug 1848
Jones George P. to Dashiell Polly G. 10 Jun 1823
Jones George T. to Windsor Mary K. 7 Feb 1866
Jones George W. to Dashiell Peggy Ann 9 May 1818
Jones George W. to Dunn Polly 21 May 1827

Jones George W. to Carew Arianna 31 May 1864
Jones Hamilton to Puzey Leah 2 Jan 1822
Jones Henry to Jones Elizabeth 1 Jul 1797
Jones Henry to Cannon Leah J. 4 Mar 1862 C
Jones Henry to Duncan Isabella 26 Feb 1866
Jones Henry to Turpin Maria F. 18 Dec 1867 C
Jones Henry A. to Jones Roxanna 9 Dec 1864 C
Jones Henry A. to Price Julia F. 19 Dec 1865
Jones Henry A. to Jones Sally W. 3 May 1870 C
Jones Isaac to Shield Charlotte 8 Mar 1870 C
Jones Isaac H. to Crouch Sally F. 27 Mar 1866
Jones Isaac J. to Hemonds Sarah J. 28 Oct 1856
Jones Jacob to Dashiell Sally Anne 15 Mar 1865 C
Jones James to Follen Loveth 23 Aug 1803
Jones James to Smith Leah 23 Jan 1810
Jones James to Jenkins Milly 5 Feb 1811
Jones James to Juett Sally 29 Aug 1814
Jones James to Byrd Elizabeth 2 Oct 1819
Jones James to Bozman Elisabeth 11 Mar 1833
Jones James to Turner Louisa 28 Apr 1846
Jones James to Bussells Eleanor 28 Jan 1862
Jones James to Riggin Mary J. 4 Mar 1862
Jones James to Toadvine Milly 9 Sep 1865 C
Jones James to Waters Mary 26 Dec 1866 C
Jones James to Smith Henrietta 14 Jun 1869 C
Jones James to Nace Julia Ann 21 Jun 1871 C
Jones James A. to White Eliza 18 Dec 1871 C
Jones James W. to Walston Elizabeth 5 May 1870 C
Jones John to Moore Sarah 6 Sep 1797
Jones John to Taylor Patty 11 Feb 1800
Jones John to Venables Leah 29 Dec 1807
Jones John to McGee Betsy 29 Jun 1808
Jones John to Cullen Kessy 22 Oct 1814
Jones John to Covington Rebecca 19 Dec 1815
Jones John to Jones Zipporah W. 17 Nov 1818
Jones John to Murrill Sally 9 Oct 1821
Jones John to Adams Amelia 31 Oct 1826
Jones John to Parks Bridget A.E. 11 Sep 1849
Jones John to Horner Susan Anne 21 May 1855
Jones John (of Geo.) to Crockett Elizabeth 1 Aug 1821

Jones John (of Jas) to Waltes Nancy A. 23 Apr 1822
Jones John (of Thomas) to Johnson Charlotte 24 Dec 1828
Jones John B. W. to Hall _____ 8 Nov 1840
Jones John H. to Rowe Milcah Anne 18 Oct 1832
Jones John H. to Waters Margaret 18 Sep 1852 C
Jones John H. to Parks Mary Ann 27 Jul 1854
Jones John H.D. to Hall Elizabeth 11 Jun 1835
Jones John Smith to Brewington Caroline 7 Nov 1860
Jones John T. to White Charlotte 7 Feb 1871 C
Jones John Washington to White Drucilla 27 Jan 1859
Jones Joseph to Jones Nelly 1 Sep 1808
Jones Joseph to Webster Milcah Ann 30 Jan 1828
Jones Joseph to Murrell Mary Ann 27 Aug 1828
Jones Joseph to Lemmon Jane 22 May 1855
Jones Joseph to Elzey Martha 31 Mar 1866 C
Jones Joshua T. to Johnson Matilda 30 May 1871 C
Jones Josiah D. to Lowes Elizabeth 24 Jun 1823
Jones Leonard C. to Mason Jurina F. 12 Sep 1866
Jones Levin to James Elizabeth 10 Dec 1796
Jones Levin to James Nancy 31 Oct 1809
Jones Levin to Evans Sarah Matilda 2 Jul 1822
Jones Levin D. to Smith Mary 9 Jan 1810
Jones Levin D. to Hyland Matilda 1 May 1821
Jones Lewis to Follin Betsy 2 Sep 1800
Jones Lewis to Rider Betsy 19 Jan 1804
Jones Littleton to Heath Leah 29 May 1798
Jones Marcellus to Hughes Mary 31 Jan 1815
Jones Marcellus to Jones Mary 1 May 1844
Jones Marcellus to Phoebus Sally Anne 8 Jun 1846
Jones Matthias to Cha---milcha Gale 5 Aug 1797
Jones Mitchel to Hardy Priscilla 7 Jan 1851
Jones Mitchell to Garretson Elizabeth 14 Apr 1854 C
Jones Mitchell to Beckett Milcah A. 5 Oct 1869 C
Jones Nehemiah to Bozman Adeline 22 Sep 1858
Jones Nicholas to Martin Mary 28 Feb 1825
Jones Nicholas H. to Parks Sarah R. 4 Sep 1849
Jones Perry to Jones Betsy Jane 3 May 1856 C
Jones Purnell to Mitchell Polly 6 Apr 1819
Jones Robert to Wood Mary J. 16 Mar 1820
Jones Robert to Shores Emily 21 Aug 1860

Jones Robert to Byrd Mary 31 Dec 1867 C
Jones Robert (of Geo.) to Fleming Sarah Ann 23 May 1823
Jones Robert (of Geo.) to Gilliss Elizabeth McC 13 Jan 1829
Jones Robert (of Geo.} to King Henrietta 22 Jan 1833
Jones Robert H. to Evans Harriet J. 4 Oct 1842
Jones Robert V. to Waller Eleanor 2 Jun 1832
Jones Rufus P. to Webster Mary E. 14 Sep 1858
Jones Samuel to Bedsworth Polly 4 Nov 1811
Jones Samuel to Gibson Nancy 23 Jun 1823
Jones Samuel to Parker Catty 17 May 1825
Jones Samuel to White Maria E. 16 Jun 1859
Jones Samuel to Winright Nervey 24 Mar 1864 C
Jones Samuel to Smith Mary R. 21 Jun 1864
Jones Samuel to Jones Esther 13 Jan 1868 C
Jones Samuel B. D. to Jones Maria S. 10 Nov 1835
Jones Samuel B.D. to Horsey Eglantine 20 Feb 1855
Jones Samuel H.W. to Merrill Lucinda A. 5 Sep 1846
Jones Samuel M. to Jones Sally A. 4 Jan 1859
Jones Samuel W. to Jones Mary H. 28 Apr 1830
Jones Samuel W. to Stewart Sally R. 21 Mar 1832
Jones Sneed to Carol Octave 3 May 1870 C
Jones Solomon W. to Scott Leah E. 3 May 1866
Jones Stephen A. to Bloodsworth Rebecca J. 14 Feb 1854
Jones Sydney to Powell Sally 28 Feb 1865 C
Jones Sydney to Dennis Margaret 27 Dec 1869
Jones Thomas to Dunn Priscilla 19 Dec 1797
Jones Thomas to Leatherbury Nelly 24 Dec 1799
Jones Thomas to Reddish Eleanor 15 Aug 1804
Jones Thomas to Long Rachel 21 Feb 1810
Jones Thomas to Covington Eleanor 18 Jan 1826
Jones Thomas to Kelly Mary Ann 18 Sep 1827
Jones Thomas to Dorman Harriet 29 Oct 1833
Jones Thomas to Messick Eliza J. 27 Nov 1849
Jones Thomas (K. T.) to Handy Martha 26 Feb 1811
Jones Thomas (of Jno} to Hitch Sarah Cathell 2 Oct 1821
Jones Thomas (of Thomas} to Gibbons Priscilla 25 Sep 1828
Jones Thomas (of Thomas} to Jones Maria S. 22 Dec 1830
Jones Thomas (Shad Pt} to Jenkins Betsy 18 Nov 1814
Jones Thomas M. to Furniss Elizabeth 20 Apr 1815
Jones Washington to Dashiell Terissa 28 Jul 1809

Jones Washington to Wainright Martha 20 Sep 1869
Jones William to Laws Sarah 4 Oct 1797
Jones William to Hayward Nelly 15 Dec 1798
Jones William to Holbrook Prissy 16 Feb 1802
Jones William to Horsey Molly 22 Dec 1812
Jones William to Wallace Margaret 28 Aug 1838
Jones William to Leonard Emeline 8 Jan 1839
Jones William to Turner Hetty Anne 25 Nov 1845
Jones William to Marshall Darkey 21 Jan 1853
Jones William to Murray Sallie Anne 26 Apr 1854
Jones William to Shores Margaret 13 May 1856
Jones William to Smith Leah J. 15 Feb 1871 C
Jones William (Shad Pt) to Smith Milly 6 Sep 1814
Jones William C.E. to Curtis Sarah 27 Jan 1830
Jones William Edgar to Bird Maria E.H. 28 Jan 1863
Jones William G. H. to Holbrook Julianna 24 Apr 1826
Jones William H. to Jones Sarah L. 18 Jul 1839
Jones William H.H. to Kelly Almira J. 23 Jan 1868
Jones William J. to Ewell Hester J. 13 Jan 1863
Jones William L. to Jones Margaret H. H. 8 Nov 1826
Jones William M. to Jones Sally D. 16 Sep 1823
Jones William N. to Harris Mary M. 14 Jul 1851
Jones William R. to White Sarah E. 23 Aug 1849
Jones William T. to Pusey Sarah Ann Cathrine 4 Nov 1861
Jones William Thomas to McCready Gatty 23 Mar 1858
Jones William W. to Jones Adaline 11 Oct 1870 C
Jones Zachariah to Black Emily Virginia 15 Mar 1864 C
Jones Zebedee to Waters Nancy 11 Apr 1871 C
Jordan John to Livingston Mary A. 15 Jan 1851
Joursan John to Cox Jenny 21 Feb 1803
Judah Henry R. to Reece Mary J. L. 28 Aug 1820
Juett William to Cullen Betsy 31 Dec 1808
Juit Kellum to Selva Matilda A. 5 Feb 1858 C
Justin Joseph C. to Parramore Sally 1 Jun 1858
Justis James to Rich Sarah 5 Mar 1859
Kelley George to Dorman Charlotte -- Sep 1839
Kelley Samuel H. to Callaway Sarah Ann 8 Sep 1841
Kellip Seth to Follen Louisa F. 15 Aug 1865
Kelly Henry to Howard Sarah 1 Sep 1801
Kelly Isaac to Beauchamp Hetty 20 Oct 1824

Kellum John H. to Dougherty Sarah A. 26 Feb 1833
Kellum William C. to Hitch Sarah 9 Feb 1837
Kelly Charles to Bradley Mary E. 29 Aug 1865
Kelly Elijah W. to Barkley Maria P. 12 May 1863
Kelly George to Dorman Mary Ann 11 Sep 1827
Kelly George to Rion Mary E. 22 Oct 1857
Kelly James to Jones Catey 24 Feb 1801
Kelly James to Williams Felitha C____ 25 Jun 1839
Kelly James F. to White Mary A. 3 Feb 1824
Kelly James F. to Simpkins Anne 1 Oct 1844
Kelly James F. to Jones Margaret M. 8 Dec 1858
Kelly John to White Sarah 31 Jan 1797
Kelly John to Puzey Susan 28 Dec 1830
Kelly John to White Eleanor Anne 5 Jan 1833
Kelly John F. to Giles Anne M. 9 Jun 1863
Kelly John S. to Warren Zippirah 19 Mar 1824
Kelly John W. to Benton Jane 5 Aug 1858
Kelly Marcellus G. W. to Webster Mary C. 6 Jul 1869
Kelly Noah to Daniel Elizabeth 13 Jul 1825
Kelly Noah T. to Parks Roxanna 17 Jan 1871
Kelly Pasquel V. to Handy Eliza 17 Aug 1810
Kelly Thomas J. to Jones Eliza 10 Jan 1843
Kelly Thomas W. to Scott Louisa A. 10 Aug 1865
Kelly Washington to Mister Caroline 11 Jun 1833
Kelly William to Kelly Anna 13 Jan 1801
Kelly William to Goslee Elizabeth 14 Mar 1815
Kelly William D. to Shores Catherine T. 17 Jan 1863
Kelly William H.W. to Howard Margaret J. 14 Aug 1863
Kelly Zedekiah to Young Susan M. 5 Jul 1859
Kemp George to Jurt Permelia 16 May 1871
Kemp John to Brown Betsy 25 Apr 1804
Kemp Matthew to Cannon Eliza 26 Oct 1813
Kemp Matthias to Benson Margaret 3 Aug 1819
Kemp Theophilus to Larmore Matilda 3 Jan 1826
Kenner George D. to Horsman Margaret A. 3 Jun 1862
Kennerly Barnardton to Drura Mary Jane 29 Sep 1836
Kennerly Caleb to Bounds Priscilla 17 Jan 1805
Kennerly Caleb to Goslee Juliann 18 Jul 1826
Kennerly Columbus to Walter Mary A. 14 Dec 1848
Kennerly Columbus to Twilley Jane 8 Feb 1859

Kennerly Everton to Gupton Mary 28 Oct 1840
Kennerly George to Barkley Mary Ann 26 Apr 1830
Kennerly Henry to Venables Mary A. 27 Nov 1823
Kennerly Irving to Jones Margaret 27 Nov 1849
Kennerly Irving to Covington Mary C. 26 Feb 1864
Kennerly Isaac to David Nancy 6 Oct 1816
Kennerly Isaac to Robertson Elizabeth 5 Dec 1820
Kennerly Isaac to Graham Mary 24 Mar 1840
Kennerly James W. to White Adeline 18 Dec 1865
Kennerly John to Howard Mary 2 Feb 1857
Kennerly Joseph to Hurley Betsy 18 May 1802
Kennerly Peter to Kennerly Anne 23 Apr 1799
Kennerly Thomas to Walker Elizabeth 30 Nov 1841
Kennerly Thomas to Graham Elizabeth 1 Nov 1852
Kennerly Wm. A. to Wilson Eleanor W. --(?) 1837
Ker Samuel I. S. to Davis Louisa A. 22 Oct 1833
Kersey John to Harper Narcissa 13 Dec 1825
Kersey John to Harper Narcissa 13 Dec 1825
Kersey Noah to Kersey Mary 10 Jan 1827
Kersey Peter to Riggin Nancy 18 Jan 1823
Kersey Sidney T. to Dennis Nancy 17 Jul 1866
Kerwin Soveren to Bugan Elizabeth 6 Mar 1805
Kesterson John to Webster Deborah W. 27 Oct 1847
Ketchum Charles E. to Parks Mary A. 18 Apr 1865
Kibble George to Collins Rosetta 23 Jan 1798
Kibble George W. to Wheatley Dorothy A. 12 Dec 1860
Kibble John W. to Fields Eliza E. 30 Jan 1866
Kibble Willian to Malone Anne 7 Jan 1817
Kibble William to Smith Ann Maria 19 Dec 1826
Killam John H. to Dougherty Christiana 16 Oct 1856
Killiam George W. to Lowe Mary H. 17 Mar 1862
Killim John to Porter Gertrude 4 Feb 1803
Killman John W. to Evans Betsy 15 Aug 1853
Kimberly Lazarus H. to Ford Esther I. 19 Jul 1867
Kimley David to Ford Elizabeth Anne 19 Sep 1838
King Alexander H. to Jones Sarah E. 15 Mar 1871
King Alfred J. to Bell Sarah E. 13 Sep 1869
King Arthur to Whitney Leah J. 25 Feb 1867 C
King Benjamin to Malcomb Martha 20 Feb 1868 C
King Edward to Hayman Margaret E. 29 May 1865 C

King Hamilton to Furniss Leah 9 Feb 1867 C
King Henry to Donoho Priscilla A. 30 Nov 1852
King Henry to Parsons Mary 6 Mar 1866 C
King Henry N. to Covington Mary L. 20 Dec 1860
King James to Wright Jane 30 Jan 1869 C
King James G. to Blain Martha Jane 16 Jan 1838
King John to Jones Harriet 5 Mar 1867 C
King John to Turner Matilda 28 Jun 1870 C
King John H. to Crockett Sally E.J.C. 27 Nov 1827
King John H. to Dove Charlotte 13 Mar 1833
King John T. to Hyland Sallie A. 20 Apr 1854
King John W. to Waters Sarah A. 27 Jan 1821
King Joseph to Haron Mary 29 Nov 1809
King Joseph to Lemmon Maria C.W. 11 Feb 1817
King Joseph to Walston Anne 9 Jan 1821
King Levin M. to Duer Sally --(?) 1838
King Planner H. to Fountain Sally Anne 13 Mar 1832
King Planner H. to Dix Catharine 16 May 1837
King Robert to Gibbons Juliana 19 Feb 1834
King Robert J. (Doctor) to Hobbs Sally 23 May 1818
King Robert J.H. to Handy Aurelia 17 Aug 1826
King Robert J.H. to Handy Matilda 31 Dec 1834
King Robert J.H. to Broughton Mary Ann 2 Jan 1849
King Samuel to Covington Nancy 1 Dec 1807
King Samuel to Bonnawell Esther A. 8 Apr 1851
King Sydney C. to Powell Priscilla I. 4 Dec 1866
King Thomas to Malcomb Peggy 18 Aug 1801
King Whittington to Willing Mary 10 Jan 1821
King William to Taylor Polly 9 Jul 1799
King William to Dickerson Lanty 13 Jul 1826
King William to Jones Maria 10 Dec 1838
King William T. to Stevens Clarietta 8 Sep 1852
King William W. to Cox Amanda R. 8 Jun 1864
Kinney James E. to Wilson Maria E. 17 Oct 1866
Kinney Josiah to Powell Peggy 3 Jul 1804
Kirby William F. to Heath Charlotte R. 11 Feb 1833
Kirgan John to Holland Mary Ann 24 Oct 1804
Kirwan Elliott to Bloodsworth Sarah 24 Jun 1833
Kirwan Elliott to Jones Elizabeth 27 Jul 1847
Kirwan James H. to Green Martha A.J. 13 Jan 1866

Kirwan John to Bounds Mary 13 Dec 1831
Kirwan Zebedius to Harris Jane F. 15 Jun 1858
Kirwin Alexander to Benton Elizabeth J. 27 Nov 1855
Kirwin Elliott to Nutter Tempy 18 May 1808
Kirwin Isaac H. to Holland Sally 20 Dec 1870
Kirwin John to Horner Susan 24 Sep 1824
Kirwin Philip to Whitley Elizabeth 6 Jul 1825
Kitchens John to Collins Mary J. 30 May 1868 C
Knight Samuel B. to Crockett Matilda 4 Jan 1843
Knowles George R. to Russell Mary J. 24 Jan 1860
Knowles Rufus D. to Connolly Esther A. 2 May 1864
Knowles Thomas to Bradley Matty Anne 26 Jan 1833
Laird Benjamin W. to Newman Leah 27 Apr 1842
Laird Franklin to Wilson Mary E. 12 Jan 1870
Laird Gilbert N. to Landing Jane 18 May 1855
Laird James to Winder Dorothy Arietta 24 Nov 1802
Laird John S. to Riggin Keziah 12 Apr 1842
Laird John T. to Wilson Anna E. 25 Jul 1867
Laird John W. to Nicols Mary E. 3 Feb 1870
Laird William M. to Ward Maria A.D. 27 May 1863
Lambdon Thomas J. to Campbell Virginia 10 Feb 1869
Land Noah W. to Stevenson Cornelia W. 25 Dec 1871
Landen Ephraim to Davis Polly 24 Mar 1801
Landen Ezekiel to Walston Prissy 22 Sep 1801
Landen Ezekiel to James Emily 15 Dec 1855
Landen Francis to Dykes Matilda 20 Sep 1814
Landen Franky to McGrath Grace 7 Apr 1831
Landen Henry to Landen Dolly 27 Nov 1798
Landen Henry to Outerbridge Peggy 20 Jun 1818
Landen Isaac to Dise Peggy 4 Dec 1804
Landen John to Dougherty Jemima 23 Jun 1852
Landen Joseph to Mills Alice 11 May 1803
Landen Josiah to Gibson Ally 9 Dec 1830
Landen Michael to Trehern Sally 11 Jun 1800
Landen Richard to Muir Polly 26 Dec 1815
Landen Samuel to Perkins Harriet 17 Aug 1819
Landen Samuel J. to Ford Eliza J. 18 Jun 1839
Landen Solomon to Ford Polly 27 Feb 1813
Landen Thomas to Dize Anne Maria 14 Jan 1829
Landen William to Carson Mary Ann Prishy 16 Aug 1836

Landin William to Smith Sarah Priscilla 14 Mar 1844
Landing Francis to Nicholas Matilda 28 Jul 1812
Landing James to Ross Margaret 17 Jun 1857
Landing John H. to Hunley Nancy 15 Jul 1863
Landing John T. to Ford Sophia E. 2 Sep 1856
Landing Lancely to Summers Margaret 26 Jun 1821
Landing Richard E. to Maddux Elizabeth 14 Jun 1842
Landing Thomas W. to Blake Alice Jane 1 May 1862
Landon Edward L. to McDaniel Virginia E. 6 May 1862
Landon Francis W. to Cox Margaret 21 Feb 1865
Landon Jesse to Mitchell Peggy 22 Jan 1801
Landon Richard to Ritchie Sarah E. 7 May 1861
Landreth John to Gilliss Peggy 1 Aug 1797
Landroth John to Wright Sarah 13 Feb 1809
Lane John H. (Capt.) to Scott Ann M. 10 Apr 1855
Lane William to Waters Maria E. 21 Dec 1871
Langford Aaron C. to Moore Allazan --(?) 1838
Langford John to Langford Matilda 28 Apr 1823
Langford Joseph to Summers Joseph 25 Oct 1814
Langrall Samuel A. to Roberts Mary J. 30 Jun 1857
Langrall William J. to Absalom Mary E. 31 May 1853
Langsdale Henry to Porter Elizabeth 9 Feb 1798
Langsdale Henry J. to Brattan Ann M. 3 Feb 1862
Langsdale Hurt to Bird Polly 15 Mar 1808
Langsdale James R. to Hopkins Elizabeth J. 13 Mar 1838
Langsdale John to Hopkins Elizabeth 29 Feb 1828
Langsdale Joshua W. to Larmore Mary J. 4 Nov 1845
Langsdale Peter W. to Farrington Elizabeth A. 27 Aug 1832
Langsdale Robert to Dean Elizabeth 6 Jul 1809
Langsdale Robert to Bedsworth Eleanor 8 Aug 1837
Langsdale Robert to Bounds Biddy L. 16 Jul 1844
Langsdale Robert to Brown Roxanna V. 9 Feb 1866
Langsdale Thomas to Stevens Mary Anne D. 25 Feb 1835
Langsdale William to Porter Ebby 11 Sep 1809
Lankford A.J.H. to Brewington Mary E. 18 Jun 1862
Lankford Aaron C. to Shockley Molly 14 Feb 1826
Lankford Abraham to Whaley Nancy 26 Feb 1822
Lankford Alexander to Moore Elizabeth 23 Jun 1863
Lankford Alfred to Crosswell Keziah 15 Jul 1851
Lankford Anthony to Gale Leah A. 22 Apr 1869 C

Lankford Arthur to Cluff Sarah A. 22 Jan 1861
Lankford Arthur to Hall Kitturah 19 Jan 1869 C
Lankford Arthur H. to Berkhead Henrietta 14 Dec 1824
Lanhford Arthur H. to Crockett Emily M. 22 Sep 1859
Lankford Azariah P. to Coulbourn Esther L.A. 16 Aug 1865
Lankford Benjamin to Holland Patty 24 Dec 1816
Lankford Benjamin to Gibbons Mary 15 Oct 1833
Lankford Benjamin (of Benj) to Porter Susan 22 Jan 1822
Lankford Benjamin F. to Porter Amanda E.S. 20 Dec 1859
Lankford Benjamin F. to Dryden Matilda J. 16 Feb 1863
Lankford Charles to Elzey Charlotte 27 Feb 1865 C
Lankford Charles to Cornish Amy A. 9 Oct 1867 C
Lankford Coulbourn to Lankford Mary 23 Apr 1816
Lankford David to Long Betsy 9 Oct 1798
Lankford David to Gibbons Esther Ann 28 Oct 1823
Lankford Edward F. to Howard Julia 4 Jan 1868
Lankford Edward K.B. to Denson Esther A. 29 Jan 1866
Lankford Elijah to Adams Peggy 19 Apr 1797
Lankford Elijah to Hopkins Hannah 6 Dec 1803
Lankford Ezekiel to Campbell Esther 11 Mar 1800
Lankford Ezephan to Miles Elizabeth 5 Jan 1832
Lankford George H. to Puzey Adaline J. 4 Sep 1865
Lankford George W. to Tull Elizabeth Anne 11 Sep 1834
Lankford George W. to Lankford Juliann 30 Nov 1841
Lankford Henry to Dakes Nancy S. 5 Sep 1810
Lankford Henry W. to Miles Esther A. 30 Jun 1863
Lankford Hiram to Hitch Letty 29 Aug 1820
Lankford Isaac S. to Coulbourn Harriet 11 Mar 1845
Lankford Isaac Smith to Coulbourn Sarah S. 15 Mar 1836
Lankford Isaac T.D. to Kellum Sarah J. 27 Aug 1866
Lankford Isaac W. to Adams Eliza A. 26 Jan 1836
Lankford James to Sterling Harriet S. 20 Nov 1832
Lankford James to Adams Mary 4 Dec 1839
Lankford James to Reece Catharine 10 Jan 1851
Lankford John to Odear Leah 9 Oct 1798
Lankford John to Lankford Nancy 30 Sep 1817
Lankford John to Haley Laura Anne 9 Feb 1858
Lankford John to Turpin Henny 29 Jan 1867 C
Lankford John A. to Broughton Augusta 3 Apr 1822
Lankford John H. to White Mary G. 11 Dec 1851

Lankford John H.O. to Lankford Mary C. 28 Mar 1865
Lankford John L. to Lankford Mary 15 May 1856
Lankford John S. to Corbin Juliet 13 Jun 1860
Lankford John T.P. to Johnson Mary E. 10 Feb 1863
Lankford Joseph to Coulbourn Nancy 9 Jul 1798
Lankford Joseph to Moore Nancy 19 Aug 1816
Lankford Joseph C.C. to Dyze Clementina 1 Oct 1866
Lankford Joseph W. to Garrison Agnes M. 16 Feb 1864
Lankford Joshua to Leach Hetty 18 Jan 1827
Lankford Lazarus to Miles Marcilla 16 Jan 1821
Lankford Lazarus to Milbourne Mary Ann 15 Jul 1836
Lankford Littleton to Townsend Adaline 20 Mar 1827
Lankford Nathan J. to Wilson Eliza W. 10 Mar 1832
Lankford Noah to Bozman Mary Ann 28 Oct 1800
Lankford Noah T. to Marshall Mary Jane 14 Apr 1858
Lankford Noah T. to Boatman Annie 7 Sep 1864
Lankford Robert to Potter Polly 22 Mar 1809
Lankford Robert to Hall Margaret 26 Dec 1848
Lankford Robert H. to Cottingham Sally L. 18 Dec 1829
Lankford Samuel to Ingersoll Euphamia 9 Feb 1813
Lankford Smith to Miles Caroline W. 4 Jun 1832
Lankford Smith to Green Alice K. 9 Jan 18b6
Lankford Stephen to Tully Polly 11 Nov 1802
Lankford Stephen to Beauchamp Leah 9 Jun 1821
Lankford Thomas to Swift Sally 10 Feb 1827
Lankford Thomas to Boston Mary 10 May 1831
Lankford Thomas to Boston Mary 10 May 1831
Lankford Thomas to Maddux Rosy 10 Sep 1851
Lankford Thomas W. to Heighe Elizabeth 26 Aug 1856
Lankford Tubman C. to Bunting Mary 14 May 1835
Lankford Tubman C. to Rollins Hannah A. 28 Jan 1869
Lankford Uriah to Bounds Priscilla E. 23 May 1866
Lankford Washington to Ennis Susanna 28 Jan 1869
Lankford William to Hall Zipporah 17 Feb 1801
Lankford William to Barrett Betsy 15 Feb 1803
Lankford William to Dunn Priscilla 29 Apr 1857
Lankford William to Adams Josephine 3 Jun 1857
Lankford William to Bailey Rachel D.D. 5 Jan 1860
Lankford William D. to Holland Mary Jane 11 Nov 1845
Lankford William D. to Adams Annie 21 Nov 1859

Lankford William H. to Lankford Sarah A.S. 16 Jun 1822
Lankford William H. to Burkett Elizabeth 17 Feb 1835
Lankford William H. to Pollitt Sally 21 Dec 1837
Lankford William H. to Sterling Grace T. 10 Aug 1855
Lankford William to How Hayman Lydia 9 Dec 1800
Lankford William S. to Adams Amelia E. 8 Jul 1856
Lankford Zephen to Ward Mary Jane 27 Jul 1839
Lansing Isaac T. to Holland Hester A. 31 May 1853
Laramore Eben to Dunn Rosetta 16 Jan 1810
Larimore Henry to Street Elizabeth 9 Oct 1832
Larimore John to Walter Priscilla 28 Oct 1840
Larimore William N. to Blake Elizabeth E. 26 Aug 1835
Larmore Charles W. to Jarrett Sarah R. 23 May 1865
Larmore Ebenezer to Horsman Mary A. 19 Sep 1844
Larmore Ebenezer to Landen Margaret A. 4 Nov 1851
Larmore Elihu to Winright Leah 13 Nov 1822
Larmore Elihu to Winright Sarah 15 Jun 1830
Larmore Esau to Green Priscilla 16 Nov 1816
Larmore Esau to Covington Louisa 20 Jun 1865
Larmore Francis G. to Horsman Mary E. 15 Jan 1850
Larmore George E. to Walter Mary J. 22 Dec 1841
Larmore George H. to Hemons Mary E. 28 Nov 1866
Larmore George R. to Horseman Mary W. 16 May 1865
Larmore Hezrow to Williams Sally 9 Dec 1851
Larmore Isaiah to Hobbs Elizabeth 4 Feb 1809
Larmore Isaiah to Howard Polly 22 Jan 1811
Larmore Jackson to Parks Zaris 9 Jan 1835
Larmore Jacob to Jarrett Comfort 18 May 1813
Larmore Jacob to Jackson Charity M. 11 Mar 1856
Larmore James to Nelson Mary 8 Aug 1829
Larmore James to Salisbury Mary 4 Aug 1830
Larmore James A. to Roberts Susan 15 Feb 1836
Larmore James M. to Wilson Margaret E. 30 Nov 1852
Larmore John to Jones Mary Ann 7 Oct 1823
Larmore John to Walston Leah Jane 3 Nov 1847
Larmore John to Larmore Betsy 23 Sep 1851
Larmore John A. to Cantwell Rebecca A. 15 Jun 1870
Larmore John R. to Dunn Hester A. 2 Feb 1864
Larmore John S. to Adams Mary E. 13 Jul 1856
Larmore Joseph to Horsman Susan 26 Nov 1861

Larmore Louther to Robertson Polly Wells 11 Nov 1823
Larmore Marcellus W.J. to Larmore Sarah 15 Jan 1858
Larmore Raymond to Larmore Lurania 22 Feb 1842
Larmore Reuben to Dashiell Nancy 24 Nov 1818
Larmore Reubin T. to Bennett Mary E. 22 Feb 1864
Larmore Richard to Street Margaret 9 Nov 1830
Larmore William M. to Larmore Anne 26 Aug 1833
Larramore William to Libby Sarah 21 Jul 1801
Latchum George to Benata Polly 30 Jan 1821
Launder Edward to Whaler Harriet J. 12 Oct 1831
Laurence Joseph to Jones Mary Anne 19 Dec 1833
Laurence William to Shepherd Mary Anne 5 Aug 1834
Lawes Thomas to Long Nelly 12 Jan 1801
Lawes William to Aries Amelia 1 Aug 1809
Lawrence Elijah to Nicholson Esther 27 Sep 1815
Lawrence Garratt to Dickerson Emeline H.M. 11 Jan 1844
Lawrence Jonadab to Dubberly Hesse 16 Oct 1821
Lawrence Purnell to White Sarah 16 Oct 1838
Lawrence Wesley to Bozman Hester 12 May 1866
Lawrence William B. to Hopkins Annie R. 17 Dec 1867
Lawrence William John to Bounds Selah 9 Aug 1859
Laws Edward to Lawson Grace 21 Jan 1845
Laws John to Gunby Mary 28 Aug 1819
Laws John Q. to Hewitt Mary Anne 14 Jun 1853
Laws William to Wilson Sarah 11 Jun 1816
Lawson Augustus B. to Lawson Nancy 30 Jul 1855
Lawson Elijah to Johnson Jane 15 Jun 1824
Lawson George L. to Sterling Emily 7 Dec 1853
Lawson George W. to Lawson Maria W. 12 Jan 1864
Lawson George W. to Riggin Elizabeth A. 27 Dec 1864
Lawson Hance to Sterling Emeline 22 May 1846
Lawson Isaac to Tyler Nancy 7 Feb 1809
Lawson Isaac to Sterling Hannah 4 Feb 1812
Lawson Isaac to Lankford Sally 15 Aug 1815
Lawson Isaac to Moore Nancy 8 Jun 1827
Lawson Isaac to Taws Nancy 27 Dec 1839
Lawson Isaac to Somers Mahala 3 Nov 1840
Lawson Isaac to Nelson Mary A. 17 Feb 1851
Lawson Isaac to Sterling Sarah A.B. 23 Feb 1864
Lawson James to Nelson Mary 8 Aug 1829

Lawson James P. to Sterling Melissa 2 Aug 1864
Lawson John to Sterling Mary 18 Dec 1798
Lawson John to Summers Sally 15 Jan 1822
Lawson John to Sterling Grace 21 Oct 1825
Lawson John H. to Taws Casey Anne 14 Mar 1854
Lawson John H. to Sterling Nancy W. 6 Apr 1871
Lawson John J. to Sterling Mary 11 Sep 1838
Lawson John W. to Dougherty Margaret U. 22 Sep 1870
Lawson Lorenzo D. to Davey Sally R. 21 May 1840
Lawson Noah M. to Ward Nancy W. 4 Nov 1851
Lawson Samuel to Taws Eleanor 16 Sep 1851
Lawson Thomas H. to Tyler Mary A. 26 Jul 1964
Lawson Travers to Lawson Sarah Anne 1 Jul 1845
Lawson William to Lawson Caroline 1 Jul 1845
Lawson William H. to Sterling Julia A. 17 May 1864
Layfield Alfred to Bishop Elizabeth 27 Nov 1865
Layfield Edward to Atkinson Elizabeth (Mrs.) 9 Jan 1851
Layfield Ezekiel to Adams Sarah Elizabeth 18 Oct 1854
Layfield George to Carroll Sally 26 Jan 1808
Layfield George to Winright Mary 22 Dec 1840
Layfield George W. to Adams Elizabeth 2 Apr 1839
Layfield George W. to Ford Mary W. 15 Sep 1853
Layfield Isaac to Layfield Sally 21 Jan 1833
Layfield James to Beachamp Polly 19 Jul 1825
Layfield James to Blain Elizabeth J. 6 Feb 1838
Layfield Jesse to Staplefort Levisa 26 Jun 1813
Layfield John to McDaniel Priscilla 26 Apr 1808
Layfield John to McGee Elizabeth 3 Aug 1824
Layfield John to Layfield Sally 22 Dec 1827
Layfield John to Brewington Elizabeth 5 Jan 1847
Layfield John to Jenkins Drucilla 17 Jun 1851
Layfield Levin to Warwick Anne 26 Dec 1842
Layfield Peter to Barnes Mary E. 6 Dec 1860
Layfield Peter to Barnes Emily F. 24 Oct 1871
Layfield Robert to Nicholson Mary 9 Apr 1817
Layfield Solomon to Fox Sarah Ann E. 19 Sep 1836
Layfield Thomas to Bayley Sally 22 Nov 1804
Layfield Thomas to McClain Anne 10 Feb 1818
Layfield Thomas to Downing Anne 13 Mar 1838
Layfield William to Newman Leah 22 Feb 1817

Layfield William to Montgomery Molly 15 Jan 1828
Layfield Wm. to Warwick Elizabeth 21 Feb 1837
Layton James B. to Taylor Martha A. 9 Feb 1847
Leach George to Maddux Mary Jane 4 Aug 1838
Leapingcott Samuel to Smith Polly 29 Jan 1799
Leard Thomas W. to Dougherty Elizabeth Anne 30 Nov 1846
Leary William to Tull Zipporah 19 Oct 1855
Leatherbury Asa to Huffington Polly 6 Dec 1808
Leatherbury Ebin to Pincket Matilda 21 Mar 1865 C
Leatherbury George to Harris Delia 9 Jan 1855
Leatherbury George P. to Cullen Virginia 6 Jan 1858
Leatherbury James Littleton to Wingate Matilda F. 11 Jan 1858
Leatherbury John to Jones Mary 27 Oct 1824
Leatherbury John to Jones Mary 10 May 1831
Leatherbury John to Jones Mary 10 May 1831
Leatherbury John to Denson Maria 24 Nov 1834
Leatherbury John (Jr) to Hopkins Peggy 16 Jan 1815
Leatherbury Levin to Leatherbury Elizabeth 8 Sep 1818
Leatherbury Levin K. to Pollitt Priscilla 24 Apr 1822
Leatherbury Peregrine to Handy Betsy 30 May 1807
Leatherbury Samuel to Done Mary 18 Dec 1817
Leatherbury Stephen to Barkley Esther 10 Sep 1868 C
Leatherbury Thomas to Dorman Leah 20 Feb 1810
Leatherbury William to Ballard Anne 1 Dec 1813
Lecates Charles W. to Prier Matilda 16 Dec 1848
Lecates Elijah to Hall Esther 2 Oct 1845
Leckie John Q. to Porter Sallie P. 14 Sep 1863
Lecompte Hanson A. to Hull Mary S. 17 Mar 1837
Lecompte James M. to Owens Elizabeth W. 18 Aug 1852
Lecompte Samuel to North Esther 14 Nov 1826
Lecompte Solomon S. to Lowe Margaret E. 29 Jul 1864
Lecompte William to Lewis Jane 3 May 1854
Lee George T. to McDorman Annie F. 29 Jun 1870
Leech George E. to Hewitt Permelia A. 16 Jul 1861
Leech Robert to Beauchamp Priscilla F. 1 May 1871
Leonard George to ______ Margaret A. 15 Mar 1866 C
Leonard George W. to Williams Mary J. 20 Jan 1852
Leonard Isaac to Maddox Mary 18 Sep 1810
Leonard John to Jackson Sarah 13 Jan 1801
Letts James to Hall Harriet S. 3 Jul 1834

Levingston Stephen to Taylor Sarah 30 Oct 1827
Lewhit Louis to Morgan Lucy J. 31 Jan 1865
Lewis James to Gibbons Anne 4 Mar 1822
Lewis James to Horner Sarah J. 7 Oct 1856
Lewis John to Dunn Milly 28 Jun 1845
Lewis John A.W. to Elliott Sally 6 Jul 1869
Lewis John W. to Ward Margaret 2 Mar 1861
Lewis Minos to Wroten Sally 21 Dec 1835
Lewis Minus to Matthews Sally 28 Aug 1838
Lewis Paton to Small Charlotte 16 May 1870 C
Lewis Rayman to Marshall Catherine 30 Dec 1858
Lewis Teackle to Cooper Polly 18 Feb 1800
Lewis William to Thomas Polly 20 Aug 1824
Lewis William to Dorman Emeline 13 Oct 1835
Lewis William to Crockett Elizabeth J. 23 Jun 1860
Lewis William J. to Phoebus Mary J. 26 Jan 1870
Lewis William R. to Russell Sarah 15 Jun 1848
Lewis William T. to Adams Susan M. 10 Sep 1858
Lewis Wingate to Russell Kate 28 Dec 1871
Linton Elijah to Robertson Eleanor 29 Sep 1801
Linton Jacob to Evans Nicey 24 May 1836
Linton Major to Pharks Euphemia 22 Nov 1826
Linton William W. to Bennett Caroline 31 Oct 1864
Livingston John to Hillman Elizabeth A.W. 11 Jan 1848
Lloyd Amon to Sewell Mary Elizabeth 3 Jan 1851
Lloyd Barney B. to Webster Lucretia 24 Jul 1814
Lloyd Edward to Olpha Nancy 16 Dec 1801
Lloyd Edward B. to Drura Elizabeth 19 Apr 1843
Lloyd Israel to Moore Margaret Anne 8 Nov 1851
Lloyd James to Russell Priscilla 24 Dec 1798
Lloyd James to Rhodes Rachael R. 27 Jun 1834
Lloyd John to Kersey Sarah 24 Dec 1798
Lloyd John to Phillips Jane 13 Feb 1839
Lloyd Levin W. to Flowers Susanna M. 5 May 1868
Lloyd Mitchell to Powell Elizabeth 11 Dec 1837
Lloyd Mitchell to Green Mary Jane 17 Feb 1840
Lloyd Moses to Jones Annie M. 9 Jul 1870 C
Lloyd Peter to Smith Priscilla 30 Aug 1842
Lloyd Peter to Majors Elizabeth 2 Jun 1849
Lloyd Ralph to Wilson Susan E. 17 Apr 1860

Lloyd Samuel to Cox Sally 6 Apr 1836
Lloyd Thomas to Jones Susan I. (or J.) 5 Feb 1831
Lloyd Thomas to Middleton Luraney 6 Mar 1845
Lloyd William to English Priscilla 24 Jul 1810
Lloyd William to Mezick Esther 10 Jul 1827
Lloyd William to Lloyd Mary Jane 11 May 1841
Lloyd William S. to Elliott Emily 5 Jun 1866
Lockerman Francis S. to Ballard Annie D. 9 Feb 1870
Lockerman Thomas to Bayly Peggy 1 May 1804
Lokey Benjamin to Ford Margaret 20 Jun 1848
Lokey Dingley to Williams Mary 23 Aug 1836
Lokey Francis to Shores Emily 13 Feb 1861
Long Aurelius to Cluff Susannah 25 Dec 1860
Long David to Elzey Henrietta 13 Aug 1818
Long David to Miles Anne 1 Dec 1823
Long David to Gibbons Sarah 15 Oct 1834
Long Edward to Roach Aurelia Anne 21 Jun 1843
Long Edwin M. to Benson Mary A. 11 May 1842
Long Edwin M. to Hawks Emily A. 29 Oct 1857
Long George W. to Taylor Margaret 18 Dec 1869
Long Henry to Sturgis W. 30 May 1871 C
Long Henry K. to Curtis Susan H. 17 Mar 1819
Long Henry W. to Jones Henrietta S. 14 Jun 1832
Long Henry W. to Mitchell Maria 16 Dec 1845
Long James W. to Powell Mary H. 3 Nov 1851
Long John to Gibbons Anne 28 Jun 1827
Long John S. to Covington Emily 8 Jan 1862
Long Josiah to Miles Elizabeth 23 Aug 1825
Long Levin to Whittington Maria A. 20 Jul 1818
Long Levin T. to Stevenson Elizabeth 12 Jan 1864
Long Littleton to Tull Anne 31 May 1808
Long Littleton to Coston Anne 14 Mar 1821
Long Littleton (Sr.) to Jones Sarah L. 5 Jul 1858
Long Samuel to Killum Elizabeth 21 Jun 1804
Long Santa Anna to King Mary A.P. 10 Mar 1863
Long Sewell to Powell Mary 22 Sep 1801
Long Solomon to Matthews Nelly 25 Jun 1803
Long Solomon to Carver Mary 3 Jun 1815
Long Stephen to Collins Polly 2 Feb 1866 C
Long Sydney C. to Wilson Mary A.S. 14 Feb 1849

Long Sydney C. to Hayman Josephine 4 Oct 1865
Long Theodore to Gibbons Cenia Anna 29 Oct 1860
Long Thomas N. to Riggin Mary Anne 23 Mar 1835
Long Thomas W. to White Louisa V. 11 Feb 1863
Long William to Miles Priscilla 29 Dec 1802
Long William to Banks Polly 11 Jun 1807
Long William to Adams Mary Anne 26 Apr 1836
Long William H.C. to Broughton Mary S. 7 Apr 1847
Long William M.P. to Matthews Sally J. 6 Jun 1865
Long Zadoc Rufus to Gibbons Maria 18 Dec 1867
Lord Aaron to Horsey Mary 30 Aug 1836
Lord Asbury to Davis Keziah 16 Jul 1868
Lord Elijah to Hull Maria 21 Jul 1863 C
Lord Elsby to Hearn Charlotte 2 Feb 1835
Lord Jesse to Jones Milcah 15 Dec 1800
Lord John to Harris Mary 21 Nov 1853
Lord John W. to Johnson Sarah J. 13 May 1862
Lord Levi to Johnson Sally 18 May 1832
Lord Severn to Dougherty Patty 4 Jul 1848
Lord Stephen to Riggin Jemima 6 Oct 1801
Lord Thomas to ______ Betsy 17 Jan 1797
Lord Thomas W. to Dougherty Angeline 1 Oct 1858
Lord William to Duncan _____ 8 Oct 1846
Lore John Q. to Nelson Jane 10 May 1870
Lowe Cyrus to Elliss Leah Jane 9 Dec 1850
Lowe E. Louis to Polk Esther Wanda 29 May 1844
Lowe George to Bounds Mary Anne 14 Jan 1845
Lowe George R. to Taylor Sarah S. 7 Mar 1865
Lowe James R. to Disharoon Esther A. 9 Feb 1864
Lowe John to Fitcheh Shada (?) 2 Feb 1819
Lowe Levin to Weatherly Matilda 4 Mar 1828
Lowe Levin R. to Waller Elizabeth E. 26 Nov 1855
Lowe Ralph to Bounds Bridget 15 Nov 1819
Lowe Ralph to Evans Elizabeth 29 Jul 1834
Lowe Robert to Mills Isabella 29 Jan 1822
Lowe William W. to Dashiell Mary Catherine 18 Feb 1862
Lowes Tubman to Dashiell Sarah 30 Apr 1816
Lowrie James to Kennerly Luvisa 4 Jun 1833
Loyd Curtis to Owens Lizzy 28 Apr 1820
Lynch Joseph E. to Moore Sarah R. 29 Aug 1853

Macca James Smith to Handy Seusan Dashiell 16 Apr 1803
Mack Samuel to Conway Hester 15 Nov 1865 C
Maddox Hannibal to Hull Hester 12 Mar 1870 C
Maddox Samuel to Silverthorn Amelia 29 Mar 1803
Maddux Benjamin to Holland Elizabeth Anne 23 Feb 1848
Maddux Charles T. to Cottman Mary 18 Oct 1831
Maddux Daniel H. to Ballard Susan M.N. 17 May 1836
Maddux Daniel J. to Hall Elizabeth P. 17 Feb 1864
Maddux Edward S. to McDaniell Lydia M. 6 May 1846
Maddux Elijah to Collins Hetty 10 Jan 1815
Maddux Ezekiel to Reddish Zipporah 21 Jan 1824
Maddux George to Riggin Mary 23 Jan 1812
Maddux George to Somers Rebecca 6 Jan 1813
Maddux George to Sheehee Hetty 7 Jan 1823
Maddux George to Davy Mimy 22 Nov 1866 C
Maddux George to Turpin Henny 19 Oct 1867 C
Maddux Gustavus A. to Maddux Elizabeth D. 15 Feb 1858
Maddux Henry to Johnson Arracada 22 Apr 1817
Maddux Henry to Turpin Ann 23 Sep 1823
Maddux Henry to Anderson Margaret 14 Jan 1834
Maddux Isaac to Hurst Betsy 10 Jan 1809
Maddux James to Ellis Leah J. 9 Dec 1850
Maddux Jesse to Cahoon Zipporah 14 Jun 1803
Maddux John to Milligan Sally 2 Feb 1809
Maddux John to McDaniel Jane 23 Jul 1816
Maddux John to Harris Nancy 7 Sep 1841
Maddux John to McDaniel Sarah J. 14 Feb 1849
Maddux John H. to Waters Caroline 18 Feb 1868 C
Maddux Joseph G. to Ballard Sallie G. 9 Nov 1871
Maddux Lazarus to Bayley Peggy 6 Dec 1808
Maddux Lazarus C. to Adams Leah J. 15 Jul 1852
Maddux Levin L. to Nance Julia A. 22 Feb 1848
Maddux Littleton to Long Lydia 26 May 1868
Maddux Littleton D. to Maddux Leah 18 Aug 1813
Maddux Luther M.H. to Williams Arietta 18 Dec 1838
Maddux Robert to Tull Martha 21 Oct 1845
Maddux Samuel H. to McDaniel Mary 24 Dec 1829
Maddux Samuel W.S. to Mills Lavinia A. 20 Nov 1861
Maddux Samuel W.S. to Mezick Sarah C. 8 Jul 1867
Maddux Stoughton to Maddux Betsy 9 Nov 1812

Maddux Thomas J. to Wheyland Lucinda 12 Feb 1850
Maddux William to Miles Leah 9 Dec 1797
Maddux William to Waters Rachael 19 Jun 1858 C
Maddux William to Fontaine Priscilla F. 6 Jun 1866 C
Maddux William H. to Ward Sarah 25 Dec 1849
Maddux William H. to Small Henrietta 1 Mar 1870 C
Maddux William S. to Tull Mary M. 4 Jun 1820
Maddux William W. to Dashiell Jane 9 Mar 1830
Majors Kendal to Alpha Aurelia 20 Dec 1847
Majors William to Russell Esther 20 Jan 1862
Malcomb Elias to Windsor Sarah 29 Apr 1816
Malcomb Elias to Durham Sally 16 Feb 1822
Malcomb George to Anderson Leah 5 Sep 1809
Malcomb George to Noble Elizabeth 2 Jul 1821
Malcomb Levin to Davis Betsy 16 Jan 1804
Malcomb Robert to Green Sally 28 Dec 1802
Malcomb Tubman to Gilliss Elizabeth 18 Dec 1804
Malcomb William to Harris Ritty 6 Jun 1821
Malone Alexander to Crouch Julia 2 May 1837
Malone David to Williams Nancy 25 May 1839
Malone George (Jr) to Porter Elizabeth W. 30 Oct 1832
Malone George W. to Denson Mary V. 26 Jan 1864
Malone John to Blyden Elizabeth 28 Aug 1838
Malone Lemuel to Gunby Julia 9 Jan 1866
Malone Levi to Pryor Lysia 17 Dec 1850
Malone Levin W. to Standford Sarah G. 16 Oct 1849
Malone Purnell Wesley to Booth Mary Anne 6 Mar 1860
Malone Robert to Disharoon Harriet 2 Mar 1841
Malone Sidney G. to Goslee Mary E. 4 Jun 1868
Malone Stephen to Hitch Dolly 12 Oct 1842
Malone Sydney G. to Stevens Ellen 3 Apr 1861
Malone Thomas to Cheetham Nancy 12 Jan 1842
Malone William to Goslee Frances 5 Nov 1799
Malone William to Dorman Eliza 1 Mar 1836
Malone William to Prior Sally 6 Feb 1849
Marble James to Hearn Julia Ann 16 Mar 1847
Marian James to Robertson Rhoda 23 Jan 1833
Mariner John O. to Taylor Priscilla A. 15 Jun 1869
Mariner Matthew W. to Bloxson Margaret 4 Dec 1822
Mariner White to Matthews Sarah Anne 25 Feb 1851

Mariner Whitty J. to Beauchamp Eliza Anne 31 Oct 1855
Mariner William T. to Matthews Sally Ann 2 Jan 1849
Marriner Edward James to Trehern Adaline 1 Apr 1847
Marriner John H. to Beauchamp Sarah M. 12 Jan 1842
Marriner William T. to Jones Sarah L.M. 11 Dec 1855
Marsh Walter H. to Evans Rhoda 2 May 1826
Marshall Adrian to Bedsworth Nelly 26 Dec 1843
Marshall Charles T. to Porter Priscilla M. 3 Apr 1849
Marshall Effraim to Mathews Sarah A. 11 Jun 1853
Marshall Ephraim to Noble Polly 30 Jul 1799
Marshall Ephraim to Saulsbury Casey 5 May 1836
Marshall George to Kelly Mary 16 May 1820
Marshall George D. to Marshall Jane 13 Jan 1857
Marshall George W. to Smith Surania C. 13 Nov 1863
Marshall Henry J. to Burnett Mary 9 May 1867 C
Marshall Isaac T. to Milbourn Peggy 25 Oct 1831
Marshall James A. to Garrison Isabella S. 20 Feb 1866
Marshall John to Banks Nancy 9 Nov 1802
Marshall John P. to Handy Martha W. 24 Apr 1811
Marshall John R. to Crockett Eliza A. 2 Feb 1858
Marshall Lewis F. to Miles Mary E. 14 Dec 1866
Marshall Matthias to Hopkins Esther A. 15 Oct 1859
Marshall Robert to Hall Esther 11 Jul 1803
Marshall Robert H. to Cox Mary E. 9 Feb 1835
Marshall Samuel to Smith Nancy 15 Jan 1828
Marshall Stephen to Coulbourn Esther 13 Feb 1802
Marshall Thomas to Milbourn Sarah 24 Nov 1807
Marshall Thomas to Hopenole(?) Elizabeth 3 Mar 1812
Marshall Thomas to Benson Sarah 25 Apr 1848
Marshall William to Conner Nelly 13 Jan 1801
Marshall William to Milbourn Sarah 6 Dec 1803
Marshall William to Adams Margaret 2 Dec 1812
Marshall William to Beard Mary 25 Mar 1816
Marshall William to Sparrow Rachel 16 Sep 1848
Marshall William S. to Burgess Mary R. 6 Jan 1865
Martha John to Dorman Oris 28 Dec 1819
Martin Daniel to King Polly 4 Oct 1816
Martin Daniel to King Elizabeth 10 Nov 1831
Martin George to Dryden Sally 24 Nov 1823
Martin Henry J. to Ross Mary E. 15 Feb 1871

Martin John to Ward Elizabeth 6 Jun 1802
Martin Luther to Thomas Sally 15 Sep 1832
Martin Thomas to Mungar Polly 30 Mar 1802
Martin Thomas to Horner Rhoda 28 Jan 1812
Martin Thomas to Hill Anne 28 Jan 1818
Martin Thomas to Somers Emeline 1 Aug 1827
Martin Thomas to Parks Eliza 19 Jun 1845
Martin William to Redden Peggy 29 Mar 1802
Martin William to Williams Eleanor 28 Dec 1840
Martin William to Walker Emeline 12 Aug 1845
Martin William to Pusey Margaret 12 May 1860
Martin William W. to Mezick Martha J. 12 Mar 1867
Marvel Ephraim to Freeny Eliza Jane 25 Mar 1848
Marvell Thomas to Nelson Priscilla 11 Mar 1835
Mash Charles to Parks Charity 2 Mar 1829
Mason Alfred to Ewell Lizzie 21 Mar 1871 C
Mason Bennett to Trehern Elizabeth T. 11 Nov 1845
Mason Bennett to Trehearn Sally 13 Apr 1852
Mason Edward to Dougherty Anna 26 Jun 1860
Mason Ephraim to Linton Sirah 3 Jun 1834
Mason Ephraim H. to Shores Virginia F. 29 Jan 1867
Mason George to Sterling Milcah 5 Jun 1812
Mason George to Conner Polly Jul 1812
Mason George S. to Taws Elizabeth 21 Dec 1846
Mason George S. to Cullen Lovey A. 10 Aug 1869
Mason James K. to Blades Adeline D. 1 Sep 1845
Mason John to Evans Jemima 24 Nov 1815
Mason John to Hanby Elizabeth 24 Feb 1835
Mason John to Moore Magilla 19 Jun 1839
Mason John T. to Thomas Lauretta D. 13 Nov 1866
Mason Lawson J. to Parks Emma J. 16 Aug 1870
Mason Middleton to Tyler Rosey Ellender 13 Apr 1802
Mason Middleton T. to Lankford Henrietta 14 May 1862
Mason Riley to Dashiell Margaret 28 Jun 1854
Mason William to Lankford Alice Ann 7 Jan 1852
Mason William C. to Wilson Sally J. -- Nov 1865
Massey Wilbur F. to Phoebus Sarah E. M. 1 Apr 1861
Mathews George W. to Howard Rebecca P. 11 Jun 1853
Mathews Levin to Rencher Louisa 9 May 1849
Mathews William W. to Odian Sarah M. 6 Jun 1853

Matthews Bartholamew to Bacon Mary G. 23 Nov 1854
Matthews Charles L. to Corbin Mary A. 23 Dec 1868
Matthews Elijah Z. to Kellum Harriet E.T. 29 Jul 1868
Matthews George to Mezick Jane 27 Aug 1816
Matthews George to Carsley Sally 22 Oct 1816
Matthews Henry to Melvin Sarah 15 Jan 1839
Matthews Henry W. to Walston Nancy 30 Jan 1832
Matthews Henry W. to Riggin Margaret 12 Jun 1843
Matthews Isaac to Lankford Sophia 4 Sep 1804
Matthews Isaac to Kersey Nancy 16 Sep 1815
Matthews James to Curtis Sarah M. 16 Sep 1857
Matthews Jesse to Austin Martha 29 May 1809
Matthews Jesse to Kelly Nelly 4 Jun 1816
Matthews John to Taylor Milly 31 Dec 1816
Matthews John to Nelson Esther 19 Nov 1834
Matthews Joshua to Lord Polly 28 Jan 1805
Matthews Joshua J. to Beauchamp Sarah E. 16 May 1864
Matthews Levi to Dickerson Nancy 3 Apr 1811
Matthews Levin to Majors Sarah C. 5 Dec 1865
Matthews Samuel to Adams Sally 4 Dec 1828
Matthews Samuel to Mills Nancy J. 2 Aug 1831
Matthews Samuel to Hudson Amelia Anne 26 Mar 1839
Matthews Samuel to Hudson Mary G. 3 Feb 1845
Matthews Thomas to Muir Betsy 11 Oct 1826
Matthews Thomas to Henderson Matilda 22 Apr 1851
Matthews Thomas H. to Phobus Margaret A. 11 Jun 1844
Matthews Thomas K. to Dorman Sarah E. 29 Jun 1841
Matthews Whittington to Muir Sarah 15 Feb 1820
Matthews William to Mills Ebby 21 Feb 1797
Matthews William to O'dear Martha 4 Oct 1810
Matthews William to Hobbs Mary 22 May 1821
Matthews William to Bridle Mary Anne 21 Jan 1854
Matthews William (Sr.) to Tull Agnes 2 Jan 1854
Matthews Zachariah to McCready Lotty 28 Jan 1804
Mayne David to Parks Arianna 22 Jun 1859
McAlister Alfred E. to Bennett Emily E. 15 Apr 1856
McBride William to Riggin Emily F. 13 Jan 1864
McBryde Charles to Jones Annie 15 Nov 1870 C
McBryde Elijah to Jones Sarah 24 Jun 1869 C
McBryde Samuel to Townsend Elizabeth A. 9 Mar 1813

McClain John E. to Williams Sally A. 19 Jun 1849
McClain Levin to Catlin Sarah C. 29 Jan 1845
McClannon Benjamin to Venables Anne 17 Apr 1804
McClean James to Tull Harriet 6 Feb 1816
McClemy George T. to Fisher Martha A. 23 Apr 1860
McClemmy John to Taylor Mary C. 19 May 1863
McClemmy Thomas to Brown Harriet 3 Mar 1829
McCollister James to Cordray Angeline 27 Jan 1840
McCollister Joseph F. to Briddell Julia A. 10 Feb 1863
McCollister Spencer E. to Brown Sarah E.J. 20 Mar 1849
McCormack John P. to Cottman Elizabeth Anne 22 Mar 1830
McCormick William L. to Cottman Esther H. 14 Mar 1826
McCoy Henry C. to Todd Leah Anna 20 Dec 1859
McCready Benjamin to Thomas Elizabeth 12 Jan 1819
McCready Benjamin to Bloyd Amanda 28 Feb 1856
McCready Benjamin F. to Lawson Mary Jane 23 Feb 1858
McCready Colemore A. to Carver Dolly Anne 10 Apr 1847
McCready George S. to Ward Lovey 13 Sep 1859
McCready George S. to Somers Sidonia V. 6 Nov 1866
McCready Harvey J. to Conway Fennitte J.A. 2 Dec 1853
McCready Isaac to Riggin Gertrude 15 Oct 1808
McCready John to Carvender Nelly 10 Sep 1817
McCready John D. to Parker Esther A. 18 Dec 1871
McCready Riley to McCready Sally 10 Jan 1837
McCready Robert H. to Sterling Sarah E. 19 Nov 1859
McCready Robert H. to Johnson Leah 22 Nov 1871 C
McCready Solomon to Carsey Polly 11 Aug 1807
McCready Thomas to Nelson Patty Ann 30 Jan 1849
McCready William Henry to Marshall Susan G. 2 Oct 1863
McCreddy Isaac to White Mathew 28 Mar 1797
McCree James to McBryde Frances 23 Dec 1801
McCreedy Benjamin to Revill Amelia 13 Apr 1852
McCulloh William to Merchant Betsy 27 Jan 1797
McDaniel Alfred to Carew Biddy 30 Nov 1859
McDaniel David to White Sebrew 18 Mar 1800
McDaniel Henry D. to Mills Elizabeth 18 Dec 1821
McDaniel James to Long Elizabeth 8 Jul 1823
McDaniel James to Heath Leah Anne 12 May 1847
McDaniel John to Williams Leah 11 Jul 1804
McDaniel John to Handy Eleanor 13 Aug 1816

McDaniel John to Layfield Maria 29 Feb 1860
McDaniel John F. to Henderson Adaline C. 4 Feb 1862
Mddaniel John H. to Parsons Mary Elizabeth 18 Feb 1868
McDaniel Marshall to Harris Maria 10 Jun 1819
McDaniel Marshall to Anderson Eliza 22 Jul 1830
McDaniel Peter to White Matilda 27 Feb 1827
McDaniel Peter to Beauchamp Mary 29 Aug 1838
McDaniel William to Maddux Sally 13 Feb 1801
McDaniel William to McDaniel Sarah 6 Aug 1838
McDaniel William to Wallace Sarah Elizabeth 26 Jun 1850
McDaniel William to Wallace Mary 30 Jun 1855
McDorman George to White Rebecca 3 Dec 1799
McDorman George to White Rebecca 8 Jan 1838
McDorman George to Townsend Frances C. 7 Sep 1865
McDorman James to McDorman Elizabeth 31 Dec 1822
McDorman James T. to White Martha A. 3 Aug 1848
McDorman James T.S. to White Virginia E. 25 Aug 1863
McDorman James T.S. to White Helen A. 25 Jul 1865
McDorman John H. to Davis Anna 18 Feb 1863
McDorman Lewis to Wallace Sally 26 Jul 1803
McDorman Lewis to _____ _____ 26 May 1818
McDorman Rufus A. to Price Beulah S. 13 Dec 1870
McDorman William to Dorman Rebecca 16 Sep 1846
McElhiney George to Bell Jane 1 Dec 1830
McGee James to Layfield Peggy 26 May 1812
McGee Peter to Layfield Leah 4 Feb 1817
McGlottan James H. to Game Harriet E. 29 Jan 1864
McGrath Asbury to White Julia A. 28 Oct 1856
McGrath David to Dorman Eliza 25 Jun 1800
McGrath David C. to Ross Eleanor 23 Nov 1813
McGrath Jesse H. to Dize Elizabeth 7 Aug 1847
McGrath John to Smith Anne 14 Feb 1797
McGrath John to Foxwell Grace 17 Jan 1826
McGrath John to Marshall Nancy 11 Jun 1828
McGrath John to Banks Rebecca 17 Jan 1832
McGrath John to Turner John 7 May 1839
McGrath John K. to Fitzgerald Sarah 30 Jun 1841
McGrath Joseph I. to Bloodsworth Mary A. 18 Jan 1870
McGrath Levin to Walter Betsy 19 Oct 1816
McGrath Lewis to Bloodsworth Rachael 16 Dec 1839

McGrath Thomas to Jones Arlita 7 Feb 1832
McGrath Thomas to Holder Sally A. 10 Apr 1844
McGrath Tubman to Covington Margaret 6 May 1817
McGrath William to M---(?) Dolly 29 Dec 1819
McGrath William to Wilkinson Mary R. 18 Apr 1837
McGrath William J. to Stewart Sarah R. 17 Nov 1863
McGrath William James to Parks Eliza Anne 20 Apr 1858
McGrawth Arthur W. to White Nelly 1 Dec 1863
McIntrye Jesse to Kerwin Eleanor 24 Sep 1824
McIntyre Columbus to Simms Alphonzo 3 Sep 1868
McIntyre John to Jones Mary Ellen 9 Dec 1850
McJones James to Anderson Mary Anne 11 Apr 1848
McKay Elijah to Price Mary 6 Apr 1819
McKensey Isaiah to Philips Betsy 10 Oct 1812
McKenzie James K. to Jones Mary W. 23 Jun 1846
McKinsey Isaiah to Wainright Betsy 25 Sep 1810
McKinzie Stephen to Gilliss Eleanor 21 May 1839
McLally Thomas to Tolly Anna 22 Feb 1803
McLane James to Parks Harriet Anne 23 Dec 1846
McLean William to Riggin Fanny R. 11 Jun 1855
McLewis Kendal to Covington Amanda M. 19 Dec 1839
McNamara John to Carey Margaret 9 Aug 1849
McNamara Patrick to Hollin Mary A. 8 Oct 1862
McNeal George W. to Durham Eliza 22 Dec 1855
McNeal William to Smith Mary Anne 17 Aug 1842
McNeill William to Ellis Matty 30 Jan 1821
Mcrea William to Jones Elizabeth 28 Oct 1867 C
Mears Isaac to Haywood Laura 21 Oct 1871 C
Melson Edward to Nicols Lida A. 24 Nov 1869
Melson Elijah to Tignall Sally 17 Nov 1813
Melson George H. to Tyson Anne E. 5 Sep 1867
Melson Joseph W. to Windsor Hester 30 May 1866
Melson Levin H. to Evans Elizabeth A. 22 Apr 1868
Melson Washington to Weatherly Julia Anne 15 Dec 1835
Melson William to Robertson Polly 31 Jan 1809
Melvin Alfred J. to Jones Mary E. 28 Feb 1865
Melvin David S. to Maddux Sarah M. 22 Oct 1857
Melvin Thomas to Glasgow Nancy 17 Mar 1818
Melvin Thomas to Williams Sally 26 Mar 1822
Melvin William Wesley to Beauchamp Harriet 30 Sep 1846

Meredith Daniel to Blake Rachel Ann 15 Aug 1848
Meredith Thomas to Gibson Nancy 28 Apr 1804
Meredith Thomas to Evans Mary Thomas 11 Dec 1821
Merrill George to Rounds Matilda J. 12 Feb 1861 C
Merrill Henry L. to Sterling Henrietta 20 Sep 1859
Mesick Aaron to Wailes Elizabeth 21 Jul 1812
Mesick Benjamin to Adams Rody 16 Jul 1812
Messick Daniel to Winright Priscilla 21 Feb 1797
Messick James to Parks Mary --- --- 1850
Mexick Littleton to Turner Mary 17 Nov 1828
Mezick Affra D. to Kelly Annie S. 10 Feb 1863
Mezick Alexander C. to Harrington Mary 5 Feb 1866
Mezick Benjamin to Wainright Anne E. 5 Jul 1842
Mezick Benjamin to Insley Betsy 6 May 1845
Mezick Benjamin F. to Porter Mary E. 19 Apr 1865
Mezick Bradshaw to Smith Eleanora 21 Dec 1865
Mezick Columbus to Venables Marietta 17 Dec 1862
Mezick Covington to Mezick Leah 9 Jan 1810
Mezick Daniel to Dashiell Sarah 10 Jan 1867 C
Mezick Dickerson to Bedsworth _____ (?) 15 Jun 1816
Mezick Elijah T. to Wilson Media M. 14 Feb 1865
Mezick Francis to Denson Sarah Anne 1 Jan 1834
Mezick Francis to Stevenson Ann 12 Jul 1843
Mezick Francis A. to Harris Matilda F. 10 Nov 1857
Mezick George to Anderson Leah A. 21 Nov 1865
Mezick George W. to White Julian 11 Oct 1847
Mezick George W. to Evans Matilda F. 30 Oct 1854
Mezick Henry to Barkley Mary E. 19 Nov 1861
Mezick Henry to Graham Harriet A. 14 May 1866
Mezick Isaac to Selby Leah 28 Nov 1832
Mezick Jacob to Hunpriss Jane 22 Jul 1817
Mezick James to Hopkins Elizabeth 2 Feb 1819
Mezick James to Elzey Caroline 27 Feb 1828
Mezick Jewell to Larramore Katherine 24 Sep 1799
Mezick John to Dorman Sarah 15 Jul 1800
Mezick John to Vinson Polly 31 Dec 1821
Mezick John to Downing Amelia 1 Feb 1853
Mezick John to Todd Permelia 29 Oct 1857
Mezick John to Collins Elizabeth 20 Jul 1858
Mezick John (Nanticoke) to Green Mary 21 Jun 1815

Mezick John A. to Tyre Lovey H. 19 Jun 1866
Mezick John F. to Brewington Emily F. 28 Jan 1862
Mezick John R.D. to Catlin Mary W. 9 Sep 1865
Mezick John S. to Dashiell Mary 31 Oct 1854
Mezick John W. to Denson Alice Jane 5 Jan 1858
Mezick John W. to Barkley Mary Eliza 4 Jul 1865
Mezick Joshua to Anderson Susan 25 Jan 1847
Mezick Levin to Mezick Eleanor 20 Feb 1819
Mezick Littleton to Anderson Margaret 5 Sep 1825
Mezick Merrill to Downing Writta Ann 19 Feb 1849
Mezick Nehemiah to Lord Jemima 29 Jun 1820
Mezick Nehemiah to Watlow Susan 25 Jul 1854
Mezick Nelson to Bennett Jenny 28 Jul 1801
Mezick Nelson to Taylor Susan E. -- Sep 1839
Mezck Nelson to Phillips Margaret 26 Jan 1849
Mezck Nelson to Venables Margaret 9 Dec 1851
Mezick Newton W. to Donoho Margaret 26 Jan 1813
Mezick Philip to Dryden Nelly 2 Jul 1839
Mezick Philip N. to Turner Martha E. 27 Nov 1866
Mezick Robert to Harris Olivia 9 Jun 1866
Mezick Samuel to Denson Drusilla 15 Dec 1835
Mezick Samuel W. to Barkley Martha A. 12 Jan 1863
Mezick Thomas to Jones Anne 12 Jun 1816
Mezick Tubman to Jones Nancy 17 Mar 1827
Mezick Tubman to Jones Eleanor 2 Feb 1841
Mezick Warren to Kennerly Octavia E. 6 Feb 1866
Mezick William to Handy Eleanor 26 Jul 1814
Mezick William to Hopkins Mary E. 27 Oct 1829
Mezick William to Phillips Esther A. 10 Dec 1833
Mezick William to Phillips Arietta 10 Jul 1838
Mezick William F.P. to Hopkins Henrietta 9 Feb 1858
Milbourn Benjamin to Cottingham Mary Anne 20 Jun 1826
Milbourn Charles D. to Broughton Henrietta 19 Jan 1848
Milbourn Elijah to Mitchell Nelly 3 Nov 1807
Milbourn Francis to Elliss Leah E. 8 Sep 1868
Milbourn Francis W. to Milbourne Arminta J. 26 Oct 1841
Milbourn George to Williams Sarah 6 Aug 1869 C
Milbourn Gilbert to Parks Susan 11 Jan 1798
Milbourn Jacob to McCready Hannah 25 Jun 1801
Milbourn Jacob to Catlin Peggy 5 Jan 1811

Milbourn James to Mason Nancy 15 May 1810
Milbourn James to Bonnewell Nancy 13 Dec 1843
Milbourn James to Paden Elizabeth 14 Feb 1855
Milbourn James M. to Dashiell Harriet 1 Oct 1867
Milbourn John to Merrill Nancy 3 Sep 1815
Milbourn John W. to Marshall Elizabeth H. 18 Mar 1845
Milbourn Lawrenson to Jewett Nelly 17 May 1859
Milbourn Levin to Riggin Rosy 23 Nov 1851
Milbourn Nathan to Mills Mary A. 26 Aug 1862
Milbourn Nathaniel to Bell Polly 18 Jan 1805
Milbourn Ralph to Grayham Sally 24 Feb 1801
Milbourn Ralph T. to Broughton Sarah A. 14 Aug 1866
Milbourn Robert to Riggin Anne 1 May 1804
Milbourn Robert to Davis Caroline 18 Jan 1854
Milbourn Robert H. to Bonnawell Elizabeth A. 13 Oct 1847
Milbourn Robert H. to Wilkins Mary E. 30 Mar 1861
Milbourn Samuel to Adams Harriet 9 Jul 1822
Milbourn Samuel to Davis Hetty W. 13 Mar 1832
Milbourn Samuel to Spencer Esther M. R. 13 Feb 1855
Milbourn Spencer to Handy Elissa 5 Mar 1867 C
Milbourn William to Paden Mary 16 Oct 1827
Milbourne _____ to Dise Audrey J. 26 Nov 1850
Milbourne Charles to Wood Nancy 9 Sep 1869
Milbourne John W. to Winder Eliza 25 Oct 1867 C
Milbourne Littleton to Beauchamp Margaret J. 4 Dec 1861
Milbourne Lodowick J. to Milbourn Sally D. 6 Mar 1827
Miles Alfred M. to King Aurelia 30 Oct 1851
Miles Alfred M. to Jones Virginia W. 14 Dec 1858
Miles Benjamin to English Molly 16 Aug 1808
Miles Daniel to Maddux Milcah Anne 4 Mar 1833
Miles Daniel to Hall Leah 26 Jul 1864
Miles George D. to McCready Sally 2 Aug 1842
Miles Henry to Ward Rachel 10 Mar 1798
Miles Henry to Adams Ann W. 13 Jun 1820
Miles Henry to Roach Hetty 6 Apr 1833
Miles Henry to Pusey Angeline 5 Oct 1854
Miles Hewett to Laws Hannah 30 Jan 1867 C
Miles Isaac to Davy Jane 16 Jun 1818
Miles Isaac to Boston Esther 21 Aug 1867 C
Miles Isaac T. to Adams Aurelia A. 24 Oct 1871

Miles Jacob to Hall Waife 4 Aug 1831
Miles James to Thomas Louisa 4 Jun 1829
Miles James E. to Hayward Amanda 11 Apr 1871 C
Miles Jesse to Shores Matilda A. 2 Feb 1858
Miles John to Michdanel Sally 13 Mar 1804
Miles John to Powell Catherine 18 May 1813
Miles John to Stevenson Hannah N. 3 Jul 1834
Miles John (of Wm.) to King Mary 10 Nov 1827
Miles John B. to Fontaine Sally Anne 10 Jun 1834
Miles John H. to Nelson Lovey W. 10 Feb 1851
Miles John H. to Mason Mary J. 16 Jan 1867
Miles Joseph Henry to Horner Sarah E. 6 Mar 1860
Miles Joshua H. to Croswell Henrietta W. 20 Feb 1838
Miles Lazarus A. to Miles Sarah E. 22 Feb 1854
Miles Levin to Mure Milcah A. 5 Aug 1851
Miles Levin to Wailes Eliza 31 Jan 1866 C
Miles Louis to Beckett Alice 1 Nov 1867 C
Miles Luther T. to Handy Anne E. 15 Oct 1856
Miles Matthias to Taylor Caroline 19 Nov 1856
Miles Matthias (Jr} to Pollitt Nancy 25 Jun 1807
Miles Poulson J. to Hall Sarah E. 4 Dec 1866
Miles Raymond to Houston Maria A. 11 May 1841 C
Miles Robert H. to Lankford Mary M. 18 Dec 1860
Miles Samuel to Lawson Polly 22 Jun 1808
Miles Samuel to Cox Hannah N. 4 Jul 1848
Miles Samuel to Stevens Chloe 26 Dec 1868 C
Miles Samuel to Barnes Mary 26 Sep 1870 C
Miles Samuel G. to Lankford Sarah A. 25 Oct 1853
Miles Samuel J. to Coulbourn Elizabeth 12 Jul 1843
Miles Southy to Roach Christianna 12 Oct 1846
Miles Stephen to Johnson Betsy 15 Jun 1808
Miles Stephen to Brown Eleanor 20 Jul 1808
Miles Stephen to Johnson Margaret 14 Jul 1846
Miles Stephen Revil to Ward Polly 5 May 1835
Miles Thomas to McDaniel Sally 25 Dec 1804
Miles Thomas to Holland Eliza J. 16 Oct 1855
Miles Thomas to Costen Matilda F. 10 Feb 1857
Miles Thomas to Ward Sarah 24 Jul 1866
Miles W.F.W. to Coston Sallie E.S. 8 Jun 1859
Miles Washington to Lankford Henrietta B. 14 Apr 1848

Miles Washington to Wood Caroline E.A. 23 Jun 1852
Miles Washington C. to Wards Ann 22 Nov 1869 C
Miles Whittington to Lamden Elizabeth 7 Apr 1849
Miles William to Ballard Peggy 3 Nov 1801
Miles William to Robertson Mary 17 Jun 1803
Miles William to Davy Elizabeth 8 Mar 1819
Miles William to Sterling Priscilla 4 Sep 1866 C
Miles William to Miles Mary A. 2 Jun 1869 C
Miles William F.W. to Dickerson Caroline V. 27 Apr 1847
Miles William R. to Dougherty Louisa 12 Feb 1868
Miller Isaac to Culver Elizabeth 2 Apr 1800
Miller James to Lankford Mary 23 Mar 1830
Miller James to Henderson Sarah Ann 21 Mar 1871
Miller John to Fisher Sally 11 May 1799
Miller John J. to Gibbons Marietta 29 Mar 1870
Miller Josephus to Marriner Leah G. 14 Jun 1870
Miller Levin to Smulling Nancy 24 Feb 1801
Miller Levin M. to Porter Sarah Anne 11 Aug 1847
Miller Levin T. to Powell Emeline E. 23 Nov 1857
Miller Nathaniel C. to Brown Elizabeth J. 19 Jan 1841
Millican Henry to McDaniel Peggy 6 Jan 1801
Milligan Edward (Capt.) to Holland Charlotte T. 5 Jan 1853
Milligan Edward W. to Tull Elizabeth A. 10 Dec 1867
Milligan Eli to Dorman Lizzy 5 Sep 1815
Milligan Eli M. to Somers Sarah Anne 23 Jun 1845
Milligan Isaac to Tull Mary J. 10 Jun 1856
Milligan John to Stevens Sally 1 Jan 1799
Milligan John to Cullen Louiza 2 Apr 1828
Milligan Josiah to Riggin Elizabeth 6 Oct 1828
Mills Benjamin to Dennis Mary Anne 13 Dec 1853
Mills Clayton H. to Wilson Hester 16 Mar 1863
Mills Edward W. to Henderson Mary A. 4 Jan 1859
Mills George L. to McCollister Mary 16 Jan 1867
Mills George W. to Anderson Louisa 11 Apr 1843
Mills Henry C. to Mills Palmira B. 16 Dec 1856
Mills Isaac to Hastings Mary A. 30 Jul 1844
Mills Isaac to Jenkins Charlotte A. 25 Apr 1864
Mills James B. (or P.) to Lankford Betsy 28 Jan 1797
Mills Jehu M. to Freeney Amelia 17 Dec 1832
Mills John to Milbourn Margaret 28 Aug 1866

Mills John H. to Powell Laura V. 11 Jan 1871
Mills Josiah D. to Wright Margaret 19 Oct 1858
Mills Littleton P. to Henderson Elizabeth 30 Apr 1856
Mills Stephen to Donoho Mary 2 Mar 1847
Mills Stephen to Phillips Anne 21 Dec 1852
Mills Stephen to Jackson Mary A. 28 Sep 1858
Mills Stephen D. to Williams Ann Eliza 12 Nov 1846
Mills William to Patterson Sarah M. 20 Jul 1831
Mills William to Phillips Patty 7 Jan 1845
Minnish Richard to Gilliss Eleanor 28 Jul 1797
Minson John T. to Ward Cecelia I. 28 Jul 1869
Mister Bennett to Parks Brittania 13 Aug 1828
Mister Bennett to Daniel Mary 25 May 1838
Mister Charles E. to Byrd Julia A. 12 May 1863
Mister George W. to Rowe Anne K. 20 Mar 1855
Mister Jacob to Wilson Virginia 7 Mar 1865
Mister James H. to Lawson Anna M. F. 27 Feb 1866
Mister John to Conner Serena 3 Nov 1871
Mister Planner to Whitelock Amanda 23 Jun 1859
Mister Richard J. to Webster Malinda J. 2 Aug 1864
Mister Thomas to Johnson Euphamia 29 Aug 1843
Mister William M. to Thomas Ann Maria 20 Jun 1839
Mitchell David C. to Ward Mary Jane 16 Sep 1834
Mitchell Francis A. to Dashiell Harriet L. 22 Feb 1842
Mitchell Henry J. to Catlin Emma F. 20 Apr 1861
Mitchell Henry T. to Curtis Mary H. 26 Jul 1825
Mitchell Isaac to Jones Maria H. 8 Nov 1837
Mitchell Isaac to Hearn Betsey L. 13 Dec 1852
Mitchell James to Mesick Anne 13 Jan 1824
Mitchell James E. to Slemons Priscilla F. 10 Feb 1857
Mitchell James M. to Dashiell Sally E. W. 5 Mar 1849
Mitchell John to Bounds Elizabeth 22 Apr 1823
Mitchell John to Long Martha 17 Dec 1834
Mitchell John F. to Tull Mary E. 2 Jul 1862
Mitchell Joseph W. to Price Sarah E. 2 Feb 1855
Mitchell Purnell T. to Hitch Rebecca E. 8 Aug 1853
Mitchell Thomas to Jackson Nancy 2 Jan 1798
Mitchell Thomas to Gale Cerinda 10 Mar 1828
Mitchell Thomas to Moore Sally 23 Sep 1833
Mitchell Thomas W.H. to White Sarah E. 29 Nov 1853

Mitchell Tubman to Tull Sally 25 Jan 1804
Mitchell William to Smullin Sally 18 Dec 1798
Mitchell William to Smith Peggy 31 Aug 1813
Mitchell William to Toadvin Nelly 28 May 1816
Mitchell William to Booth Elizabeth 29 Dec 1849
Mitchell Zadoc to Venables Sally 17 Jan 1797
Mizick James to Anderson Catherine 5 Aug 1825
Mizick James to Cantwell Mary Anne 10 Jul 1832
Moger Gehial to Evans Ellen 27 Dec 1859
Mongar Zorobable to Martin Peggy 12 Nov 1800
Monroe Henry A. to Wilson Christianna A. 28 Dec 1868 C
Monroe Neal to Rogers Hester A. 27 Jan 1864
Monroe William W. to Moore Susan A. 6 Nov 1856
Montgomery James to Jaffreys Patty 22 Dec 1807
Montgomery James to Dickerson Patty 6 Sep 1808
Montgomery James to Miles Nancy 11 Dec 1810
Moon John S. to Bounds Kitty P. 1 Jun 1831
Moore Benjamin to Bayly Hetty 16 Feb 1813
Moore Caleb S. to Covington Martha W. 24 Sep 1861
Moore Charles to Dickerson Rebecca 11 Dec 1821
Moore Charles to Mezick Eleanor 7 Aug 1827
Moore Elijah to McClemmy Sally 6 Feb 1808
Moore Elijah to Jackson Eleanor 8 Mar 1825
Moore Elijah R. to Moore Lucretia 14 Dec 1818
Moore George to Bounds Ann Maria 13 Apr 1847
Moore George to Abbott Louisa 9 Jan 1849
Moore George to Horner Nancy 23 Feb 1864
Moore George W. to Tilghman Harriet A. 9 May 1861
Moore Hamilton to Lawson Sally R. 6 May 1839
Moore Hance L. to Sterling Mary W. 24 Dec 1870
Moore Henry to Giles Elizabeth 29 Aug 1809
Moore Henry Haw to Moore Fanny 8 Nov 1864
Moore Isaac to Green Nancy 19 May 1811
Moore Jacob to Crouch Lucretia A. 26 Oct 1852
Moore Jacob T. to Shelton Virginia 2 Apr 1867
Moore James to Roberts Sally 3 Apr 1821
Moore James to Wilson Emeline 16 Aug 1853
Moore James to Sturgis Priscilla 23 Apr 1856
Moore James C. to Handy Peggy 19 Sep 1821
Moore James F. to Larmore Sarah G. 21 Jul 1846

Moore James I. to Evans Grace 27 Nov 1867
Moore James K. to Sterling Serena 19 Dec 1865
Moore Job to Lawson Leah 12 Jul 1823
Moore Job to Sterling Sally 20 May 1845
Moore John to Bowen Sally 21 Oct 1799
Moore John to Coulbourn Elizabeth 12 Nov 1839
Moore John to Coulbourn Amelia 14 Oct 1846
Moore John R.P. to Toadvine Margaret G. 10 Nov 1855
Moore John W. to Mazick Elizabeth 1 Dec 1815
Moore John W. to Riall Delia E. 19 Dec 1854
Moore Jonathan to Pollitt Sarah Ann 2 Aug 1836
Moore Jonathan to Shores Rebecca E.E. 3 Jan 1838
Moore Joseph to Whayland Rebecca 3 Jun 1817
Moore Joseph (or Moose?) to Darby Peggy 18 Jan 1803
Moore Joshua to Collins Margaret 23 Jan 1827
Moore Joshua to Ker Elizabeth H. 13 Sep 1827
Moore Levin to Standford Betsy 1 Dec 1801
Moore Nicholas to Wilson Margaret E. 27 Nov 1866
Moore Noah to Mills Margaret 6 Aug 1860 C
Moore Samuel J. to Robertson Sarah A.C. 8 Jan 1851
Moore Samuel W. to Horner Ameliaanne Crawford 26 Jan 1848
Moore Solomon to Humphreys Sarah Ann 28 Nov 1831
Moore Stephen to Bennett Elizabeth 11 Apr 1837
Moore Thomas to Byrd Polly 14 Jun 1825
Moore Thomas to Dorman Elizabeth 12 Jun 1827
Moore Thomas A. to Street Charlotte V. 16 Feb 1857
Moore Thomas B. to Lowe Rachel W. 14 Nov 1848
Moore Vincent to Gordy Leah E. 10 Jun 1856
Moore William to Colbert Nancy 5 Jan 1802
Moore William to Howard Anne 26 Mar 1804
Moore William to Sterling Deborah 28 Jul 1818
Moore William to Dickerson Ruth 10 Dec 1822
Moore William D. to Gosley Ardilla 29 Jan 1850
Moore William G. to Hobbs Milly Ann 5 Jan 1847
Moore William J. to Barkley Mina 9 Jan 1855 C
Moore William S. to Griffin Laura C. 14 Jan 1869
Moore William W. to Green Esther 17 Dec 1822
Moore William White to Adams Sally 2 Oct 1811
Morgan Henry James to Gravenor Luvena 23 Aug 1851
Morgan R. Reese to Collier Louisa A. 22 Oct 1860

Morgan William E. to Matthews Harriet A. 7 Jul 1842
Morgin Thomas W. to Darby Harriet H. 11 Dec 1849
Morris Cornelius to Green Maria 15 Oct 1845
Morris George R. to Simms Mary E. 4 May 1870
Morris Henry to Gale Jane 12 Mar 1868 C
Morris Henry E.L. to Pollitt Emeline 23 Mar 1844
Morris Isaac to Wright Elizabeth S. 11 Jun 1856
Morris Jacob to Benson Nancy 22 Jan 1822
Morris Jacob to Morris Anne Eliza 5 Mar 1855
Morris James to Disharoon Sally 7 Jan 1833
Morris James to Huffington Sally 16 Jun 1834
Morris John to Pollitt Anne 23 Aug 1825
Morris John B. to Ward Sally 5 Dec 1848
Morris John H. to Cottman Biddy 19 Sep 1820
Morris Joshua to Kibble Henrietta 13 Jun 1820
Morris Joshua to White Emeline 6 Aug 1830
Morris Joshua B. to Weatherly Elizabeth A. 24 Mar 1857
Morris Levin to Craft Mary R. 10 Jan 1815
Morris Levin to Jones Elize Ann F. 22 May 1821
Morris Lewis W. (Dr.) to Somers S. Annie 20 Feb 1849
Morris Louis W. (Dr.) to Slemons Clara E. 1 Nov 1856
Morris Nehemiah to Codrey Polly 2 Sep 1829
Morris Robert to Collins Rebecca 7 Oct 1828
Morris Robert to Malone Henrietta 7 Jan 1845
Morris Samuel to Furbos Eleanor 11 May 1829
Morris Samuel J. to Coulbourn Emeline 14 Nov 1864
Morris Thomas to Graft Ann 25 Jan 1819
Morris Thomas to Anderson Lucinda 21 Feb 1837
Morris William to Harris Nancy 4 Jul 1803
Morris William to Disharoon Charlotte 12 Jan 1808
Morris William to Disharoon Esther 10 Dec 1811
Morris William to Maddux Jane --(?) 1837
Morris William (Senr.) to Hastings Mary Anne 20 Sep 1842
Morris William B. to Stevens Mary E. 24 Sep 1855
Morris William P. to Stanford Mary C. 17 Jan 1843
Morrison George to Milbourn Lovey 30 Mar 1865 C
Morrison James to Riggin Eleanor 4 Oct 1797
Morton John B. to Done Elizabeth 3 Apr 1816
Moseby Cornelius to Wright Leah 5 Feb 1823
Mosely John to Dashiell Matilda 24 Dec 1863 C

Muir Arnold to Howarth Permelia 29 Jul 1828
Muir Charles to Walston Sally 5 Jan 1803
Muir George to Curtis Ramelia 25 Jan 1823
Muir George to Wilcott Hannah 4 Oct 1824
Muir Hamilton to Powell Peggy 10 Nov 1827
Muir Henry to Matthews Elizabeth 27 Oct 1818
Muir James Cash to Windsor Anne Maria 23 Jun 1852
Muir John to Howell Hetty 11 Jan 1825
Muir John H. to Ward Cornelia C. 28 Jun 1859
Muir Joseph to Bozman Anne 30 Jul 1822
Muir Lambert to Heath Nancy 16 Dec 1858
Muir Lambert W. to Evans Mary V. 1 Jun 1864
Muir Robert to Warbleton Emeline 13 Feb 1834
Muir Robert H. to Oats Louisa 20 Feb 1868
Muir Thomas to Brown Margaret 15 Nov 1848
Muir William to Howarth Betsy 12 Jun 1827
Muir William to Evans Maria 6 Aug 1860
Muir William A. to Lord Mary W. 1 Apr 1867
Muir William E. to Howarth Malissa A. 21 Jun 1864
Muirr Lambert W. to Howerth Mary E. 18 Oct 1854
Mumford John to Marshall Henrietta Anne 3 Jan 1865
Mungar Zorobabel to Landen Betsy 18 Jan 1809
Mure George W. to Lord Lurana 19 Oct 1870
Murphey Edward to Dean Catherine 11 Jun 1862
Murphey Robert W. to Bloodsworth Sarah Jane 19 Aug 1867
Murphy James to Taylor Rachel 23 Nov 1847
Murphy Jno. to Horseman Kitturah 22 Feb 1831
Murphy John to Hopkins Eleanor 20 May 1826
Murphy John T. to Collier Mary E. 11 Mar 1865
Murphy Joseph to Adams Priscilla 2 Aug 1831
Murra Thomas to Murrell Elizabeth 9 Sep 1823
Murray Ebben W. to Austin Mariana 12 Jan 1869
Murray Francis to Webb Sarah 21 Apr 1858
Murray Henry to Stephenson Ann Eliza 20 Oct 1846
Murray Henry to Sims Virginia 23 Aug 1865
Murray Isaac to Jones Nancy 13 Jan 1851
Murray James B. to Kelly Charlotte P. 29 Apr 1835
Murray John Thomas to Adams Kezziah 6 Sep 1847
Murray Michael J. to Bounds Elizabeth 16 Sep 1862
Murrel George to Chatam Leah 30 Nov 1847

Murrel John to McGee Lucretia 28 May 1822
Murrel John W. to Porter Sarah R. 11 Feb 1856
Murrell Michael to Leonard Eleanor 12 Feb 1833
Murrell Michael to Sims Sarah 29 Mar 1859
Murrell Samuel S. to Bloodsworth Rebecca 21 Dec 1868
Murrill Alexander to Price Sally Anne 5 Jan 1858
Murrill William J. to Prior Mary J. 10 Jan 1855
Murry Michael to Sims Polly 3 Apr 1797
Murry Michael to Maddux Nancy 16 Feb 1801
Muse John H. to Gunby Hester A. 4 Feb 1870 C
Nelson Alexander to Selby Elizabeth 21 Oct 1834
Nelson Alonzo B. to Sterling Sally L. 4 May 1847
Nelson Andrew A. to Bracher Nancy A. 16 Oct 1866
Nelson Azariah to McCready Mary Catherine 10 Jul 1849
Nelson Cyrus to Nelson Sarah H. 13 Dec 1836
Nelson David M. to McCready Julian 23 Jul 1844
Nelson David to Miles Margaret E. 28 Jun 1870
Nelson Edward L. to Newman Nancy 5 Mar 1869
Nelson Edward R. to Mezick Mary E. 30 Nov 1857
Nelson Elijah C. to Hall Sally J. 23 Feb 1848
Nelson Elijah W. to Sterling Nancy E. 11 Jun 1860
Nelson Ephraim to Nelson Mary King 9 Jan 1812
Nelson Francis to Mitchell Nancy 14 Feb 1815
Nelson George to Sterling Rose Anne 15 May 1855
Nelson George T. to Moore Rieta A. 25 Feb 1868
Nelson Isaac J. to Lawson Emeline 10 Jun 1836
Nelson James to Somers Mary 22 Jan 1835
Nelson James C. to Sterling Nancy E. 4 Feb 1864
Nelson James T. to Dashiell Leah 8 Sep 1812
Nelson James T. to Venables Charlotte 6 Sep 1815
Nelson James W. to Sterling Henrietta 1 Jun 1855
Nelson John to Maddux Hetty 5 May 1821
Nelson John to Costen Sarah 24 Jan 1826
Nelson John to Lawson Mary 16 Jan 1829
Nelson John to Gray Mary 22 Nov 1830
Nelson John to Somers Kessey 26 Jan 1841
Nelson John L. to Davis Willianna 11 Dec 1866
Nelson Lorenzo T. to Lawson Harriet A. 3 Jun 1867
Nelson Oliver P. to Leatherbury Eleanor 15 Feb 1842
Nelson Sacker to Juett Rhoda 8 Jul 1809

Nelson Samuel to Brewington Casey 9 Apr 1867 C
Nelson Samuel J. to Bozman Mary E. 19 May 1863
Nelson Theophilus to Lankford Susan 23 Apr 1844
Nelson Thomas to Lawson Susannah 10 Jun 1836
Nelson Tubman to Donoho Rebecca 31 Jan 1823
Nelson William to Benson Emeline 8 Jun 1825
Nelson William to Mister Ellen 14 May 1827
Nelson Zachariah to Dorsey Harriet 22 Dec 1846
Netter Jesse to Elzy Rhoda -- May 1850 C
Newball William to Cottingham Elizabeth 2 May 1797
Newcomb Jesse to Hall Milcah 18 Jul 1801
Newman Henry to Wallace Emeline 22 Feb 1825
Newman Isaac to Shipham Mary 16 Jan 1798
Newman Isaac to Balson Harriet 10 Feb 1825
Newman John to Davis Polly 30 Apr 1798
Newman John to Harris Rachel 19 Jun 1827
Newman John to Handy Margaret 8 Feb 1848
Newman Sidney C. to Price Virginia E. 31 Aug 1861
Newman Thomas to Hayman Nancy 10 Feb 1820
Newman Thomas to Hayman Elizabeth 14 Feb 1849
Newman William G.H. (Dr.) to Rider Mary A. 13 Nov 1850
Newton Levin B. to Catlin Sarah Jane 14 Jul 1857
Newton Thomas to Brerwood Emeline 9 Oct 1827
Nicholas Rozel to Hitch Lotty 22 Feb 1800
Nicholls James to Mezick Mary 10 Apr 1804
Nichols Isaac to Russum Hetty 15 Apr 1811
Nichols Isaac to Stocks Mary Ann 14 Oct 1823
Nichols J. W.C. to Maddux Josaphine F. 4 Dec 1855
Nichols James to Mills Sarah 5 Feb 1822
Nichols John to Hitch Betsy 28 Aug 1811
Nichols Levin to Jenkins Elizabeth 20 Mar 1855
Nichols Theophilus to Vincent Grace 9 Mar 1825
Nicholson Charles to Hitch Ebby 2 Jan 1797
Nicholson George to Dormen Leah 7 Sep 1813
Nicholson Henry to Harris Amelia W. 18 Nov 1813
Nicholson Isaac M. to Hearn Amanda 29 May 1856
Nicholson Jacob E. to Quarles Susanna F. 4 Apr 1825
Nicholson James to Green Anne 12 Jul 1803
Nicholson John to Fletcher Mary 3 Sep 1804
Nicholson Jonathan A. to Bradley Margaret S.E. 15 Dec 1854

Nicholson Thomas F. to Mills Louisa A. 5 Oct 1858
Nicols Alexander to Waters Rachel 13 Apr 1869 C
Nicols Isaac to Hopkins Leah 26 Jan 1836
Nicols John to Walker Elizabeth 19 Mar 1844
Nicols William E. to Cooper Mary W. 11 May 1869
Nicolson Elias to Hitch Mary 20 Dec 1845
Niskey Charles to Hayman Rebecca 22 Dec 1866 C
Noble Edward to Smith Leah Campbell 9 Jun 1863
Noble George A. to Bourbon Mary Jane 4 Mar 1834
Noble George A. to Dorman Charlotte 17 May 1853
Noble James to Goddard Sally 10 Apr 1810
Noble John to Gunby Sally 23 Sep 1823
Noble Thomas to Miller Nancy 14 Mar 1800
Noble Thomas to Ballard Sarah 27 Jun 1800
Nock John W. to Henderson Elexine 28 Aug 1867
Norris Robert to Brimingham Mary 5 Apr 1817
North Edward to Dunn Priscilla 26 Feb 1822
North Edward to Somers Anne 13 Feb 1828
North George T. to Lewis Sarah J. 8 May 1860
Northam James to Dix Catharine 5 Oct 1814
Northam Thomas A. to Hindman Vernitta A. 22 Nov 1853
Nutter Caleb W. to Lawrence Henrietta A. 5 Jun 1860
Nutter Charles to Handy Sally 8 Feb 1810
Nutter Charles I. to Phoebus Indiana 5 Nov 1866
Nutter Gabriel to Elzey Sarah 7 Jan 1851
Nutter Henry to Evans Leah 10 Feb 1840
Nutter Hezekiah to Gale Leah Jane 13 Jan 1855 C
Nutter John to White Georgianna 14 Dec 1866 C
Nutter Morris to Cottman Ellindra Dec 1871 C
Nutter Stephen to Hardy Matilda 2 Jul 1845
Nutter Stephen to Conway Sarah 3 Oct 1851
Nutter William to Rogers Sarah 13 Nov 1800
Nutter William to Elzey Alice 21 Oct 1862 C
Nutter William Pitt to Dashiell Mary Hester 1 Apr 1863 C
Nutter Zachius to Cornish Henrietta 16 Jul 1856
O'Brien Daniel to Howers Hester Ann 13 Oct 1871 C
O'Conner Eugene to Chue Fanny 13 May 1802
O'Dear James to Hudson Nancy 30 Sep 1825
O'Dear Kendall to Pusey Nancy 12 Jan 1814
O'Dear Kendall to Dubberly Sally 28 Feb 1821

Oakes Francis F. to Scott Eliza Anne 23 Sep 1834
Odear Andrew to Dashiell Adeline 17 Jun 1856
Olter William F. to Revill Margaret 6 Mar 1826
Oneil Michael to Mills Catherine W. 19 Nov 1867
Onions George to Ward Kessey E. 17 Dec 1869
Onions John to Daugherty Harriet 26 Jun 1832
Onions William to Wilson Nancy E. 12 Jan 1861
Only Smith to Staunt Elizabeth 27 Feb 1866
Opper Conrad to Hayman Eliza I. 19 Nov 1868
Orem John H. to Brown Eliza E. 23 May 1867
Overly Thomas W. to Marshall Martha S.J. 27 Sep 1837
Overton Lester D. to Harris Mary E. 19 Jun 1856
Owens Elisha to Davis Mary 10 Apr 1832
Owens Elisha to Graham Sarah Anne 17 Sep 1839
Owens James to Matthews Sally 22 Dec 1796
Owens James to Nelson Betsy 17 Apr 1804
Owens Jesse to Philips Eleanor 24 Jan 1821
Owens John to Green Betsy 6 Dec 1808
Owens Joshua to Brooks Hetty 23 Jul 1799
Owens Josiah E. to Bradley Priscilla B. 6 Oct 1852
Owens Marcellus to Venables Mary E. 26 Apr 1854
Owens Peter to Nelson Elizabeth 20 Jan 1840
Owens Peter to Bradley Jane 31 Dec 1855
Owens Thomas to Benson Louisa 30 Apr 1822
Owings James to Abbet Polly 18 Jun 1801
Owney Ephraim to Moore Margaret 28 Apr 1801
Packard C.S.W. to Jones Elizabeth 28 Jan 1850
Packard Charles A. to Dory Elizabeth A. 13 Dec 1866
Packer John to Jones Margaret 9 Dec 1871 C
Paden Henry to Lankford Elizabeth 1 Feb 1831
Paden James to Matthews Eleanor 19 Jul 1808
Paden John to Benston Suesey 25 Aug 1801
Paden John R. to Murray Charlotte 12 Jul 1860
Paden Sydney to Powell Susan 5 Jan 1869
Paden William to Purkins Esther Long 26 Jan 1822
Palmer Brennus to Robertson Dolly C. 17 Dec 1850
Palmer Charles to Hayes Frances W.E.L. 19 May 1818
Palmore Charles to Newman Elizabeth S. 26 Apr 1825
Palmore Peter to Collier Mary 21 Jul 1856
Pane Levin D. to Henderson Sally J. 19 Jul 1864

Parker Albert to Hickman Adda 25 Apr 1865
Parker Elisha to Weatherly Polly 19 May 1810
Parker George to Marchant Rebecca 14 Jun 1803
Parker George to Stanford Amelia 6 Jan 1823
Parker Henry S. to Leonard Matilda 30 Aug 1845
Parker Isaac W. to Stewart Mary Jane 1 Aug 1846
Parker James to Coulbourne Zipporah 22 Oct 1810
Parker James to Mills Polly 7 Mar 1866
Parker John to Dunning Kitty 22 Feb 1820
Parker John to Baily Harriet 27 Jan 1826
Parker John to Jones Harriet 24 Feb 1840
Parker John to Johnson Mary 3 Jul 1851
Parker John R. to Ward Anne L. 21 Jun 1825
Parker Levin to Beauchamp Susan 13 Mar 1838
Parker Levin T. to Dryden Margaret 2 Jan 1867
Parker Lorenzo D. to Parker Elizabeth 24 Sep 1833
Parker Richard to Fowler Charlotte 3 Oct 1866 C
Parker Robert R. to Horsey Mary Jane 1 May 1836
Parker Samuel to Bounds Jane 25 Oct 1831
Parker Samuel to Miles Esther 28 Dec 1869 C
Parker Thomas H. to Jones Maria V. 28 Jan 1869
Parker William to Roach Betsy 5 Nov 1799
Parker William S. to Irving Betsy 6 Dec 1809
Parks Abel to Parks Lavina 8 Jan 1811
Parks Arthur to Mitchell Nancy 24 Jul 1801
Parks Arthur to Nutter Polly 27 Aug 1804
Parks Arthur to Williams Leah 27 Jul 1808
Parks Charles to Evans Lovey 2 Jun 1830
Parks Edward W. to Townsend Miranda J. 2 Feb 1864
Parks Elias to Evans Eleanor 28 Jun 1831
Parks Gabriel T. to Roberts Martha S. 26 Nov 1846
Parks Geo W. to Tyler Jane E. 10 May 1870
Parks George to Jones Emaline 18 Sep 1847
Parks George W. to Ford Elizabeth C. 18 Nov 1856
Parks George W. to Revill Mary E. 19 May 1858
Parks Hance L. to Howeth Harriet 25 May 1870
Parks Henry to Landen Anna 12 Jan 1813
Parks Hesekiah S. to Colbert Amelia 26 Aug 1850
Parks Isaac to Lankford Esther 15 Feb 1828
Parks Isaac to McDaniel Elizabeth 13 Oct 1835

Parks Isaac to White Nancy E. 15 Sep 1857
Parks Isaac H. to Adams Maria H. 11 Jul 1854
Parks Isaac T. to Wallace Anna P. 12 Jun 1866
Parks Jacob to Daniel Juliann 2 Jul 1828
Parks James to McDaniel Jane --(?) 1837
Parks James to Collins Emma 9 Feb 1870
Parks James K. to White Polly 17 Feb 1837
Parks Jesse to Mezick Eliza 15 Sep 1854
Parks Jesse J. to Todd Ealien 17 Jun 1862
Parks Job to Williams Bridget 22 Jan 1817
Parks Job to David Charlotte 4 Aug 1821
Parks Job T. to Disharoon Virginia 9 Jan 1855
Parks John to Trehern Matty 24 Aug 1802
Parks John to Rumley Amey 11 Jul 1821
Parks John E. to Emmerson Netta 1 Mar 1870
Parks John Edward to McDaniel Nancy 6 Jul 1841
Parks John Edward to Spence Mary Jane 10 Jun 1859
Parks John H. to Parks Amelia 3 Jun 1845
Parks John H. to Whitelock Mary E. 30 Aug 1862
Parks John H. to Somers Mary E. 12 Jun 1866
Parks John T. to Walston Milcah Anne 31 Oct 1864
Parks John T. to Crockett Sarah 30 May 1871
Parks John W. to Mure Elizabeth 10 Feb 1847
Parks John W. to Mure Williamanna 22 Dec 1869
Parks John W. to Barclay Sarah Victoria 18 Oct 1871
Parks Reuben to Mason Julia 18 Jan 1842
Parks Revill to Blake Rachel 12 Jan 1828
Parks Riley to Evans Aurelia 18 Feb 1868
Parks Robert to Windsor Ibby 14 Jun 1831
Parks Robert to Davis Mary 15 Feb 1859
Parks Robert F. to Landon Virginia E. 11 Feb 1868
Parks Severn to Sparrow Matilda 28 Dec 1869
Parks Solomon to Bedsworth Mary Anne 22 Jul 1834
Parks Thomas to Dorman Nancy 20 Mar 1810
Parks Thomas to Catlin Susan 5 Aug 1822
Parks Th(imas to Cullen Sally Anne 15 Aug 1853
Parks Thomas J. to Lewis Sarah A. 19 May 1857
Parks Tubman L. to Landon Mary E. 15 Aug 1862
Parks William to Gibson Sarah 4 Jan 1803
Parks William to Williams Elizabeth 20 Jul 1833

Parks William A. to Bradshaw Margaret 6 Jun 1854
Parks William E. to Parks Mary W. 22 Mar 1859
Parks William H. to McDaniel Matilda 6 Jun 1838
Parks William H. to Muir Malissa C. 10 Nov 1863
Parks William J. to Drummond Elizabeth 1 Oct 1846
Parks William L. to Williams Isabell B. 4 Apr 1860
Parks William W. to Blake Sarah Jane 20 Dec 1853
Parks Wm. R. to Crockett Amanda 9 Apr 1867
Parks Zebulin to Parks Susan 26 Jul 1814
Parks Zebulum to Walston Charlotte 3 Apr 1799
Parmer James to Givans Mary 12 May 1812
Parr James to Hunt Elizabeth 9 Mar 1813
Parramore William A. to Turpin Elizabeth A.S. 22 Nov 1815
Parritt Hofer to Mason Sarah J. 21 Jun 1859
Parrott George W. to Bell Arianna 17 Apr 1866 C
Pars Samuel to Carey Priscilla 5 Nov 1804
Parsons Benjamin to Owens May 25 Sep 1827
Parsons Elijah to Mitcalf Sally 18 Aug 1808
Parsons Elijah to Parsons Charlotte 29 Dec 1865 C
Parsons George to Disharoon Prissey 18 May 1797
Parsons George (Jr) to Stewart Elizabeth 21 Apr 1829
Parsons George G. to Peacock Amelia A. 1 May 1860
Parsons Henry to Leatherbury Elizabeth 21 May 1812
Parsons Isaac to Culver Polly 16 Nov 1813
Parsons James A. to Sirman Esther E. 25 Mar 1862
Parsons Jehu to Somers Esther 8 Dec 1813
Parsons Jehu to Johnson Sarah J. 16 Dec 1868
Parsons Jehu H. to King Leah Jane 4 Aug 1864
Parsons John (Jr) to Merrill Nancy 31 Dec 1833
Parsons Jordon to Ford Mary E.J. 7 Jan 1840
Parsons Kandall B. to Noble Sally 12 Oct 1830
Parsons Leonard to White Hannah 6 Apr 1866 C
Parsons Levin A. to Parvin Anne E. 15 Jan 1856
Parsons Lowdan to Smith Ann 31 Dec 1836
Parsons Milton A. to Williams Caroline T. 6 Apr 1852
Parsons Rufus M. to White Charlotte J. 21 Apr 1841
Parsons Samuel T. to Ellit Margaret E. 3 Jan 1850
Parsons Silas E. to Kelly Mary Elizabeth 16 May 1848
Parsons Theodore to Bell Margaret H. 15 Jan 1839
Parsons William to Bowland Margaret Anne 8 Feb 1842

Parsons William to Prior Caroline 9 Dec 1851
Parsons William A. to Lankford Elizabeth A. 30 Sep 1862
Parsons William S. to Rider Elizabeth E. 24 Nov 1856
Parsons William W. to Robertson Mary H. 11 Nov 1856
Pasquith Charles E. to Todd Maria E. 25 Aug 1868
Patrick Levin H. to Byrd Sarah Anne 15 Jun 1824
Patterson Jacob to Rounds Charlotte 10 Sep 1817
Patterson Revil A. to Whittington Sally R. 24 Feb 1868
Patterson Robert to Stayton Elen 5 May 1823
Patterson Robert to White Helen S. 20 Jul 1846
Paul George W. to Gibson Margaret 12 Jan 1847
Payne Joshua A. to Johnson Sarah A. 27 Oct 1853
Peacock William to Scott Henny 18 Sep 1860
Pennel Josiah W. to Maddux Ellen 20 Mar 1856
Pennywell Isaac F. to Jackson Leah 13 Oct 1834
Pepper William H. to Robertson Sally 14 Jan 1840
Perdeau Lemuel H. to Marval Ellen A. 21 Nov 1860
Perkins William to Hall Milly 26 Mar 1833
Perry Ishmael to Anderson Peggy 23 Nov 1797
Peters Benjamin to Hill Martha 27 Nov 1860 C
Peters George to Morris Amanda 20 Jan 1862 C
Peters Levin to Robertson Elizabeth 7 Nov 1860 C
Peters Samuel Q. to Peters Sarah M. 11 Apr 1860 C
Peters William J. to Ayres Mary F. 1 Jan 1866 C
Peterson John to Jones Nancy 26 Jan 1813
Petty Jesse to Pryer Mary 4 Jan 1797
Peyton James to Austin Mary 5 Feb 1861
Peyton John to Foxwell Eliza 16 Jan 1833
Phebus James to Howard Elizabeth R. 13 Jan 1825
Phebus James to Willing Anne 2 Apr 1829
Phebus William to Ross Jane 30 Nov 1824
Philipps Jacob to Jackson Sarah C. 12 Dec 1863
Philips Day to Jorret Peggy 7 Jul 1804
Philips Day to Guptin Molly 19 Dec 1812
Philips Day to Tully Frances 26 Apr 1816
Philips Elihu to Porter Hetty 10 May 1808
Philips Elijah to Donoho Mary 17 Mar 1812
Philips James to Hattan Esther 16 Feb 1813
Philips Jesse to Dear Nancy 14 Sep 1818
Philips Jesse to Heath Hetty 5 Aug 1825

Philips Jonathan to Taylor Elizabeth H. 31 Jan 1826
Philips Noah to Philips Nelly 27 Feb 1816
Philips Robert to Howard Peggy 1 Jan 1811
Philips Samuel B. to Howard Eleanor 30 Nov 1824
Philips Thomas to Dulany Rhoda 17 Dec 1811
Philips William to Robertson Betsy 6 Nov 1804
Philips William to Dashiell Elizabeth 28 Feb 1822
Phillips Asa L. to Russell Martha J. 16 Dec 1848
Phillips Collins to Jackson Margaret 5 May 1835
Phillips Elijah to Taylor Harrietta 9 Oct 1867
Phillips James to McCollister Maria 5 Jan 1847
Phillips James R. to Bennett Mary Jane 8 Feb 1842
Phillips James R. to Standford Nancy 19 Jan 1847
Phillips James W.T. to Donoho Elizabeth A. 6 Dec 1859
Phillips John M. to Bounds Virginia F. 5 Apr 1859
Phillips John T. to Freeney Julia A.L. 26 Feb 1861
Phillips Joseph A. to Bennett Mary 21 Feb 1842
Phillips Joshua W. to Crockett Nancy 19 Oct 1841
Phillips Joshua W. to Dashiell Maria E. 30 Apr 1850
Phillips Levin to Gunby Mary A.J. 20 Aug 1839
Phillips Noah to Elzey Rachel 13 Nov 1850
Phillips Roger to Taylor Sarah 15 Dec 1835
Phillips Roger to Gravener Maria 23 Oct 1843
Phillips Samuel J. to Bailey Elizabeth E. 4 Jan 1860
Phillips Theodore A. to Mills Martha J. 9 Mar 1859
Phillips Thomas to Adams Polly 24 Oct 1810
Phillips Thomas to Hopkins Mary Jane 18 Jan 1841
Phillips Thomas C. to Walker Lena 19 Jan 1863
Phillips Thomas J. to Hurt Rebecca 3 Nov 1858
Phillips Thomas W. to Vincent Sally A. 22 Oct 1849
Phillips Whitty to Robertson Ellenor 5 Jan 1842
Phillips William to Reddish Elzenian 23 Aug 1841
Phillips William M. to Howard Sally E. 16 Mar 1852
Phillips William R. to Jackson Matilda A. 13 Dec 1853
Phillips William R. to Byrd Eliza A. 21 Apr 1863
Phillips William T. to Price Esther L. 21 Dec 1866
Phills Absalon to Calhoon Elizabeth 10 Oct 1826
Phippin Thomas to Hopkins Mary Elizabeth 16 Apr 1858
Phoebus Edward to Hill Anne 25 Jun 1829
Phoebus Edward to Tyler Julia A. 30 Jun 1863

Phoebus George A. to Massey Virginia C. 22 Nov 1856
Phoebus Isaac J.A. to Jones Elizabeth M. 3 Mar 1863
Phoebus James to Muir Betsy 26 Mar 1799
Phoebus James to Townsend Sally 20 Jun 1832
Phoebus James A. to Webster Elenora 19 Dec 1865
Phoebus John W. to Massey Mary P. 22 Nov 1859
Phoebus Lewis to Austin Polly 20 Nov 1802
Phoebus Lewis to Rose Sally 20 Sep 1816
Phoebus Louis S. to Loga Sallie 16 Sep 1857
Rhoebus Thomas to Smith Sally 15 Jul 1820
Phoebus Thomas to North Leah E. 11 Sep 1844
Phoebus Thornton to Wilson Mary 18 Jun 1832
Phoebus Thos. to Phoebus Sarah S. 29 Sep 1831
Phoebus William to Ford Elizabeth 1 May 1833
Phoebus William A. to Somers Jane 20 Dec 1853
Pincket Elijah C. to Slemons Maria E. 24 Apr 1866 C
Pinket Adam to Toadvine Jane 6 Feb 1867 C
Pinto John V. to Long Leah W. 4 Apr 1822
Pinto Thomas J. to Pinto Matilda W. 15 May 1856
Pinto Thmas J. to Long Aurelia A. 20 Dec 1871
Piper George S. to Costen Elizabeth --(?) 1837
Pitts William R.T. to Dixon Mary Ella 5 Jul 1871
Planter Isreal to Long Sarah 4 Apr 1801 C
Plumer Joseph L. to Kelly Rachel E. 4 Oct 1855
Poe George to Bradshaw Levina 22 Dec 1841
Polk Alfred to Polk Esther 3 Jul 1867 C
Polk Benjamin to McColloch Betsy 8 Sep 1801
Polk Benjamin to Catlin Mary 4 Jun 1867
Polk Isaac to Whithear Rebecca 25 Apr 1809
Polk James to Merchant Polly 11 Jan 1803
Polk James to Stuart Anna M. 27 Mar 1817
Polk James to Wilson Elizabeth 8 Jul 1845 C
Polk John to Nelson Polly 16 Mar 1825
Polk Morris to Black Rebecca C. 11 Mar 1856 C
Polk Whittington to Chapman Rebecca 5 Dec 1797
Polk Whittington to Adams Rebecca C. 7 Jan 1823
Polk Whittington to Stevenson Sarah A. 14 Nov 1860
Polk William T. to Harcum Louisa J. 3 Jun 1826
Polk William T. to Turner Elizabeth L. 19 Nov 1861
Polk William T.G. to Woolford Elizabeth 21 Feb 1832

Pollitt Anthony to Huffington Henrietta 15 Jan 1856
Pollitt Anthony to Anderson Mary V. 11 Mar 1868
Pollitt Daniel to Fooks Hester 11 Dec 1867
Pollitt Frost to Stewart Priscilla 12 Mar 1867
Pollitt George to Black Margaret 2 Jan 1862
Pollitt Gilliss to Ballard Esther Jane 18 May 1826
Pollitt Henry to Morris Jane 18 Mar 1817
Pollitt Henry to Harris Susan 16 Aug 1833
Pollitt Henry James to Jones Gatty 23 Apr 1867 C
Pollitt James to Levingston Maria 21 Apr 1819
Pollitt John E. to Jones Sarah D. 3 Mar 1815
Pollitt John E. to Foxwell Susan 6 Jan 1846
Pollitt Joseph to White Henny 24 Jan 1865 C
Pollitt Levin to Sloan Sarah 9 Jan 1797
Pollitt Levin to Morris Elizabeth 12 Apr 1825
Pollitt Levin to Jackson Harriet 20 Feb 1868 C
Pollitt Levin I. to Culver Charlotte 23 Feb 1841
Pollitt Littleton to Jones Elizabeth 16 Oct 1812
Pollitt Littleton to King Maria 4 Feb 1824
Pollitt Louis A. to Williams Martha Jane 1 Nov 1865
Pollitt Morris W. to Cannon Hester 25 Oct 1853
Pollitt Nehemiah to Blake Lizzie 7 Oct 1865 C
Pollitt Robert to Hayman Drucilla 16 Jan 1827
Pollitt Samuel to Disharoon Nancy 18 Dec 1798
Pollitt Samuel to Kellum Charlotte Anne 21 Aug 1828
Pollitt Sovereign to Dorman Peggy 25 May 1802
Pollitt Thomas to Cantwell Rebecca 23 Jul 1818
Pollitt Thomas to Silverthorn Maria 13 May 1845
Pollitt Thomas J. to Byrd Sarah A. 3 May 1861
Pollitt William to Irving Sally 10 Jun 1803
Pollitt William to Hayland Elizabeth R. 11 Jul 1827
Pollitt William to Seabreeze Margaret 20 Dec 1859
Pollitt William to Hayman Charlotte 27 Dec 1865 C
Pool George W. to Clogg Sarah E. -- Jul 1867
Poole John to Revel Betsy 29 Jun 1813
Poole Whittington to Lippincott Polly 26 Mar 1816
Pope George T. to Reece Olivia G. 28 Dec 1870
Pope Isaac to Matthews Esther 28 Feb 1811
Porter Alpheus to Fooks Letitia 31 Jan 1865
Porter George to Twilley Isabella A. 18 May 1841

Porter George (of Alexr) to Disharoon Betsy D. 14 Mar 1809
Porter George W. to Shreeves Elizabeth 9 May 1816
Porter Hugh to Winright Peggy 14 Nov 1797
Porter James to Hobbs Jane 10 Jan 1809
Porter James to Mungar Anne 15 Jul 1816
Porter John to Allen Polly 3 Aug 1801
Porter John S. to Langford Amanda J.D. 4 Jun 1856
Porter Joseph to Smith Peggy 17 Sep 1801
Porter Levi to Nelson Hetty 15 Jun 1804
Porter Levi to Hayman Leticia 12 Dec 1853
Porter Levi H. to Twigg Martha E. 15 Feb 1870
Porter Levin D. to Malone Rebecca W. 21 May 1833
Porter McKeemey (?) to Moor Ebby 13 Aug 1804
Porter Robert H. to Toadvine Amanda 13 May 1862
Porter Samuel I. to Langford Sarah A. 21 May 1839
Porter Theodore to Brewington Hellen 30 Oct 1827
Porter Theodore to Mezick Mary A. 24 Nov 1835
Porter William to Johnson Anne 1 Nov 1796
Porter William to Miles Sally 3 Feb 1829
Porter William I. to Dashiell Helen E. 22 Mar 1869
Porter Wrixham Lewis to Riggin Priscilla 30 Jul 1799
Potter David to Adams Mary 9 May 1797
Potter Elijah to Maddux Eleanor 23 Jan 1824
Potter Elijah to Johnson Patty 2 Aug 1825
Potter Elijah (Jr) to Benson Elizabeth 23 Nov 1819
Potter Henry W. to Foreman Anne M. 27 Nov 1855
Potter Isaac J. to Ward Sarah 9 Jan 1868
Potter John to Wilson Harriet 17 Feb 1824
Potter John Q. to Tull Eliza O. 13 Dec 1871
Potter Levin to Simms Mary 10 Jan 1837
Potter Luther to Sterling Emeline 26 Aug 1854
Potter Salathiel S. to Dorsey Sarah E. 11 Dec 1855
Potter Salathiel S. to Dorsey Margaret M. 19 Dec 1859
Potter Thomas to Wilson Charity 16 Jan 1797
Potter Thomas to Linton Rachael 15 Dec 1801
Potter Thomas to Price Jemima 22 Aug 1809
Potter Thomas H. to Parks Sarah E. 6 Feb 1867
Potts William to Hasty Sarah Ellen 20 Feb 1864
Powell Arthur M. to Bevans Emeline 11 Oct 1840
Powell Britain to Gibbens Polly 27 Dec 1803

Powell Elijah to Smulling Sally 23 Dec 1812
Powell Elijah A.J. to Hitch Amelia E. 9 Jun 1857
Powell Elijah F. to Puzey Sally A. 9 Jan 1866
Powell George to Harris Nancy 19 Jan 1830
Powell George to Williams Drucilla 19 Jul 1831
Powell George C. to Dryden Mary E. 18 Mar 1856
Powell George W. to Adams Priscilla A. 5 Apr 1825
Powell George W. to Dryden Martha 15 Mar 1866
Powell Henry to Renshaw Esther Anne 14 May 1840
Powell Henry E. to Howard Susan A. 24 May 1866
Powell James to Williams Prissey 7 Apr 1804
Powell James to Smulling Henrietta 30 Jul 1816
Powell James H. to Corbin Leah L. 19 Dec 1870
Powell Jesse to Adams Maria 1 Oct 1834
Powell John to Luke Elizabeth 16 Dec 1824
Powell John to Howard Elizabeth 16 Sep 1871
Powell Joshua T. to Miles Caroline 8 Jan 1863
Powell Lazarus to Moore Kitturah P. 27 Jan 1840
Powell Lendora to Dougherty Ann Eliza 20 Feb 1861
Powell Levi to Powell Betsy 5 Jun 1798
Powell Levin to Robertson Priscilla 23 Sep 1819
Powell Levin W. to Cluff Mary Elizabeth 31 Aug 1848
Powell Peregrine to Webster Emeline 15 Apr 1840
Powell Richard to Windsor Sarah 12 Feb 1862
Powell Robert to Sterling Mary 8 Apr 1837
Powell Robert H. to Sanders Adaline 30 Jan 1867 C
Powell Robert J.W. to Parks Rebecca F. 21 Aug 1868
Powell Samuel to Long Matilda 15 Jan 1802
Powell Samuel to Adams Amelia J. 21 Nov 1833
Powell Samuel to Moore Elizabeth 2 Aug 1836
Powell Samuel H. to Trehern Mary A. 12 Nov 1846
Powell Thomas L. to Whittington Sarah E. 24 Oct 1859
Powell Walter to Rencher Mary E. 1 Mar 1837
Powell Walter to Renshaw Jane R. 5 Dec 1855
Powell William A. to Adams Sarah A. 5 Aug 1867
Powell William N. to Trehearn Julia A. 23 Dec 1869
Powell William W. to Lankford Rosanna 9 Mar 1852
Powell William W. to Hitch Leah J. 21 Dec 1859
Power Edward J. to Harding Matilda K. 22 Jul 1839
Power Edward J. to Jones Julia M. 4 Nov 1863

Powley Nicholas to Bloodsworth Nancy 28 Dec 1843
Prewitt Edward to Crockett Emma 10 May 1870
Price Abraham W. to Jones Angelina M. 19 May 1865
Price Asa to Jenkins Martha 5 Feb 1828
Price Charles H. to Phillips Demanas 16 Dec 1851
Price Charles W. to Dashiell Martha A. 17 Jul 1860
Price Ephraim to Bloodsworth Nancy 17 Jul 1798
Price Ephraim to Parks Leah Anne 31 Jan 1854
Price George to Riggin Polly 18 Jan 1803
Price George to Fletcher Zipporah 21 Dec 1831
Price George to Malone Anne 28 Aug 1832
Price George to Fletcher Sarah R. 18 Feb 1851
Price Isaac to Foster Anne E. 26 Dec 1865
Price John to Mister Eleanor 30 Oct 1833
Price John Marcellus to Scott Lotty A. 20 Dec 1871
Price John R. to Harris Sarah 31 Jul 1834
Price Joseph to Barbon Mary 13 Nov 1850
Price Louday to Sutton Anna 6 Oct 1801
Price Louther to White Milcah 3 Aug 1820
Price Peter to Mister Sally 20 Apr 1829
Price Peter to Jones Elizabeth 2 May 1842
Price Philip C. to _____ Louisa 2 Aug 1852
Price Robert to Riggin Mary Anne 21 Mar 1837
Price Rufus M. to Twigg Almira A. 23 Fep. 1864
Price Severn to White Charlotte 24 Aug 1858
Price Severn M. to Todd Ruth Ann 21 Nov 1865
Price Thomas to Mezick Ketturah 20 May 1828
Price Thomas to Anderson Martha 12 Oct 1852
Price Wesley to White Mary E. 31 Jul 1856
Price William A. to White Anne R. 24 Feb 1857
Price William H. to Williams Annie M. 12 Jun 1871
Prior Alexander to Disharoon Nelly 11 Feb 1803
Prior Alexander to Jones Matty 14 Nov 1815
Prior Alexander to Parker Sally 11 May 1825
Prior Columbus to Stewart Elizabeth 2 Mar 1864
Prior Francis to Cullen Sarah 6 Nov 1838
Prior John S.C. to Foreman Mary Jane 20 Mar 1860
Prior William A. to Price Charlotte 1 Oct 1833
Pritchell Thomas to Dorman Rebecca G.W. 20 Nov 1834
Pritchett James to Horseman Molly 7 Apr 1808

Pritchett James to Harris Betsy 9 May 1815
Pritchett Robert to Webster Sina G. 30 Aug 1860
Pritchett Thomas to Phoebus Sarah E.J. 10 Jun 1856
Pritchett Zebulon to Moor Rebecca 18 Jan 1810
Pruett George to Evans Leah 28 Jan 1801
Pruitt Elijah H. to Sterling Cornelia C. 22 May 1866
Pruitt Gabriel to Cullen Nelly 17 May 1836
Pruitt George to Crockett Eliza Ann 18 Jun 1844
Pruitt John to Johnson Elizabeth 30 Dec 1861
Pruitt Robert to Lawrence Sarah 13 Oct 1863
Pruitt Thomas to Smith Elizabeth 4 Oct 1837
Pruitt William H. to Sterling Marietta 9 Sep 1862
Pryor James to Ballard Eleanor 27 Jul 1802
Pryor John to Malone Harriett 22 Apr 1845
Purnel Levin W. to Brickel Sophia A. 7 Sep 1867 C
Purnell John to Cox Beersheba 11 Sep 1829
Purnell John F. to Hickman Nancy 8 Jan 1861
Purnell William to Dutton Sarah Jane 17 Jun 1856 C
Purnell Wrixam to Shreeves Maria 23 Nov 1824
Purner John M. to Wood Martha E. 11 May 1866
Purse Joshua Y. to Revill Alice 21 Jun 1856
Purss Gilbert to Dickerson Susan 25 Sep 1820
Pusey Henry to Stevens Sally Ann 14 Nov 1855
Pusey Littleton H. to Pusey Sally Anne 6 Nov 1860
Pusey Peter to Ruark Elizabeth 6 Dec 1854
Puzey Benjamin to Hayman Sally 11 Nov 1824
Puzey Edward F. to Jones Elizabeth 25 May 1858
Puzey George W. to Powell Martha W. 9 Jan 1866
Puzey Jeptha to Townsend Matilda 14 Oct 1835
Puzey John to Trehearn Lydia 28 Feb 1838
Puzey John to Trehearn Clarissa 10 Feb 1841
Puzey Josiah to Miller Mary 25 Jan 1837
Puzey Josiah to Parsons Sarah 7 Feb 1844
Puzey Littleton H. to Richards Eliza M. 29 Dec 1840
Puzey Nathaniel to Smulling Betsey 6 Nov 1833
Puzey Parker to Gates Elizabeth 27 Jan 1832
Puzey Planner to Hayman Sally 14 Mar 1797
Puzey Puah to Leonard Sally 4 Sep 1816
Puzey Puah(?) to Chipman Emeline 30 Oct 1841
Puzey Purnell to Lankford Susan 31 Dec 1816

Puzey Thomas to Smulling Sarah Anne 23 May 1833
Puzey William to Riggin Henrietta 1 Jul 1865
Quigg Thomas to Cullen Hannah 12 Dec 1826
Quinn John W. to Long Allen W. 13 Dec 1836
Quinn Samuel S. to Atkinson Sallie A.Q. 11 Jun 1861
Quinton Charles D. to Sampson Emily 10 Jan 1862 C
Quinton John H. to Brown Sarah E. 4 Mar 1862 C
Quinton Samuel to Cook Nancy E. 2 Jan 1865 C
R_____ William to Beachamp Elizabeth 20 Mar 1827
Rainey Patrick to Price Elizabeth 3 Nov 1835
Ralph Thomas to Weatherly Nancy 17 Dec 1850
Randolph Thomas to Anderson Elizabeth A.G. 13 Oct 1834
Rayfield James K. to Sterling Amelia S. 10 Feb 1843
Rayfield Peter H. to Hickman Susan J. 21 Jun 1871
Rayfield William A. to Ward Isadora F. 26 Jun 1866
Rayfield William C. to Porter Virginia A. 21 Apr 1859
Redden James to Landon Elizabeth 26 Apr 1801
Redden Littleton J.D. to Waller Whilmina E.W. 5 Jan 1836
Redden Teagle to Windsor Eliza 10 Apr 1804
Reddin John to Martha Leah 2 Apr 1805
Redding Littleton to Leatherbury Mary H. 1 Sep 1830
Redding William T. to Fleming Julia 1 Mar 1848
Reddish George to Holland Eliza Ann 24 Jan 1825
Reddish John to Goddard Eliza 1 Jan 1810
Reddish Nicholas to Elzey Mary 24 Oct 1832
Reden Nehemiah to Dreden Anna 17 Jan 1804
Reding Teagle to Puss Peggy 1 Aug 1799
Reece Joshua to White Louisa 5 Apr 1824
Reece Rufus S. to Muir Harriet E. 4 Feb 1864
Reece William H. to Parsons Mary E. J. 1 Jun 1847
Reed Robert to Jones Elizabeth E. 10 Jun 1829
Reed William to Ross Harriet 20 Dec 1849
Reese George A. to Somers Sarah E. 19 Dec 1865
Reese Joshua to Gale Mary Hayward 18 Nov 1799
Reese William to Townsend Esther A. 31 Mar 1824
Reese William to Glascow Elizabeth 23 Feb 1858
Reid Edwin A. to Powell Mary E. 9 Aug 1871
Reid Won to Johnson Elizabeth 15 May 1871 C
Rencher George H. to Harris Mary 28 Feb 1837
Rencher George T. to Barbon Anastatia 5 Mar 1849

Rencher Hardy to Simms Sarah Anne 12 Jul 1831
Rencher Henry C. to Manson Margaret C. 15 Feb 1859
Rencher Henry C. to Bounds Alice 26 Mar 1867
Rencher John to Harris Elizabeth 13 Jun 1826
Rencher Thomas (Jr) to Ballard Priscilla 8 Dec 1801
Rencher William to Wright Polly 10 Dec 1799
Renshaw Thaddeus W. to Hitch Alice 17 Nov 1859
Renshaw Thaddeus W. to Bounds Mary E. 16 Mar 1864
Renshaw William T. to Murry Nancy 23 Feb 1858
Retze Justus F. to Jarvis Annie L. 10 Oct 1871
Revell Charles to Taylor Polly 27 Mar 1812
Revell David to Ford Aley 25 Jul 1814
Revell John to Abbott Sally 29 Jan 1799
Revell William to Mills Nancy 27 Feb 1798
Revil David to Lankford Esther 15 Feb 1804
Revill Curtis to _____ Gibson 17 Jan 1826
Revill David J. to Parks Mary W. 13 Jun 1848
Revill George R. to Ford Mary E. 3 Jul 1860
Revill Isaac to Gibson Nancy 5 May 1826
Revill James H. to Whittington Sally Elizabeth 20 Jan 1852
R£vill James S. to Benson Henrietta B. 7 Nov 1860
Revill John to Ford Sarah 21 Jan 1861
Revill John C. to Revell Maria J. 26 Mar 1821
Revill John C. to Matthias Nancy 5 Mar 1833
Revill John H. to Willing Dolly C. 15 Aug 1860
Revill Samuel E. to Somers Esther Anne 17 May 1859
Revill William to Powell Eleanor 23 Jan 1821
Revill William to Mason Nancy 23 Jan 1839
Revill William to Peacock Maria 23 Aug 1859
Revill William James to Mariner Nancy 5 Aug 1857
Reynoa Pierre J.C. to Broughton Susan A. 13 Sep 1831
Rhoads Benjamin to Taylor Mary Ann 15 Sep 1849
Rhodes Beacham to Wilson Charlotte W. 8 Sep 1835
Rhodes Joshua to Gibson Bolly 1 Oct 1811
Rial George to Larmore Louisa 24 Jun 1826
Riall George H. to Mezick Harriet K.W. 14 Dec 1852
Riall James H. to Carey Mary Anne 10 Jan 1854
Riall John to Smith Martha M. 9 Jan 1850
Riall William to Walter Mary 10 Dec 1833
Riall William P. to Wallace Mary E. 20 Apr 1842

Richards John S. to Powell Maria H. 30 Oct 1838
Richards John W. to Cantwell Esther A. 29 Mar 1865
Richards Joseph to Dryden Sarah 28 Mar 1816
Richards Joseph T. to McKonekin Harriet 25 Apr 1843
Richardson Charles to O'Dear Nancy 27 Oct 1801
Richardson George H. to Dailey Mary A. 9 Jan 1855
Richardson George S. to Toadvine Eleanora E. 21 Nov 1848
Richardson John to Matthews Susan E. 14 Apr 1863
Richardson Nathan to Bradshaw Matilda 29 May 1857
Richardson Thomas to Ellis Hetty 5 Sep 1825
Richs Thomas J. to Collins Mary E. -- Sep 1839
Rickoaf Alexander to Wilson Sarah Ann 6 Apr 1840
Rider Charles to Fontaine Anne M. 19 Mar 1833
Rider Charles E. to Purnell Margaret L. 21 Dec 1852
Rider Henry to Shiler Hester 8 May 1867 C
Rider James to Maddux Nancy 17 Dec 1804
Rider James to Armstrong Betsy 6 May 1813
Rider James M. to Moore Elizabeth 31 Aug 1830
Rider John N. to Hayward Sarah Anne H. 2 Apr 1835
Rider Noah to Bird Elizabeth 11 Nov 1817
Rider William H. to Rider Margaret A. 17 Feb 1840
Rider William P. to Elligood Margaret A. 14 Apr 1856
Rider Wilson to Maddux Henrietta 19 Feb 1833
Riech Elisha M. to Abbott Margaret A. 6 Mar 1858
Riggen Elisha to Mister Martha 24 Aug 1818
Riggen Elisha to Cullen Amelia 12 Jan 1820
Riggen Isaac to Lawson Nelly 5 Feb 1799
Riggen Isaac to Ward Polly 1 Jun 1813 C
Riggen John to Sommers Lizey 31 Dec 1817
Riggen John (Jr) to Marshall Esther 15 Nov 1803
Riggen Joseph to Brown Nancy 19 Feb 1811
Riggen Nehemiah to Lankford Polly 20 Feb 1821
Riggen Noah to Dickerson Patty 15 Feb 1808
Riggen Obediah to Newman Molly 10 Jun 1813
Riggen Pierce to Harris Betsy 16 Jan 1798
Riggen Pierce to Milbourn Anne 10 Nov 1807
Riggen Robert to Costen Peggy 30 Oct 1798
Riggin Alonzo to Blades Emily J. 27 Jul 1855
Riggin Andrew Franklin to Somers Sarah Elizabeth 21 Oct 1868
Riggin Edward to Price Nelly 3 Nov 1829

Riggin Elisha to Roach Catharine 10 Aug 1822
Riggin Elisha to Miles Hannah 15 Jan 1839
Riggin Elisha W. to Tignor Mary L. 29 May 1860
Riggin Emory to Lawson Susan 2 Jan 1828
Riggin George to Rounds Martha 4 Aug 1832
Riggin George to Wilson Sarah E. 9 Jul 1863
Riggin George W. to Adams Caroline J. 22 Jul 1862
Riggin George Washington to Bell Mary E. 10 Apr 1855
Riggin Henry to Davis Mary 6 Mar 1827
Riggin Henry to Gale Elizabeth 25 May 1831
Riggin Henry J. to Stewart Rebecca 14 Jan 1823
Riggin Isaac to Anderson Polly 9 Jan 1836
Riggin Isaac J. to Hurley Cirdelia 5 Jan 1853
Riggin Isaac J. to Dize Mary 7 Mar 1856
Riggin Jacob to Somers Mary E. 17 May 1859
Riggin James to White Emma 14 Oct 1862
Riggin James to Ward Virginia 21 May 1866
Riggin Jason Elliott to Sterling Elizabeth 5 Apr 1836
Riggin John to Jewett Maria 20 Sep 1832
Riggin John to Sterling Eliza 6 Nov 1845
Riggin John to Laws Margaret 28 Jan 1864
Riggin John T. to Adams Olivia E. 9 Nov 1869
Riggin John W. to Byrd Rosey 22 Oct 1860
Riggin John W. to Rowe Mary E. 20 Dec 1864
Riggin Jonathan to Bennett Elizabeth 31 Dec 1847
Riggin Jonathan to Bennett Matilda J. 16 Jul 1851
Riggin Joseph W. to Laws Priscilla F. 22 Oct 1855
Riggin Joshua J. to Cox Esther A. 18 Oct 1859
Riggin Nathan M. to Sparrow Ruth A. 4 Feb 1862
Riggin Noah to Nelson Hester 19 Aug 1851
Riggin Noah to Wilson Louisa 2 Jul 1855
Riggin Noah S. to McCready Margaret 19 Jan 1842
Riggin Obadiah to Perkins Amelia 8 Sep 1835
Riggin Obadiah to Kearsey Nancy 30 Jul 1839
Riggin Obed to Milbourn Lovey 7 Feb 1825
Riggin Robert to Carey Priscilla 13 May 1839
Riggin Samuel J. to Conway Anne E.W. 14 Nov 1865
Riggin Sandy to Ward Sally 26 May 1807
Riggin Seth to Sterling Mary Anne 18 Apr 1870
Riggin Severn to Thomas Elizabeth 6 Oct 1846

Riggin Stephen to Hall Margaret H. 17 Feb 1829
Riggin Stephen to Conner Margaret 25 Aug 1841
Riggin Thomas to Sterling Louisa 3 Aug 1847
Riggin Thomas to Riggin Nancy 29 Oct 1862
Riggin Washington to Dougherty Elizabeth 27 Dec 1853
Riggin William to Ward Matthew 11 Jun 1816
Riggin William to Miles Betsy B. 3 Jan 1829
Riggin William to White Polly 22 Jan 1839
Riggin William to Ward Jane 19 Feb 1844
Riggin William to Wilson Elizabeth 10 Nov 1859
Riggin William H. to Whittington Emily F. 11 Feb 1851
Riggin William H. to Dize Alice A. 25 Oct 1870
Riley Henry V. to Cannon Sally A. 23 May 1855
Riley Raymon H. to Spence Elizabeth 31 Jan 1865
Rilly William John to Evans Sarah 16 Jan 1849
Ritchie Robert to Dove Rebecca 21 Feb 1839
Ritchie Robert to Malone Elizabeth W. 26 Aug 1854
Ritchie Thomas to Goslee Betsy 21 Dec 1802
Ritchie Thomas to Parker Elizabeth 24 May 1842
Roach Augustus H. to Ward Lovey L. 5 Dec 1862
Roach Hope to Dorsey Mary 8 Oct 1868 C
Roach James to Somers Maria 18 Mar 1862
Roach Josiah to Potter Leah 15 May 1848 C
Roach Nathan to Wise Emma 29 Apr 1871 C
Roach Nehemiah James to Elzey Jane 23 Oct 1857 C
Roach Stephen B. to Waters Margaret R.H. 7 Jul 1825
Roach William to Milbourn Anne 15 Sep 1809
Roach William (Jr) to Gunby Eliza 7 Jan 1823
Roach William H. to Gunby Caroline V. 5 Nov 1849
Roads John to Lloyd Sally 27 Nov 1804
Roberts Benjamin to Robertson Elizabeth 17 Nov 1801
Roberts Benjamin to Goddard Jane Ann 10 Jan 1837
Roberts Benjamin V. to Wainright Ellen T. 19 Apr 1864
Roberts Edward to Nutter Sarah 3 Dec 1858
Roberts James A.M. to White Olivia A.H. 17 Jul 1860
Roberts John to Webster Sarah 31 Aug 1830
Roberts John to Summers Juia A. 22 Jan 1845
Roberts John E. to White Charlotte E. 11 Dec 1862
Roberts Joshua to Taylor Betsy 27 Dec 1802
Roberts Joshua B. to Russell Sally Sep 1799

Roberts Joshua W. to Roberts Mary E. 9 May 1848
Roberts Levin G. T. to Goddard Mary E. 16 Jul 1839
Roberts Thomas to Mitchell Jane 28 Jan 1811
Roberts Thomas to Foxwell Mary Eliza 1 Jan 1850
Roberts Wesley to Harris Cinderella 5 Dec 1865
Roberts William to Rencher Sarah 23 Jan 1798
Roberts William to Whayland Alsey 5 Jan 1836
Roberts William to Kennerly Caroline 25 Apr 1837
Roberts William F. to Evans Charlotte J. 3 Mar 1863
Roberts William M. to Wainright Mary 14 Nov 1837
Roberts William S. to Dashiell Eliza 13 Oct 1840
Robertson Alexander to Riley Martha M. 17 Dec 1851
Robertson Alexander M. to Walker Jane 2 Mar 1867
Robertson Alonzo W. to Melson Elizabeth 7 Jan 1840
Robertson Charles to Devereaux Henrietta 30 Dec 1823
Robertson Charles to Owens Mary 21 Feb 1832
Robertson Charles to Walker Rachael 20 Feb 1834
Robertson Dennis to Waters Tabitha 1 Jan 1870 C
Robertson Eli to Twiford Mary E. 10 Jan 1849
Robertson Elias to Silvia Nelly 9 Apr 1805
Robertson Elias to Willing Frances 11 May 1819
Robertson Elijah to Robertson Mary 28 Jun 1803
Robertson Ferdinand to Elliott Isabella 26 Feb 1861
Robertson Francis to Parsons Elizabeth 1 Jan 1845
Robertson George to Wilson Mary 16 Jan 1805
Robertson George to Powell Sarah 26 Sep 1807
Robertson George to Adams Sally 15 Sep 1831
Robertson George to Winright Leah 20 Feb 1844
Robertson George H. to Larmore Martha 20 Oct 1863
Robertson George W. to White Charlotte J. 3 Jan 1843
Robertson Henry to Carroll Sally Esther 10 Dec 1858 C
Robertson Henry C. to Kelly Sarah E. 17 Sep 1855
Robertson James to Whittington Sarah Anne 25 Apr 1854
Robertson James to Kelly Mary E. 17 Sep 1857
Robertson Job D. to Walker Sophia 18 Mar 1840
Robertson Job D.A. to Sudler Mary E. 27 Feb 1849
Robertson John to Byrd Philliss 17 Sep 1799
Robertson John to Dorithy Elizabeth 9 Dec 1799
Robertson John to Willing Eleanor 5 May 1807
Robertson John to Horner Mary 10 Feb 1817

Robertson John to Handy Priscilla C. 9 Jan 1828
Robertson John to Robertson Mahala W. 8 Dec 1829
Robertson John to Twiford Elizabeth A. 11 Feb 1840
Robertson John to Chelton Aurelia J. 1 Aug 1843
Robertson John to Robertson Dolly C. 10 Nov 1846
Robertson John D. to Mills Hannah 26 Feb 1820
Robertson John D. to Gilliss Elizabeth 29 Oct 1838
Robertson John E. to Denson Didemma 31 Jan 1837
Robertson John R. to Willing Rebecca S. 11 May 1864
Robertson John T. to Dryden Mary E. 7 Apr 1863
Robertson McKendry to Larmore Tabitha W. 18 Jun 1864
Robertson Robert to Waters Anne Hack 11 Jun 1798
Robertson Robert to Linton Lovey 23 May 1826
Robertson Robert D. to Holt Susan H. 1 Mar 1831
Robertson Robert G. to Bacon Rebecca 26 Feb 1867
Robertson Samuel to Bounds Eleanor 27 Oct 1845
Robertson Samuel to Larmore Airy J. 14 Nov 1848
Robertson Samuel A. to Covington Matilda E. 18 Oct 1842
Robertson Samuel A. to Matthews Sarah Ann 13 Nov 1849
Robertson Samuel H. (Dr.) to Ballard Margaret E. 20 Jun 1857
Robertson Thomas to Schoolfield Sarah White 3 Aug 1803
Robertson Thomas to Dashiell Kitturah 3 Dec 1810
Robertson Thomas to Denson Mary 17 Nov 1835
Robertson Thomas to Jones Elizabeth L. 8 Feb 1842
Robertson Thomas to Evans Leah E. 14 Oct 1846
Robertson Thomas (Barron Cr) to Robertson Rachel 28 Mar 1815
Robertson Thomas (Jr) to Handy Harriett 16 Mar 1809
Robertson Thomas (Sr) to Curtis Mary 22 Mar 1816
Robertson Washington H. to Evans Priscilla A. 11 Jun 1844
Robertson William to Bradley Eleanor 22 Nov 1830
Robertson William to Parsons Mary Anne 1 Nov 1842
Robertson William M. to Weatherly Leah E. 27 May 1864
Robertson William W. to Acworth Priscilla F. 21 Nov 1866
Robeson Major A. to Marain Nancy E. 30 Jan 1850
Robins James to Barnes Tabby 10 Apr 1869 C
Robinson Benjamin H. to Cooper Mary E. 12 Jan 1857
Robinson Elijah to Windsor Mary J. 15 Sep 1854
Robinson Francis H. to Sherman Priscilla S. 26 Jan 1863
Robinson James to Bradley Emeline E. 21 Feb 1849
Robinson John to Owens Angeline 24 Aug 1860

Robinson John Q. to White Margaret Ellen 26 Jun 1855
Robinson William T. to Collins Laura S. 18 Jul 1865
Rogers Alvah to Parks Elizabeth 31 Oct 1857
Rogers Frederick to Harris Joanna 6 Jan 1857
Rogers John to Shores Miranda 6 Jan 1852
Rolen John W. to Hudson Zipporah -- Jun 1837
Rollins Henry F. to Marine Martha A. 18 Dec 1855
Rolly Raymond to Crockett Emma 10 May 1870
Rook John to Winright Sarah Anne 6 Aug 1834
Rosburgh Matthias to Broughton Margaret 20 Dec 1866 C
Rose William A. to Adams Louisa N. 14 Nov 1834
Ross Asa to Tyler Annie 25 May 1820
Ross Edward W. to Shockley Sarah M. 27 May 1858
Ross Edward W. to Wilkins Emma C. 20 Nov 1869
Ross Gilbert M.L. to Dryden Anne M. 20 Jun 1860
Ross James B. to Parsons Nancy 27 Nov 1843
Ross John to Dashiell Emily 15 Feb 1859
Ross Levi to Williams Clemintine 19 Jan 1830
Ross Levin to Newman Mary Anne 14 Jul 1818
Ross Levin to Barbone Eliza M. 3 Sep 1825
Ross Levin J. to Windsor Elizabeth 21 Jan 1847
Ross Noah to Moore Betsy 15 Jan 1817
Ross Robert to Davis Catharine 23 Jun 1847
Ross Robert J. to Ford Matilda 6 Jul 1829
Ross Stoughton to Jones Elizabeth 12 Apr 1825
Ross Theodore to Adams Mary V. 3 Dec 1866
Ross William to Muir Sally 3 Dec 1818
Ross William to Smith Christianna 24 Jan 1870
Ross William H. to Adams Emiline R. 26 Mar 1851
Ross Wm. H. to Hall Margaret Esther 26 May 1868
Rounds John to Davis Anne 29 Jan 1834
Rounds William H. to Brewington Elizabeth E. 20 Jun 1867
Rowe Gabriel H. to Daniels Eleanor 27 Nov 1843
Rowe George to Webster Nancy 13 Sep 1814
Rowe George Thomas to Wallace Sarah E. 29 May 1857
Rowe George W. to White Louisa 5 Dec 1843
Rowe Henry C. to Layfield Marca J. 11 Feb 1852
Rowe John to Rowe Nancy 11 May 1808
Rowe Nicholas P. to Wilson Mary 24 Mar 1853
Rowe Samuel to Evans Betsy 5 Nov 1814

Rowe William T. to Kelly Catharine A.M. 7 Apr 1863
Rowlings William to McCready Hannah A. 12 Jan 1842
Roy A. T. to Hyland Mary G. 17 Nov 1853
Ruark Ezekiel to Jones Rachel 2 Jun 1801
Ruark George H. to Trader Nancy E. 2 Aug 1859
Ruark John to Jenkins Lucretia 25 Nov 1845
Ruark John H. to Goslee Sarah Priscilla 18 Dec 1851
Ruark Major to Williams Sally 2 Aug 1824
Ruark William M. to Hooper Nancy 8 Dec 1846
Ruark William T. to Collins Phebe 4 Feb 1864
Rucker Thomas to Adams Louisa H. 20 Jan 1835
Rud Joseph W. to Layfield Bettie 18 Dec 1866
Rue John to Summers Ephamia 30 Dec 1798
Rush J. Murray to Dennis Elizabeth A. 29 Nov 1853
Russel James to Cordray Adaline 26 Jan 1848
Russell Alza to Graham Elizabeth 18 Sep 1819
Russell Arthur to Simpkins Sarah 20 Sep 1821
Russell Curtis to Bradley Emily 25 Jan 1860
Russell Everton to Kennerly Nancy 9 Mar 1852
Russell Everton to Phillips Leah Ann 26 Jan 1859
Russell James to Twilley Molly 24 Jun 1799
Russell James to Humphreys Nelly 13 Jul 1830
Russell James T. to Lankford Mary Jane Sep 1830
Russell Joseph to Lankford Patience A. 17 Nov 1835
Russell Josiah T. to Dougherty Esther Snead 1 Jul 1851
Russell Levin to Groves Nancy 28 Jul 1797
Russell Levin to Selvey Liza 1 Dec 1799
Russell Levin to Tully Amelia 29 Aug 1835
Russell Robert to Russell Hetty 15 Jan 1828
Russell Samuel to Wheeler Elizabeth 3 Sep 1835
Russell Thomas to Seabreeze Mary Ann 15 Oct 1831
Russell William to Kennerly Elizabeth 14 Jan 1845
Russell William to Goddard Henrietta 21 Dec 1852
Ryan Thomas to Twigg Julia 18 Nov 1863
Salisbury John to Dougherty Elizabeth 7 Aug 1841
Salsbury John to Miles Leah 30 May 1826
Sammons James to Taylor Sarah J. 23 May 1848
Sampson James to Heath Betsy Wilson 27 Jun 1820
Sampson James to Turpin Milcah Ann 22 Apr 1823
Sampson Richard H. to Heath Jane M. 20 Aug 1822

Sanders Andrew K. to Dashiell Amanda E.J. 20 Apr 1836
Sanders William H. to Maddux Louisa 26 Sep 1868 C
Sasser Benjamin to Durham Polly 10 Aug 1815
Sasser Robert to Riggin Mary 6 Jul 1813
Sasser Whitty to Ballard Elizabeth 24 May 1804
Savage Joseph to Dashiell Eleanor 8 Feb 1814
Savage William to Polk Mary (Widow) 16 Apr 1813
Sawyer Henry to Evans Elizabeth 23 Jan 1853
Sayre Thomas to Scott Louisa V.L. 20 Jan 1868
Scaggs James J. to Collier Mary E.A. 26 Oct 1853
Scarborough James to Ballard Elizabeth 9 Jun 1871 C
Scarborough John to Robertson Elizabeth 2 Sep 1843
Schmidt Henry to Riggin Henrietta 13 Nov 1861
Schoolfield George to Ward Sally J. 8 Dec 1868 C
Schoolfield Joseph to Miles Jane 24 Jul 1813
Schoolfield William A. to Jones Mary 17 Mar 1801
Scott George H. to Tull Anne 9 May 1815
Scott George T.B. to Windsor Mary E. 21 May 1857
Scott George W. to McDorman Annie C. 9 Mar 1871
Scott Henry to Gunby Sarah Ann 13 Feb 1849
Scott James H. to Kelly Louisa E. 12 Dec 1849
Scott John to White Julian 15 Jan 1828
Scott John D. (Sr.) to White Julia F. 22 Nov 1866
Scott Joseph E. to Barkley William Anne 10 Sep 1867
Scott Levin to Lankford Sally Jane 21 Apr 1853
Scott Mahlon to Evans Eliza 19 Jul 1825
Scott Major to Rowe Leah 3 Oct 1843
Scott Major to Horner Sarah Ellen 23 Dec 1850
Scott Robert to Kelly Mariah 7 Aug 1827
Scott Samuel to Jones Betsy 17 Nov 1827
Scott Samuel J. to Thompson Sarah E. 29 Sep 1868
Scott William to Maddux Polly 7 Dec 1814
Scott William J. to Dryden Elizabeth M. 8 Mar 1854
Seabrease Thomas to Grant Zipporah 26 Jul 1831
Seabreese John to Hobbs Sarah 12 Sep 1820
Seabreeze John to Powell Emeline 4 Jan 1858
Seabreeze John B. to Mills Leah A. C. 13 Mar 1849
Seabreeze Richard to Adams Eleanor 30 Apr 1835
Seabreeze William to Mills Cumi 19 Oct 1858
Seabreeze William T. to Elliott Hester 1 Sep 1862

Sears Orin to Lawson Sarah A. 26 Jul 1870
Sears William A. to Nelson Mary 19 Aug 1844
Sebrease John to Cannon Mary Anne 7 Oct 1817
Sebrees William to Crocket Nancy 11 Jan 1803
Selby James E. to Phillips Sarah E.A.J. 12 Oct 1858
Selby John to Cornish Sarah 2 Jan 1867 C
Selby John to Holbrook Adelaide 16 Jan 1871 C
Selby Levin to Bounds Rebecca 17 Dec 1816
Selby Levin to King Caroline 22 Dec 1864 C
Selby Major to Larmer Leah 29 Nov 1811
Selby Major to Mezick Harriet 23 Jun 1817
Selby Robert to Twilley Leah 1 Jan 1805
Selby William H. to Austin Mary J. 8 Oct 1832
Seldom George to Hull Matilda 26 Apr 1866 C
Serman George to Brewington Mary 17 Jun 1828
Serman Isaac to _____ Elizabeth 31 Jan 1797
Serman Isaac to Cooksey Priscilla 1 Feb 1831
Sermon George to Kibble Molly 11 Jan 1814
Sermon Isaac to Smith Milcah 10 Nov 1807
Seward Thomas M.B. to Hughes Hannah G. 27 Apr 1829
Sewel Samuel to Raughley Harriet T. 7 Oct 1835
Sewell Berry to Cordray Margaret 29 Aug 1855
Sewell Peter to Rhodes Dolly 1 Jul 1819
Sewell Thomas to Russell Susanna 23 Nov 1826
Shane John H. to Evans Virginia R. 11 Mar 1864
Sharp Cyrus to Riggen Anne 2 Feb 1802
Shaw Thomas to Wilson Elizabeth 18 Jun 1832
Shay Elijah to Nelson Roze 15 Sep 1804
Sheaves James to Elliott Anne Maria 13 Jan 1853
Shehie James to Lawrence Sarah Louisa 13 Jun 1839
Shelton William to Abbott Leah 2 Jan 1821
Sheppard John D. to Hastings Levinia 7 Apr 1849
Sherfield Joseph to Hopkins Emily 7 Jan 1861
Shipham George to Hall Polly 2 Sep 1801
Shockley Christopher C. to Phillips Lavina A. 23 Mar 1863
Shockley David to Jones Mary Adeline 27 Jun 1854
Shockley Elijah to Anderson Polly 1 Mar 1815
Shockley Hamilton to Levingston Elizabeth 11 Sep 1827
Shockley John to Richardson Nancy 15 May 1798
Shockley Samuel B. to Webster Hester 19 May 1871

Shockley Steward to Sirmon Elizabeth 30 Aug 1841
Shockley Thomas to Cottinggem Betsy 9 Mar 1801
Shockley William to Phillips Eleanor 25 Jan 1864
Shores Alexander J. to McDorman Elizabeth Anne 7 Jul 1841
Shores Edward to Austen Nelly 10 May 1799
Shores George to Shores Elizabeth 13 Sep 1843
Shores George to Bozman Margaret 10 Dec 1861
Shores George H. to Jones Catharine 16 Nov 1869
Shores Henry to Webster Emily 1 Jun 1869
Shores Humphries to Polk Elizabeth 13 Jun 1866
Shores Isaac J. to Webster Margaret F. 25 May 1859
Shores John to Webster Charlotte 25 Aug 1829
Shores John S.K. to Simpkins (?) A. 21 Feb 1871
Shores John W. to Tignor Elizabeth 29 Oct 1859
Shores Lambert to Pozman Sally 2 Mar 1824
Shores Lambert H. to Webster Emeline 21 Oct 1857
Shores Lambert L. to Webster Julia Anne 5 Jun 1855
Shores Levin to Somers Mary 5 Jun 1813
Shores Levin to White Margaret 30 May 1835
Shores Levin to Windsor Elizabeth 7 Mar 1843
Shores Levin G.W. to Evans Elizabeth 11 Nov 1856
Shores Purnell to Payton Charlotte 28 Jul 1868
Shores Robert to Shores Adeline 3 Oct 1855
Shores Samuel to Parks Anne R. 24 Jul 1861
Shores Severn to Shores Margaret 10 Jul 1838
Shores Silas to Carew Martha 26 Nov 1844
Shores Silas G. to Davis Sorena A. 20 Apr 1854
Shores Solomon to Winright Elizabeth 31 Jan 1827
Shores Thomas to Wallace Polly 3 Jul 1813
Shores Thomas to Webster Mary 9 Jul 1844
Shores Thomas to Bozman Mary 2 Dec 1851
Shores Thomas to Hall Frances 26 Apr 1867
Shores William J. to Parks Leah 10 Jun 1836
Shores Zachariah to Windsor Delitha 18 Nov 1862
Short James R. to Williss Harriet E. 5 Feb 1863
Showard Joseph P. to Humphreys Serinda E. 11 Feb 1862
Showell William to Bisbie Maria Louisa 18 Aug 1856
Shreves Hancock to Hayward Anne 4 Feb 1817
Shreves James H. to Lankford Margaret 22 Oct 1863
Shreves Thomas to Shores Angeline 11 Dec 1850

Shrives Samuel to Porter Dorathy 28 Jan 1823
Silverthorn Samuel to Pollitt Martha 29 Jan 1831
Simmes Jesse to Cantwell Leah Anne 27 Sep 1853
Simms John to Murrill Adaline 5 May 1846
Simms Revill P. to Mason Sarah E. 7 Mar 1871
Simms Samuel to Simms Ellen 19 Jan 1847
Simons William to Parks Rachall 13 Feb 1838
Simonson James to Nelson Harriet 11 Mar 1841
Simonson John N. to Lawson Gussie M. 20 Jun 1865
Simpkins Charles to Roberts Elizabeth 19 Jan 1824
Simpkins Charles M. to White Eliza R. 16 Jan 1869
Simpkins Charles W. to Kelly Annie 8 Oct 1870
Simpkins Jesse to Roberts Matilda 27 Sep 1832
Simpkins Jesse to Jones Sarah A. 13 Dec 1854
Simpkins Jesse W. to Sims Rebecca A. 22 Jun 1859
Simpkins John T. to Carew Matilda E. 28 Feb 1849
Simpkins Major to Hughes Mary 31 Dec 1816
Simpkins Thomas S. to Marsh Harriet E. 9 Jan 1855
Simpkins William to Horner Julia A. 23 Mar 1858
Simple John to Sterling Rachel 25 Aug 1869 C
Simpson Benjamin to Haymon Mary 16 Dec 1828
Sims Elisha to Twilley Julia T. 6 Mar 1866
Sims James to Adams Sarah 18 Sep 1822
Sims Jesse to Simpkins Eleanor 28 Jul 1847
Sirman George to Leonard Maria 3 Sep 1839
Sirman John to Seabreeze Mary W. 11 May 1844
Skinner Peter O. to Bounds Jane 31 Jul 1827
Skinner Theodorick B. to Cottman Katharine B. 1 Jun 1842
Skinner Thomas to Rencher Eleanor B. 9 Nov 1818
Skinner William B. to Acworth Sally M. 14 Sep 1824
Slemmons John B. (Jr) to Benett Martha J. 26 Apr 1831
Slemmons John B. (Rev) to McBryde Leah 22 Jun 1801
Slemons Albert B. (Dr.) to Ker Elizabeth H. 13 Dec 1858
Slemons J. Edwin to Morris Annie W. 17 Jun 1869
Slemons James to Miller Matilda 23 Jan 1833
Slemons John B. to McBryde Mary E. 30 Jul 1844
Slemons Robert W. to Miles Classina E. 8 Jun 1843
Smart John to Dashiell Charlotte 22 Apr 1819
Smiley John to Robinson Julia 4 Sep 1866 C
Smith Benjamin to Newman Sarah Ann 5 Aug 1797

Smith Benjamin to Higgins Priscilla 5 Oct 1858
Smith Charles to Surman Betsy 8 Jan 1805
Smith Charles to Green Alley 8 Oct 1814
Smith Charles to Williams Mary 24 Jan 1837
Smith Charles to Disharoon Esther 17 Dec 1868 C
Smith David to Kennerly Peggy 1 Nov 1821
Smith Edward C. to Toadvine Virginia A. 14 Jun 1865
Smith Edward Horsey to Waller Nancy 4 Jun 1799
Smith Eliaja to Townsend Mary Anne 16 Aug 1836
Smith George to Landen Rebecca 9 Jul 1799
Smith George to Twilly Mary 5 Mar 1821
Smith George to Benson Elizabeth 6 Jun 1870 C
Smith George W. to Shockley Sarah Anne 9 Jan 1856
Smith George W. to Fields Olivia 30 Jan 1866
Smith George W. to Logan Virginia A. 26 Apr 1870
Smith Hampton H. to Sims Emily 1 Jan 1862
Smith Handy to Dashiell Indianna 5 Nov 1867 C
Smith Henry to Donoho Elizabeth 28 Feb 1809
Smith James to Rounds Betsey 16 Sep 1800
Smith James to Dougherty Sarah 4 Dec 1802
Smith James to Surman Levinah 20 Feb 1804
Smith James to Adams Eliza G. 4 Nov 1817
Smith James to Sewell Elizabeth 30 Apr 1825
Smith James to Brewington Elizabeth 3 Oct 1844
Smith James to Russell Betsy 12 Mar 1845
Smith James to Culver Elizabeth 24 Dec 1845
Smith James to Williams Margaret 6 Jan 1870 C
Smith James D. to Porter Priscilla 12 Jan 1836
Smith James H. to Adams Catharine Ann 16 Jan 1839
Smith James H. to Walston Elizabeth 8 Jun 1841
Smith James P. to Coulbourn Mary G. 21 Jan 1862
Smith James W. to Jones Lydia A. 10 Apr 1868
Smith Jeffrey to Waters Sally Jane 7 Jun 1870 C
Smith John to Covington Mary W. 16 Oct 1834
Smith John to Cornish Hester 20 May 1865 C
Smith John to Marshall Amelia 31 May 1870
Smith John H. to Kennerly Mary J. 11 Aug 1856
Smith John Henry to Roberts Elizabeth 6 Mar 1857 C
Smith John J. to Milbourn Charlotte 13 Apr 1824
Smith John S. to Parks Elizabeth A. 8 Jun 1869

Smith John W. to Wilson Nancy 3 Sep 1844
Smith John W. to Handy Esther G. 24 May 1847
Smith Joseph F. to Ballard Mary Elizabeth 29 Jan 1840
Smith Joseph Hopkinson to Handy Anne H. 30 May 1853
Smith Joshua to Fields Susan 20 Dec 1831
Smith Joshua to Jenkins Rosetta Caroline 30 Jul 1845
Smith Levin B. to Lecates Julia E. 1 Feb 1871
Smith Levin C. to Mitchell Eliza A. 18 Apr 1854
Smith Lewis to Wilkins Sally 16 Jul 1801
Smith Lewis to Hopkins Sarah 9 Jan 1826
Smith Lewis to Marshall Sarah 4 Nov 1835
Smith Littleton to Crouch Anne 13 Jul 1843
Smith Littleton to Williams Charlotte 30 Jan 1855
Smith Moses C. to Mitchell Nancy 4 Oct 1825
Smith Richard to Holbrook Keziah 25 Sep 1866 C
Smith Richard R. to Nelson Eunece 10 Jan 1843
Smith Robert T. to Disharoon Brizala T. 11 Feb 1852
Smith Samuel to Foreman Maria 17 Nov 1816
Smith Samuel to Whitelock Elizabeth 12 Sep 1832
Smith Samuel to Cottingham Nancy 25 Sep 1860
Smith Samuel J. to Waters Mary E. 1 Jan 1858 C
Smith Samuel S. to Carey Sarah D. 30 Oct 1849
Smith Stephen R. to Jenkins Miranda 5 Mar 1839
Smith Stoughton to Riggin Sally 24 Oct 1810
Smith Thomas to Vance Hetty 1 Feb 1822
Smith Thomas to Dorman Margaret 7 Mar 1825
Smith Thomas to Hopkins Mary 9 May 1854
Smith Thomas B. to Williams Margaret 23 Oct 1845
Smith Thomas W. to Phoebus Catherine 28 Oct 1867
Smith Whittington to Taylor Polly 28 May 1839
Smith William to Smith Esther 29 Jon 1811
Smith William to Kelly Elizabeth 2 Oct 1832
Smith William to Twilley Sarah Anne 24 Dec 1838
Smith William to Fields Eliza Anne 24 Dec 1839
Smith William to Haws Sally 18 Jun 1845
Smith William to Dashiell Drucilla 1 Nov 1853
Smith William to Mills Eliza 9 Apr 1863
Smith William to Wheatley Cherry 24 Jul 1868 C
Smith William S. to Giles Clara 3 Aug 1863
Smith William T. to Ford Jane 22 May 1833

Smith William T. to Beauchamp Sally 5 Dec 1861
Smith William W. to Cantwell Olivia J. 22 Dec 1852
Smith William W. to Moore Julia 11 Jan 1860
Smith William W. to Disharoon Theodoria A. 30 Apr 1866
Smith Williams to Adams Mary 19 Oct 1830
Smulling Edmond to Gibbons Sally 19 Jan 1808
Smulling James H. to Brumley Elizabeth E. 23 Feb 1864
Smulling Lambert to Emory Julia 12 Feb 1870
Smulling Nathaniel H. to Costen Elizabeth H. 28 Mar 1837
Smvlling Peter to Brooks Harriet 5 Feb 1833
Smulling William to Smulling Nancy 21 Jul 1810
Smulling William to Hayman Mary E. 1 Sep 1842
Smulling Zorobabel to Stewart Mary 27 Sep 1836
Smulling Zorohable to Gibbons Henrietta 22 Mar 1808
Snead Edward S. to Dennis Susan U. 6 Dec 1826
Snelling Richard to Stewart Mary E. 16 Oct 1844
Snow Charles to Wallace Eleanor 2 Feb 1829
Solloway William to Lloyd Sarah N.P. 20 May 1861
Somers Abraham (Jr.) to Tyler Mary 6 Jul 1842
Somers Abraham D. to Nelson Sarah A. 21 Nov 1854
Somers Algernon F. to Majors Susan A. 23 Dec 1867
Somers Benjamin to Blades Mary 13 Jan 1834
Somers Benjamin. to Miles Sarah 31 Jul 1841
Somers Benjamin to McCready Charlotte 12 Dec 1853
Somers Edward to Evans Alcey J. 16 Apr 1861
Somers Elijah to Sterling Mary 28 May 1822
Somers Elijah to Crockett Fanny 18 Jan 1842
Somers Elijah to Powell Polly 4 Aug 1846
Somers Elijah to Lankford Mary W. 21 Dec 1866
Somers Ephraim to Sterling Sally 5 Jun 1838
Somers George to Williams Drucilla E. 21 Feb 1870
Somers Gustavus E. to Benton Mary W. 15 Nov 1867
Somers Henry to Sterling Esther 22 Oct 1807
Somers Henry to Wilson Levina 19 Feb 1839
Somers Horsey to Lawson Sally 10 Mar 1829
Somers James to Nelson Grace 14 Aug 1830
Somers James to Morgan Priscilla 30 Jun 1869
Somers Jesse to Adams Jane 31 Dec 1833
Somers John to Ward Betsy 21 May 1922
Somers John to Miles Harriet 19 Oct 1841

Somers John to Ward Lovey Lee 29 Jul 1846
Somers John to Wilson Henny 8 Apr 1847
Somers John D. to Phoebus Martha E. 8 Nov 1853
Somers John H. to Ballard Susan J. 26 Dec 1854
Somers John H. to Jones Margaret R. 17 Sep 1862
Somers Jonathan to Riggin Rachel 18 Sep 1810
Somers Levi to Miles Anna 27 Apr 1941 C
Sumers Michael to Corbin Rachel H. 27 Nov 1856
Somers Nicholas to Miles Mary 17 Jul 1849
Sumers O.C. to White M.B. 19 Jul 1871
Somers Oliver C. to Sterling Emily 9 Jun 1963
Sumers Rheubin to Tawes Betsy 7 Oct 1812
Somers Samuel to Jones Nancy 23 Jan 1809
Somers Samuel to Somers Kitty 17 Sep 1840
Somers Samuel to Sterling Grace 28 Apr 1849
Somers Samuel to Thomas Maria 4 Jun 1850
Somers Samuel S. to Beauchamp Caroline 14 Aug 1867
Somers Severn to Gibson Susan 25 Jan 1842
Somers Sidney B. to Sterling Delia 21 Jul 1863
Somers Smith to Sterling Jemima 21 May 1833
Somers Stephen to Ward Mary 25 Jan 1812
Somers Thomas to Ford Milcah 1 Feb 1820
Somers Thomas to Ward Hannah 5 Feb 1833
Somers Thomas to Smith Mary 28 Nov 1848
Somers William D. to Disharoon Sarah Anne 18 May 1852
Somers William H. to Layfield Elizabeth 11 Dec 1844
Somers William J. to Bozman Elizabeth 14 Jan 1862
Somers William James to Ford Elizabeth Ann 17 May 1859
Somers William T. to Lawson Angeline 20 Aug 1867
Sorin Matthew to Robertson Maria 23 Sep 1828
Sparrow Josiah to Crockett Margaret 24 Oct 1843
Sparrow Thomas N. to Harrison Elizabeth S. 14 Apr 1852
Sparrow William to Guy Elizabeth 29 Dec 1823
Sparrow William W. to Evans Matilda A. 7 Apr 1862
Spence Benjamin to Taylor Mary 25 Oct 1819
Spence Irving to Humphreys E. Virginia 28 Jan 1864
Spence John to Guy Leah Handy 14 Sep 1818
Spence Richard A. to Dize Adeline 13 Jan 1859
Spence William to Winder Candau 8 Nov 1866 C
Spencer Benjamin to Henry Mary 7 Jan 1867 C

Spencer John to Handy Sally 22 Jun 1835
Spillane Timothy to Bright Julia Anne 20 Jun 1865
Squire Alexander to Jones Lucretia 7 Nov 1871 C
Stacks Philip to Stayton Mary 19 Jul 1803
Stafford Benjamin to Larmore Sally 18 Oct 1809
Stafford William to Insley Anne Maria 28 Mar 1833
Stanford Clement to Dashiell Anne 29 May 1802
Stanford Constant D. to Hayman Nancy 15 Mar 1830
Stanford Isaac to Moore Martha Jane 24 Jan 1843
Stanford John to Stanford Nancy 19 Apr 1803
Stanford John to Brannon Priscilla 3 May 1813
Stanford Joshua to McIntire (?) 6 Aug 1802
Stanford Obediah to Jones Mary 20 Dec 1814
Stanford William to Wailes Leah Handy 10 Dec 1804
Stant Samuel to Hay Mazy E. 19 Jul 1848
Stayton Levin to Wright Nelly 19 Feb 1801
Stayton William to Wright Rebecca 28 Jul 1798
Steele James B. to Gale Milcah 14 Apr 1819
Steppe Oscar F. to Collins Roxanna 1 Jan 1856
Sterling Aaron to Howard Betsy 16 Jul 1811
Sterling Aaron to Moore Susan 31 Dec 1816
Sterling Aaron to Johnson Myrna 2 Jul 1818
Sterling Aaron (of Ephraim) to Nelson Elizabeth 15 Aug 1820
Sterling Aaron (of John) to Lawson Grace 27 May 1850
Sterling Albert A. to Sterling Elizabeth 17 Sep 1869
Sterling Algie S. to Tyler Julia A. 17 Jan 1865
Sterling Christopher J. to Lawson Julia M. 1 Jun 1846
Sterling Clement R. to Taws Leah 7 May 1860
Sterling Cornelius W. to Hundley Mary J. 18 Jul 1865
Sterling David to Lawson Rachel 7 Mar 1848
Sterling David to Horsey Mary A. T. 19 Jan 1855
Sterling Edward to Sterling Sally J. 21 Jan 1871
Sterling Elijah to Croswell Jane 27 Jan 1818
Sterling Elijah to Lawson Mary 4 Jul 1825
Sterling Elijah to Lawson Alvertia F. 13 Dec 1869
Sterling Elijah T. to McDaniel Mary C. 3 Jan 1870
Sterling Ephraim to Bird Molly 3 Dec 1799
Sterling Ephrain to Mason Charlotte 18 May 1830
Sterling George to Moore Susan 5 Dec 1865
Sterling George B. to Sterling Nancy C. 19 Jan 1870

Sterling George R. to Ward Margaret 11 Apr 1862
Sterling George W. to Sterling Eliza E. 17 Mar 1847
Sterling George W. to Jewett Mary 17 Nov 1869 C
Sterling Gilbert to Bedsworth Mary Jane 26 Oct 1841
Sterling Hance to Bedsworth Maria H. 15 Dec 1854
Sterling Henry to Ward Mary 3 Jul 1813
Sterling Henry to Sterling Prisce 18 May 1835
Sterling Henry to Sterling Sally 28 Jun 1860
Sterling Hope W. to Riggin Sarah E. 24 Nov 1863
Sterling Isaac to Riggin Hetty 7 Jul 1815
Sterling Isaac to Ward Hetty 29 Aug 1815
Sterling Isaac to Moore Betsy 18 Jun 1833
Sterling Isaac to Sterling Peggy 5 Jun 1848
Sterling Isaac O. to Lankford Susan M. 12 Jun 1866
Sterling Isaac T. to Bratcher Mary E. 25 Mar 1861
Sterling James to Taws Grace 3 Nov 1838
Sterling James to Sterling Harriet A. 21 Feb 1861
Sterling James to Horsey Catharine 4 Feb 1870 C
Sterling Jesse to Sterling Henry 3 Jan 1826
Sterling Jesse to Nelson Sally 15 Jul 1845
Sterling Jesse to Sterling Grace L. 24 Nov 1869
Sterling John to Lawson Harriet 28 May 1844
Sterling John to Sterling Mary 22 Jul 1845
Sterling John to Mason Mary Jane 19 Jun 1850
Sterling John to Davy Sarah C. 1 Aug 1860
Sterling John to Onions Mary J. 2 Jan 1863
Sterling John (Senr) to Wilson Lovey 9 May 1842
Sterling John A. to Sterling Hannah 18 Nov 1871
Sterling John D. to Byrd Julia F. 12 Jun 1866
Sterling John E. to Sterling Angie 7 Feb 1871
Sterling John H. to Sterling Mary T. 11 Jun 1851
Sterling John H. to Miles Sarah 5 Jul 1866
Sterling John H. to Sterling Caroline 2 Oct 1866 C
Sterling John W. to Bradshaw Lovey A. 3 Dec 1861
Sterling Joseph to Lawson Kasey Ann 29 Dec 1826
Sterling Josiah to Denike Catherine 1 Apr 1856
Sterling Leonard C. to Cullen Leah J. 24 Jun 1858
Sterling Littleton to Byrd Rachael 24 Feb 1852
Sterling Littleton D.T. to Milligan Sally Ann 7 Aug 1858
Sterling Luther to Sterling Mary E. 31 May 1870

Sterling Mahlon to Sterling Esther A. 16 Dec 1856
Sterling Nathan to Nelson Hetty 22 Jan 1813
Sterling Nathan to Byrd Mary 7 Jul 1854
Sterling Nicholas P. to Adams Sarah M. 5 Jun 1860
Sterling Noah to Sterling Mary 19 Jun 1838
Sterling Noah to Evans Jane 24 Dec 1867
Sterling Noah C. to Sterling Mary Anne 30 Mar 1858
Sterling Revill J. to Thomas Margaret 13 Dec 1864
Sterling Richard to Hickman Mary 10 Sep 1825
Sterling Rufus W. to Lawson Grace C. 27 Jul 1871
Sterling Samuel to Somers Anne 18 May 1830
Sterling Severn to Blake Mary Jane 18 Jan 1848
Sterling Severn A. to Handy Harriet L. 25 Dec 1871 C .
Sterling Shadrach to Summers Prissy 25 Aug 1801
Sterling Sidney L. to Somers Rella 24 Dec 1870
Sterling Smith to Dize Elizabeth 2 Feb 1858
Sterling Southey to Taws Maria 24 Aug 1844
Sterling Southey to Dougherty Mary D. 8 Jun 1855
Sterling Thomas to Young Susan 21 Jul 1829
Sterling Thomas to Walden Sarah F. 16 Jan 1866
Sterling Thomas to Hundley Nancy 12 Jun 1866
Sterling Thomas C. to Thomas Emeline A. 16 Dec 1870
Sterling Thomas W. to Somers Dorothy C. 11 Jun 1850
Sterling Thomas W. to White Mary E. 17 Sep 1861
Sterling Travers to Ward Leah 9 Feb 1808
Sterling Travers to Somers Molly 8 Aug 1829
Sterling Travers to Lawson Grace 29 May 1833
Sterling Travers to Somers Anna 6 Sep 1837
Sterling Washington to Nelson Rebecca 3 Aug 1827
Sterling William to Nelson Sally 29 Dec 1826
Sterling William to Moore Nelly 27 May 1831
Sterling William to Moore Maria J. 27 Apr 1842
Sterling William to Sterling Susan 18 Jun 1844
Sterling William to Johnson Sarah E. 1 Feb 1853
Sterling William to Adams Julia 4 Oct 1859
Sterling William to Sterling Mary F. 8 Aug 1861
Sterling William to Moore Leah 4 Jan 1870
Sterling William C. to Somers Priscilla 2 Apr 1861
Sterling William H. to Nelson Mary E. 30 Mar 1870
Sterling William T. to Byrd Elizabeth 29 Feb 1848

Sterling William T. to Sterling Anna R. 3 Jan 1865
Sterling William T. to Dize Anne 5 Mar 1869
Sterling Wingate to Ford Virginia 19 Oct 1859
Stevens Benjamin to Vanderwolf Prissy 11 Apr 1798
Stevens Edward to Dyles Henrietta 20 Dec 1828
Stevens Edward T. to Stevenson Martha J. 14 Jan 1868
Stevens James to Ball Elizabeth 24 Oct 1865
Stevens John to Marshall Elizabeth 9 Sep 1800
Stevens John to Dorman Louisa A. 26 Jan 1860
Stevens John (Barren Cr) to Rhodes Betsy 31 Dec 1814
Stevens John S. to Polk Sarah W. 22 Dec 1829
Stevens Josiah W. to Huffington Mary E. 10 Feb 1852
Stevens Rufus H. to Lankford Matilda J. 10 Feb 1868
Stevens Samuel A. to Surman Elizabeth A. 20 Dec 1858
Stevens Silas to Clark Mary P. 31 Oct 1865
Stevens Silas J. to Lane Eleanor 3 Jan 1871 C
Stevens Thomas to Prior Henrietta 18 Jan 1865
Stevens Thomas C. to Powell Amanda L. 31 Jul 1849
Stevens William H. to Porter Henrietta J. 6 Jan 1836
Stevenson Benjamin F. to Stephenson Mary Jane 11 Mar 1867
Stevenson Benjamin T. to Ward Harriet L. 30 Dec 1831
Stevenson Edward S. to Coulbourn Sally C. 22 Nov 1860
Stevenson George F. to Todd Sarah A. 19 May 1870
Stevenson George R. to Dougherty Kessy A. 5 Oct 1838
Stevenson George R. to Porter Martha J. 31 Mar 1863
Stevenson Henry to Adams Sally W. 11 Jan 1825
Stevenson James to Willie Margaret 3 Mar 1829
Stevenson James to Stevenson Elizabeth L.J. 31 Dec 1850
Stevenson John to Ward Elizabeth 26 Jan 1827
Stevenson Joseph to Milbourn Sarah E. 3 Oct 1855
Stevenson Joseph E. to Lankford Mary Jane 13 Jun 1845
Stevenson Lycurgus H. to Porter Sarah E. 23 Jun 1856
Stevenson Lycurgus H. to Milbourn Mary Jane 3 Dec 1867
Stevenson Moses to Porter Ann 28 Nov 1837
Stevenson Prettyman L. to Cox Sally L. 19 Jan 1858
Stevenson Solon C. to Carey Sarah A. 12 Mar 1867
Stevenson Thomas to Ward Sally 4 Aug 1800
Stevenson Thomas to Miles Arinthia A. 28 Sep 1858
Stevenson Thomas to Reese Hester Anne 7 Mar 1867
Stevenson William J. to Hayman Roena 18 Feb 1868

Stewart James to Ker Nelly G. H. 21 Dec 1812
Stewart James to Johnson Mary 29 Dec 1869 C
Stewart James R. to Miles Nancy 18 May 1855
Stewart John C. to Dashiell Sally 29 Jan 1803
Stewart John C. to Aydelot Elizabeth 12 Feb 1816
Stewart John H. to Jones Mary G. 15 Apr 1839
Stewart Richard to Lankford Mary P. 20 Sep 1825
Stewart Robert (Col.) to Ker Leah J.S. 16 Dec 1839
Stewart Robert J. to Disharoon Sally A. 2 Jan 1861
Stewart William to Venables Elizabeth 5 Jan 1804
Stewart William to Hitch Juliann 2 Apr 1825
Stewart William to Washbourne Vicey 17 May 1832
Stewart William to Brewington Amanda 13 Jan 1840
Stewart William (Dr.) to Jones Henrietta H. 29 Nov 1859
Stewart William (Senr.) to Polk Margaret W. 26 Jan 1842
Stewart William C. to Dashiell Betsy 1 Sep 1801
Stewart William J. to Mezick Martha E. 16 Nov 1841
Stewart William S. to King Susan M. 8 May 1834
Stewart William T. to Ashmead Mary W. 8 Apr 1867
Stickney Ezekiel W. to Atwood Ann R. 9 Oct 1863
Stinggle James to Fairbush Sophronia 24 Jan 1871
Stokes William to Stant Levinia S. 26 Dec 1849
Stone James M. (Dr.) to Jones Lucinda G. 30 Apr 1849
Stone Thomas W. (Dr.} to Jones Leah H. 14 Apr 1849
Stradeley George W. to Ward Sarah A. 25 Jun 1866
Street James A. to Evans Mary 27 Nov 1854
Street James A. to Muley Sarah D.F. 13 Oct 1865
Street Mansfield to Willing Rosey 29 Feb 1820
Street Mansfield to Evans Rodah 13 Sep 1842
Street Samuel to Harris Sarah A.V.H. 5 Dec 1849
Street Samuel J. to Dunn Margaret E. 12 Apr 1854
Street Thomas to Williams Ann 30 Dec 1834
Street Zacheus to Baily Peggy 9 Dec 1828
Strong Nehemiah to Causey Keziah 2 Aug 1853
Strongware Simon to Bishop Nancy 10 May 1798
Stuart William B. to Dixon Ellen P. 11 Mar 1835
Stubbs John to Windsor Almira 5 Nov 1868
Stubbs John to Jones Mary A. 22 Sep 1870
Sturgeon William P. to Stevenson Catherine C. 25 Jul 1835
Sturgis Ara S. to Swift Matilda J. 1 Apr 1865

Sturgis Benjamin T. to Waters Hannah Catherine 18 Sep 1868 C
Sturgis Henry to Brereton Sarah 2 Oct 1810
Sturgis John R. to Sturgis Sarah A.P. 2 Mar 1847
Sturgis Littleton to Dreyden Priscilla L. 18 Oct 1825
Sturgis Littleton to Foster Ella 5 Jun 1867
Sturgis William to Carroll Lucy 21 Jan 1868 C
Sudler Emory to Done Elizabeth 31 Jan 1805
Sudler John to King Catharine 8 Oct 1844
Sudler John D. to Clayville Sarah A. 9 Dec 1858
Sudler Joseph to Jones Henrietta M.W. 27 Mar 1826
Sudler Joseph to Pomeroy Candace S. 23 Apr 1857
Sudler Matthias Jones to Jones Alfonza F. 31 Aug 1853
Sudler Tubman W. to Stewart Elizabeth 4 Nov 1817
Sudler William to Lester Martha 8 Aug 1811
Sudler William to Curtis Elizabeth 9 Oct 1822
Sullivan John A. to Howard Sally Elizabeth Ann 8 May 1855
Sumers Abraham to Moore Polly 31 Dec 1816
Sumers George to Nelson Leah 5 Jan 1837
Summers Abraham to Byrd Rachel 22 Aug 1820
Summers Elijah to Crosswell Betsy 23 Aug 1799
Sumers Thomas to Miles Atty 11 Feb 1818
Swan Robert to Schoolfield Margaret 30 May 1810
Swan Robert W. to Horsey Anne 2 Sep 1823
Swift Charles H. to Johnson Indianna 28 Sep 1870
Swift Francis to Matthews Mary R. 27 Mar 1862
Swift Henry. to Beauchamp Anne 17 Nov 1835
Swift Stephen to Reese Mary Anne 23 Dec 1841
Swift Theodore to Matthews Amanda M. 14 Jun 1870
Swift William to Porter Nancy 10 Jun 1823
Swigg Samuel to Beauchamp Mary J. 17 Feb 1853
Talbot William to Conaway Mary Ann 1 Jan 1838
Tall William R. to Smith Emma V. 11 Nov 1862
Tankerley Charles V. to Webster Lavina E. 10 Feb 1863
Tankerly Hyram D. to Shores Biddy A. 24 May 1860
Tankerly Thomas H. to Webster Laura C. 31 Jan 1863
Tankersley Thomas H. to Rowe Adeline F. 4 Feb 1856
Tanksley William to Maw Sarah 26 Jan 1853
Tar William E. to Tull Mary Z. 27 Jun 1860
Tarlton Joseph T. to Webster Leah P. 24 Feb 1863
Tarr Joseph to Seabreeze Sally 31 Dec 1855

Tate Joshua to Conner Pamelia 9 Sep 1835
Tatem George C. to Peers Elizabeth 20 Jul 1866
Tawes Charles R. to Evans Eliza E. 24 May 1858
Tawes Isaac to Thomas Milly 8 Sep 1835
Tawes James to Somers Charlotte 4 Aug 1834
Taws Albert to Dougherty Nancy E. 21 Jan 1862
Taws Calvin L. to Gibson Virginia E. 25 Oct 1870
Taws George W. to Carew Julia 11 Oct 1870
Taws Henry to Moore Sally 1 Apr 1829
Taws Isaac to Milbourn Priscilla 7 Jul 1815
Taws Isaac to Thomas Phema 20 Jul 1825
Taws Isaac J. to Sterling Ellie 27 Jun 1871
Taws John to Boston Leah 27 Aug 1799
Taws John to Williams Mary 25 Sep 1839
Taws John to Webster Melissa E. 21 Dec 1868
Taws Kenny to Nelson Nancy 6 Aug 1819
Taws Noah to Nelson Grace T. 17 Jul 1849
Taws Wesley to Cox Eugenia 28 Jul 1863
Taws William to Whaley Polly 16 Aug 1816
Taws William H. to Robertson Sarah E. 27 Feb 1867
Taylor Anthony M. to Malone Mary C. 4 Mar 1862
Taylor Asbury F. to Cantwell Mary Jane 22 Aug 1848
Taylor Avery M. to Layfield Margaret 4 Jul 1848
Taylor Benjamin to Kemp Zipporah 18 Mar 1822
Taylor Edward F. to Fleming Anne E.A. 5 Aug 1868
Taylor Elias to Goslee Polly May 1824
Taylor Elisha T. to Green Susan 11 Dec 1829
Taylor Ezekiel to Foxwell Charity 14 May 1799
Taylor George to Williams Rachel 20 Apr 1808
Taylor George W. to Webster Anne 26 Mar 1839
Taylor George W. to Collier Mary Alice 13 May 1863
Taylor Gilliss T. to Darby Sophronia 5 Feb 1861
Taylor Hiram to Howard Hester A. 28 May 1867
Taylor Ichabod to Phillips Emeline 24 Apr 1839
Taylor Isaac to Bull Hetty 6 Apr 1813
Taylor Isaac to Taylor Lizzy 21 Jan 1822
Taylor Isaac T. to Bennett Sally B. 20 Nov 1855
Taylor James to Basset Nancy 26 Oct 1819
Taylor James to Elliott Elizabeth 15 Dec 1835
Taylor James C. to Cooper Margaret Ellen 28 Nov 1865

Taylor James T. to _____ Ann Maria -- Jun 1850
Taylor James T. to Robinson Eleninia P.J. 16 Apr 1855
Taylor Jehu to Howard Sally 19 Nov 1817
Taylor John to Acworth Temperance 11 Dec 1797
Taylor John to Moore Anna 28 Sep 1804
Taylor John to Dunn Bridget 26 Oct 1809
Taylor John to Lankford Elizabeth 11 Sep 1832
Taylor John to Waters Mary Wesley 21 Nov 1833
Taylor John to Banks Margaret Hester 12 May 1846
Taylor John to Willing Sarah 7 Jan 1857
Taylor John C. to Bennett Nancy 20 Jan 1852
Taylor John C. to Bennett Caroline E.H. 20 Apr 1859
Taylor John H. (Dr.) to Adams Sally E. 3 Apr 1860
Taylor John K. to Lawrence Sarah J. 25 Dec 1856
Taylor John W. to White Virginia C. 23 Aug 1849
Taylor John Wesley to Whayland Louisiana 21 Dec 1852
Taylor Joshua to Adams Mary Ellen 18 Feb 1857
Taylor Josiah S. to Bennett Esther P. 3 Nov 1856
Taylor Levin to Wright Nancy 26 Aug 1812
Taylor Levin to Kindrix Mary 12 Oct 1830
Taylor Levin to Caloway Mary E. 21 Apr 1855
Taylor Levin J. to Huston Elizabeth J. 13 Apr 1852
Taylor Littleton to Culver Haldah 6 Feb 1844
Taylor Matthias to Bounds Mary 22 Feb 1826
Taylor Matthias to Elliss Sarah Anne 5 Nov 1844
Taylor Peter to Miles Matty 11 Jul 1820
Taylor Purnell to Bowles Sarah 1 Jan 1839
Taylor Richard V. to Knowles Amanda 12 Jan 1859
Taylor Robert W. to Taylor Mary Elizabeth 30 Dec 1848
Taylor Samuel to Tilghman Leah 19 Jan 1808
Taylor Samuel to Jenkins Hetty 29 Jul 1817
Taylor Samuel to Parks Mary 16 Jan 1821
Taylor Samuel to Lewis Sarah 18 Jun 1846
Taylor Samuel C. to Ewell Sarah Anne 12 Mar 1852
Taylor Samuel J. to Dougherty Mary W. 26 Apr 1863
Taylor Samuel J. to Pusey Amanda F. 29 Nov 1865
Taylor Severn to Dove Charlotte 23 Dec 1844
Taylor Sidney A. to Malone Miranda 9 Oct 1860
Taylor Stephen to Furniss Charlotte 8 Jan 1811
Taylor Stephen to Bayne Margaret 8 Sep 1818

Taylor Thomas to White Sarah Ellen 19 Jan 1853
Taylor Wesley to Robertson Mary Ellen 2 Feb 1858
Taylor Wesley to Bennett Emily 23 Jul 1862
Taylor William to Martin Nelly 4 Mar 1803
Taylor William to Banks Polly 7 Apr 1818
Taylor William to Byrd Mary 16 Jul 1822
Taylor William to Uraten Peggy 15 Feb 1831
Taylor William to Nelson Ellen 6 Oct 1840
Taylor William to Dove Leah 23 Jan 1841
Taylor William to Deer Jane 9 Nov 1847
Taylor William to Dize Polly 5 Jul 1849
Taylor William to Smith Elizabeth 3 Oct 1854
Taylor William to Hopkins Annett 9 Sep 1862
Taylor William L. to Gravenor Amada T. 13 Feb 1866
Taylor William T. to Majors Amanda 10 Mar 1869
Therogood William to Taylor Maria 28 Mar 1859
Thomas Aaron to Thomas Alcey A. 14 Nov 1844
Thomas Alexander to Horner Harriet 10 Apr 1863
Thomas Alonzo to Marshall Martha J. 8 Aug 1805
Thomas Benjamin to Dougherty Sally Ann 4 May 1847
Thomas Elisha to Parks Sally 11 Apr 1829
Thomas Elisha to Bradshaw Elizabeth 1 Jun 1840
Thomas Elisha to Moore Elizabeth 22 Feb 1842
Thomas Elisha to Tyler Ann M. 24 Aug 1858
Thomas George to Mason Sally 6 Jul 1825
Thomas George to Hamburg Mary 24 May 1836
Thomas George to Revill Nancy 11 Feb 1845
Thomas George to Crockett Mary I. 28 Dec 1869
Thomas George S. to Gibson Margaret E. 6 Jun 1865
Thomas Henry to Johnson Ritty 22 Dec 1823
Thomas Henry to Landen Esther 2 Dec 1858
Thomas John to Roach Polly 3 Jun 1800
Thomas John to Wingate Mary 2 Apr 1833
Thomas John B. to Thomas Alcey 11 Nov 1864
Thomas John C. to Revill Emily J. 21 Aug 1860
Thomas John Lybrand to Mister Theresa Jane 26 Jan 1869
Thomas John Wesley to Taylor Susan J. 9 Dec 1858
Thomas Joseph to Wingate Eliza 22 May 1838
Thomas Joshua to Bratcher Charlotte 6 Oct 1814
Thomas Noah to Landing Harriet 9 Mar 1852

Thomas Samuel to Maddux Kitty 10 Mar 1869 C
Thomas William to Lawson Martha 4 May 1826
Thomas William C.W. to Harris Alice C. 11 May 1863
Thomas William D.W. to Evans Delia 20 Jul 1858
Thomas William J. to Insley Isabella 6 Nov 1854
Thomas William S. to Dougherty Mary Anne 11 Jun 1833
Thomas William S. to Kelly Julia Ann 18 Feb 1864
Thomas William S. to Windsor Arianna R. 20 May 1869
Thomas William Snead to Mister Pamelia E. 17 Nov 1856
Thomas William T. to Jones Alice J. 5 Nov 1849
Thompson Elijah to Williams Nancy 18 Jul 1834
Thompson Elijah to Walter Mary A. 24 Mar 1852
Thompson Henry to Webster Ariana 14 Sep 1861
Thompson James to Ballard Elizabeth A. 19 Oct 1825
Thompson Robert to Ker Emily 3 Jan 1870 C
Thompson William J. to Waters Emily F. 18 Jan 1848
Thorns Stephen to Owens Sally 15 Dec 1798
Thornton James E. to Sterling Maria E. 2 Aug 1864
Thorps Joshua to Willing Betsy 17 Jun 1814
Tigner Thomas to Kelly Sarah Anne 23 Feb 1841
Tignor John to Kelly Mary C. 10 Nov 1857
Tilden Charles N. to Williams Mary P. 15 Sep 1838
Tilghman Elijah to Calloway Mary Virginia 20 Jul 1857
Tilghman George to Holbrook Harriet 12 Sep 1867 C
Tilghman George to Dennis Henrietta 22 Dec 1870 C
Tilghman George W. to Coulbourn Sarah A. 24 Dec 1858
Tilghman Henry T. to Nutter Mary C. 24 Dec 1859 C
Tilghman James to Hayward Nancy 7 Nov 1809
Tilghman James to Merrill Maria 7 Jan 1834
Tilghman James to Adams Mary Anne 28 Mar 1837
Tilghman John H. to Collins Mary J. 30 Oct 1866
Tilghman Josiah to Cluff Catharine 25 Apr 1864
Tilghman Littleton to Powell Sarah J. 4 Dec 1860
Tilghman William to Dickinson Mary 14 Jan 1812
Tilghman William to Rowley Margaret 21 Sep 1859
Tilghman William to Ballard Anne 2 Apr 1861
Tilghman William H. to Powell Mary M. 24 Feb 1857
Tillman Robert T. to Bell Maria 11 Jan 1871
Tindall David T. to Feals Patty A. 7 Aug 1860
Tipton Joshua V. to Gibbons Mary E. 13 May 1857

Tire John W. to Smith Mary E. 15 Nov 1864
Toadvine Alexander G. to Humphreys Theodora 10 Nov 1855
Toadvine Eben to Johnson Esther 2 Dec 1867 C
Toadvine Frank to Rowe Jennie 13 Oct 1871
Toadvine Henry to Disharoon Charlotte 6 Feb 1849
Toadvine John to Pollitt Sally 22 Feb 1804
Toadvine Matthias J. to Horsey Williamina 14 Sep 1852
Toadvine Matthias O. to Handy Lucretia 18 Dec 1827
Toadvine Purnell to Parsons Amanda 3 Sep 1832
Toadvine Stephen P. to Ruark Martha 12 Apr 1859
Todd George C. to Bradley Adelade 2 Oct 1866
Todd Henry L. to Fowler Julia A.W. 17 May 1852
Todd James to Parks Ruth 9 Mar 1808
Todd Major to Sampkins Esther Anne 21 May 1844
Todd Manaheim W. to Scott Emily O. 7 Sep 1858
Todd Nathan to Price Margaret 11 Oct 1833
Todd Nehemiah to Evans Elizabeth 10 Feb 1840
Todd Nehemiah S. to Douglass Mary W. 19 Nov 1860
Todd Wilson J. to Dashiell Juliet J. 12 Jan 1857
Tomkinson Theophilus L. to Hayman Laura E. 30 May 1864
Townsend Charles to Brown Drucilla J. 23 Oct 1844
Townsend Edwin J. to Brown Amanda M. 3 Jun 1851
Townsend James to Smullen Mary 14 Nov 1798
Townsend James E. to Moore Amelia J. 14 Jun 1864
Townsend James W. to Riggin Amelia 10 Dec 1863
Townsend Jesse to Williams Drusilla 4 Apr 1831
Townsend Joshua J.F. to Brown Charlotte S. 15 Oct 1844
Townsend Josiah to Moore Judith 19 Jan 1865
Townsend Levin H. to Collier Esther Ellen 20 Jan 1859
Townsend Major to Dubberly Jane 24 Dec 1822
Townsend Mitchell to Jenkins Sally 29 Mar 1836
Townsend Mitchell to Williss (alias) Sally Jenkins 29 Mar 1836
Townsend Peter to Catlin Anne 30 Jul 1825
Townsend Thomas S. to Evans Margaret E. 27 Feb 1866
Townsend William to Hargis Margaret D. 29 Mar 1844
Townsend William Henry to Malone Elizabeth Virginia 19 Dec 1866
Towsend Henry to Smulling Betsy 2 Jan 1801
Towsend Levin to Dorman Anne 22 Jul 1799
Trader Aurelius P. to Covington Mary A. 5 Jan 1870
Trader Elijah to Toadvine Caroline 14 Feb 1867 C

Trader Henry to Wilkins Sally 20 Feb 1801
Trader John to Chander Euphemia 28 Jun 1849
Trader John L. to Lowe Elizabeth E. 29 Jan 1866
Trader Levin W. to Horsey Matilda E.J. 6 Sep 1845
Trader Purnell to Garretson Leah 8 Jan 1813
Trader Stephen to Williams Amanda 28 Jan 1867 C
Travers Edward to Willing Eleanor 24 Sep 1831
Travers John to Willing Mary 8 Dec 1827
Travers John to Riggin Harriet 26 Oct 1835
Travers Joseph to Harris Rebecca 28 Nov 1864
Travers Matthias to Hopkins Jane 12 Sep 1825
Travers Thomas H. to Kelly Wilmina F. 11 Feb 1862
Traverse Edward to Mezick Margaret Anne 26 Aug 1856
Traverse George T.A. to Wilson Mary E. 10 Jan 1854
Traverse Jabus to Jones Polly 13 Jul 1814
Traverse William W. to Robertson Sarah E. 4 Oct 1865
Travis Mitchell to Fowler Ellen 8 Apr 1844
Treahearn Thomas to Dear Mary 19 Jun 1827
Trehearn Cyrus to Gunby Sally 8 May 1799
Trehearn John S. to Cantwell Emma 31 Jan 1865
Trehearn Thomas to Long Caroline 18 Jan 1870
Trehern Gellett to Green Eliza Jane 7 Aug 1849
Trehern Teagle to Lankford Leah 11 May 1802
Trewet John to Anderson Polly 11 May 1803
Trindle Thomas to Winson Charlotte 18 May 1813
Truitt Benjamin W. to Hearn Martha W. 7 Apr 1853
Truitt Rufus K. to Standford Mary Anna 26 May 1846
Tucker Lewis to Toadvine Hester 31 May 1866
Tull Alfred P. to Fitzgerald Susan 21 Nov 1849
Tull Elijah T. to Hall Harriet H. 1 Sep 1868
Tull Frederick to King Isabella F. 26 Feb 1850
Tull George to Mills Eliza 24 Jan 1832
Tull George W. to Sparrow Esther 21 Oct 1834
Tull George W. to Leech Mary E. 17 May 1870
Tull George W. to Hall Sally 16 Sep 1871
Tull Henry to Tull Ibby D. 19 Jan 1830
Tull Henry to Somers Julia 10 Apr 1867 C
Tull Henry C. to Ross Margaret E. 28 Nov 1871
Tull Henry T. to Ballard Mary D.W. 18 Dec 1838
Tull J. Francis A. to Wilson Esther A. 14 Dec 1863

Tull James to McDaniel Matilda 4 Jan 1870
Tull John to Williams Peggy 10 Dec 1827
Tull John to Laird Orpah 18 Nov 1834
Tull John to Gerald Jane 24 Feb 1835
Tull John to Jones Anne Maria 19 Feb 1839
Tull John to Revill Margaret 30 May 1865
Tull John A. to Broughton Leah 13 Jun 1849
Tull John H. to Lambdon Phebe G.H. 25 Sep 1855
Tull John K. to Marriner Ellen Frances 9 Jul 1858
Tull John S. to Covington Rebecca A. 14 Dec 1867
Tull Joshua W. to Harris Matilda A. 1 Nov 1831
Tull Joshua W. to Broughton Eliza 4 Nov 1840
Tull Joshua W. to Parks Maria Harriet 30 Apr 1859
Tull Joshua W. to Cox Louisa 3 Jan 1862
Tull Levin to Killum Molly Curtis 12 Mar 1805
Tull Levin to Lankford Rachel 6 Jan 1818
Tull Levin to Miles Rosanna 13 Jun 1820
Tull Levin to Mister Elizabeth 22 Jun 1825
Tull Levin to Riggin Mary 20 Mar 1855
Tull Nathan T. to Parker Emiline B. 17 Apr 1832
Tull Nicholas to Cheney Nelly 10 Nov 1796
Tull Peter to Holland Nancy 18 Dec 1804
Tull Richard to Catlin Elizabeth 10 Apr 1834
Tull Robert J. to Adkins Mary E. 31 Dec 1868
Tull Samuel to Byrd Nancy 21 Jan 1798
Tull Samuel to Miles Carolina 24 Jan 1805
Tull Samuel to Warrick Charlotte 1 Oct 1845
Tull Samuel L. to Gunby Maria C. 23 Nov 1853
Tull Solomon to Ward Amelia 5 Jan 1825
Tull Stephen L. to McLane Susan J. 23 Dec 1835
Tull Thomas H. to Adams Laura W. 21 Feb 1866
Tull Washington to Dorman Sarah Ellen 22 Nov 1853
Tull William to Handy Esther 17 Jan 1801
Tull William H. to Ward Sarah Anne 12 Jun 1833
Tull William M. to Whitney Elizabeth S. 10 Jul 1833
Tull William T. to Stewart Eleanor P. 11 Dec 1845
Tull William T. to Bradley Margaret V. 3 Feb 1868
Tully John to Rhodes Anne 31 May 1798
Tully Stephen to Lloyd Priscilla 28 Jan 1815
Tunis Samuel to Powell Annaretta 18 Feb 1800

Turner Asey A. to Foreman Elizabeth A. 19 Jun 1867
Turner Edward to Crouch Elizabeth C. 26 Jul 1859
Turner James to Mezick Mary J. 4 Jan 1859
Turner John to Evans Judy 3 Jan 1810
Turner John to Barkley Polly 25 Mar 1819
Turner John to Travers Alice 3 Sep 1833
Turner John W. (Capt.) to Evans Margaret 11 Jan 1859
Turner Joshua to Collins Elizabeth 18 Nov 1861
Turner Naman P. to Phillips Mary 13 Aug 1839
Turner Samuel J. to Fisher Mary Anne 20 Sep 1864
Turner Thomas V. to Prior Charlotte 17 Jun 1845
Turner William to Disharoon Sally 4 Jun 1822
Turner William to Prior Drucilla 17 Dec 1856
Turner William to Carey Mahala 26 Jul 1870
Turner William E. to Burgiss Mary A. 29 Feb 1844
Turpin Alfred B. to Beauchamp Aurelia A. 22 Jul 1862
Turpin Benjamin W. to Stanford Elizabeth A.H. 13 May 1827
Turpin Henry to Willing Betsy Jane 17 Feb 1855 C
Turpin Henry W. to Pollitt Maria H. 22 Dec 1830
Turpin Hyman J. to Kennerly Elmanda 30 Nov 1857
Turpin James E. to Windsor Charlotte A. 11 Sep 1861
Turpin John to Bell Susan W. 13 Jan 1829
Turpin John (of Wm.) to Mitchell Margaret W.B. 4 Nov 1841
Turpin John U. to Goslee Zipporah 11 May 1825
Turpin John Wesley to Gale Clara A. 5 Dec 1860
Turpin Joseph to Jenkins Annie A. 16 May 1870 C
Twiford Alfred W. to Weatherly Charlotte P. 17 Jan 1850
Twiford John B. to Bradley Eleanor Anne 25 Oct 1851
Twiford John B. to Lynch Amanda P. 9 Nov 1864
Twig Thomas to Furniss Esther 16 Oct 1811
Twigg James to McCap Elizabeth 4 Aug 1855
Twigg Thomas to Anderson Polly 26 Dec 1796
Twigg Thomas to Prior Sally 13 May 1800
Twigg Thomas M. to Hopkins Sarah P. 2 Feb 1852
Twilley Caleb D. to Huffington Esther 25 Jan 1848
Twilley George to Twilley Maria 22 Feb 1825
Twilley George W. to Walter Rebecca 4 Apr 1843
Twilley John to Wilson Nelly 15 Jul 1813
Twilley John W. to Taylor Leah C. 3 Feb 1840
Twilley Joseph P. to Wright Esther A. 5 Jan 1858

Twilley Robert to Caton Nancy 13 Dec 1796
Twilley Robert to Kelly Mary 17 Dec 1826
Twilley Robert to Dashiell Matilda 30 Nov 1847
Twilley Robert to Mezick Amelia Anne 18 Nov 1858
Twilley Thomas to Newton Esther Ann 1 Mar 1825
Twilley Thomas J. to Marine Sarah J. 31 Dec 1862
Twilley William to Crawford Maria 3 Dec 1817
Twilley William B. to Covington Carrie L. 26 Dec 1870
Twilly George W. to Elzy Elizabeth 1 Feb 1848
Twilly Joshua T. to Disharoon Sally 15 Mar 1849
Twilly Robert to Disharoon Milcah 13 Mar 1821
Twilly William to Dashiell Maria 2 Jun 1846
Tyler David to Ward Margaret 20 Jul 1849
Tyler Edward J. to Wilson Sally J. 18 Jul 1863
Tyler Ephraim to Thomas Mahala 11 Jan 1825
Tyler George to Sterling Mary J. 16 Jun 1863
Tyler George to Jubilee Arinthia 31 May 1871 C
Tyler George W. to Price Emily F. 29 May 1866
Tyler Hiram P. to Jones Louisa F. 2 Nov 1870
Tyler Isaac J. to Somers Mary Jane 19 Jun 1834
Tyler Jacob S. to Horner Anna E. 13 Dec 1871
Tyler James H. to Thomas Mary A. 6 Jun 1871
Tyler John to Tyler Anne 25 Jun 1819
Tyler John to Evans Kitturah 3 Aug 1869
Tyler John to Beauchamp Sadonia S. 5 Sep 1871
Tyler John Henry to Evans Harriett 20 Aug 1850
Tyler John W. to Anderson Rebecca 6 Jul 1852 C
Tyler John W. to Thomas Catharine S. 31 Jan 1861
Tyler John W. to Cullin Elizabeth 12 Jan 1871
Tyler Littleton T. to Sterling Hetty E. 28 Nov 1871
Tyler Noah A.W. to Evans Margaret A. 7 Jul 1871
Tyler Oliver D. to Hewitt Martha J. 10 Jun 1869
Tyler Robert E. S. to Hall Amanda S. 2 Feb 1869
Tyler Severn to Russell Ellen 27 Aug 1842
Tyler Silas to Somers Eliza Anne 13 May 1853
Tyler Thomas to Crockett Rosey 31 May 1842
Tyler Thomas to Sterling Jane 10 Apr 1851
Tyler William to Mason Maria 7 Jul 1846
Tyler William W. to Jones Esther A. 30 May 1865
Underhill Thomas to Powell Leah 30 Jan 1799

Underhill Thomas H. to Whittington Eleanor C. 1 Jun 1835
Underhill William to Buntin Polly 13 May 1835
Underhill William to Riggin Nancy 30 Nov 1842
Underhill William J. to McCready Nancy M. 24 Jul 1843
Upsher Lewis to Elligood Sally 13 May 1865
Upshur Abel P. to Dennis Elizabeth W. 24 Feb 1817
Vance David to Gray Polly 9 Feb 1808
Vance David to Storks Rosanna 19 Sep 1826
Vance George to Handy Patty 3 Mar 1800
Vance William to Maddux Esther 19 Jan 1841
Vaughan William to Giles Gainer 1 Oct 1816
Veasey William F. to Coston Laura H. 19 Dec 1868
Veazey William H. to Porter Margaret G. 20 Mar 1850
Venables Alexander to Howard Sally 15 Apr 1817
Venables Charles to Venables Amilcha 3 Feb 1801
Venables Hiram to Cornwell Rosey 17 Oct 1837
Venables John (Jr) to Phillips Polly 6 Jan 1834
Venables Josiah to Fowler Priscilla 24 Oct 1818
Venables Richard to Twilly Sarah 26 Nov 1796
Venables Robert to Ballard Sarah 8 Oct 1799
Venables Robert to Walter Biddy 28 Sep 1819
Venables Seth D. to Jones Susan 15 Feb 1849
Venables William V. to Wilson Nancy P. 16 Sep 1847
Vener Emanuel to Fips Peggy 14 Aug 1823
Vernettson William to Miles Bridget 11 Dec 1801
Vesey William to Richards Sarah Jane 6 Apr 1829
Vetra George Jones to Dorman Leah J.G. 14 Mar 1850
Vetra Henry to Kirwan Mary 18 Oct 1830
Vetra Joseph S.G. to Webster Sarah E. 26 Jun 1854
Vetre Williss L. to Powell Elizab Jane 21 Oct 1840
Vickers Elias B. to Bundick Susan 2 May 1854
Vickers James to Hillman Betsy 24 Aug 1813
Victory Thomas to Manning Priscilla 16 Mar 1797
Vinoent Ebi J. to Disharoon Elizabeth Ellen 16 Mar 1847
Vincent George M. to Mills Hetty M. 29 Oct 1856
Vincent James to Dashiell Priscilla 12 Oct 1818
Vincent James to Umstead Harriet 2 Mar 1821
Vincent John H. to Pollitt Caroline E.E. 27 Feb 1855
Vincent Matthias M. to Vincent Anne C. 13 Dec 1825
Vincent Perry to Covington Mary M. 22 Mar 1859

Vincent Perry M. to Phillips Elizabeth A. 20 Feb 1866
Vincent Solomon to Hitch Nancy 19 Dec 1815
Vincent Thomas to Taylor Sally 29 Aug 1798
Vincent William to Truitt Nancy 5 Feb 1814
Vinson Eli to Adams Comfort 11 Sep 1797
Vinson Elijah to Douglass Biddy 11 Dec 1800
Virden Moses to Vincent Sarah 24 Jul 1822
Vitry George to Roberts Maria 7 Jul 1821
Vittory John to Jones Mary 2 Aug 1800
Wailes Daniel to Bounds Polly 11 Jul 1799
Wailes Ebenezer L. to Todd Anna 7 Nov 1859
Wailes John to Mezick Betsy 12 Jan 1808
Wailes Onesimus to Walter Biddy 2 Nov 1836
Wailes Sandy to Freeney Julia A. 1 Apr 1867 C
Wailes William to Savage Eleanor 28 Apr 1818
Wailes William J. to Weatherly Julia E. 1 May 1855
Wainright Cannon to Adams Jane 4 Dec 1839
Wainright Hamilton to Larmore Mary 15 Oct 1844
Wainright Issac J. to Green Margaret 26 Jan 1858
Wainright James to Wainright Eliza 17 Oct 1842
Wainright Jesse to Walton Margaret -- Jun 1839
Wainright Jesse to Riall Esther Anne 12 Dec 1854
Wainright John to Matthews Rosa 6 Jan 1846
Wainright John A. to Bedsworth Rachael 14 Dec 1860
Wainright John E.M. to Larmore Esther Ann D. 17 Oct 1848
Wainright William H. to Wilson Georgianna 2 Apr 1867
Wainwright William to Robertson Eleanor 15 Feb 1842
Waistcoat (?) to Cox Nancy 13 Jun 1815
Walden Thomas to Smith Maria 2 Dec 1856
Wales John to Crockett Elizabeth 2 Dec 1812
Walker Allen to Beauchamp Sally A. 30 Oct 1871 C
Walker Charles to Giles Mary A. 14 Aug 1844
Walker Charles to Giles Nardilla 18 Nov 1856
Walker George W. to Fleming Amanda 1 Dec 1865
Walker Henry to Sterling Eliza 5 Sep 1846
Walker James H. to James Lydia 13 May 1865
Walker Jeremiah W. to Cooper Margaret A.Q. 10 Jan 1866
Walker John to Mason Isabella 16 Aug 1854
Walker John Curtis to Whaley Lydia 11 Jan 1821
Walker Joseph to Taylor Susan 3 Jan 1839

Walker Mimucan(?) to Dorman Molly 29 Mar 1800
Walker Nathaniel to Gravener Ardelia 28 May 1857
Walker Walter to Bennett Sally 27 Feb 1834
Walker Walter to Gravenor Mary 19 Nov 1839
Walker William to Lloyd Betsy 25 Sep 1828
Walker William to Parks Polly 31 Mar 1840
Walker Zachariah H. to Wyatt Louisa H. 5 Jul 1856
Wallace Arnold to Webster Ibby 19 Dec 1837
Wallace Arnold to Whittington Elizabeth 22 Dec 1868 C
Wallace Berry to Nutter Mary Catherine 18 Jan 1858
Wallace Charles to Wallace Grace 26 Dec 1814
Wallace Charles T. to Hughes Tabitha M. 5 Nov 1856
Wallace George to Evans Rachel 20 Apr 1801
Wallace George to Jones Emeline 22 Jan 1822
Wallace George H. to Lawson Serena M. 2 Aug 1853
Wallace James to Walston Sarah 16 May 1798
Wallace James. to Jones Elizabeth 9 Aug 1866 C
Wallace John to Shores Mary E. 27 May 1856
Wallace John to Whittington Harriet 29 Dec 1868 C
Wallace Levin to White Betsy 4 Nov 1824
Wallace Levin James to Muir Catharine 8 Aug 1859
Wallace Levin S. to Parks Maria 19 Sep 1840
Wallace Noah to Nutter Ibby 7 Jan 1851
Wallace Richard to Dorman Matilda 17 Oct 1837
Wallace Robert to Dashiell Louisa 6 Sep 1867 C
Wallace Samuel R. to Price Mary A.F. 14 Jul 1857
Wallace Stewart A. to Evans Tretia Jane 22 Apr 1851
Wallace Stewart A. to Evans Louisa E. 20 Sep 1854
Wallace Thomas to Mezick Helen 23 Feb 1859
Wallace Washington to Anderson Sophia 8 Dec 1841 C
Wallace Washington to Carroll Patty 28 Jul 1866 C
Wallace William to Jones Polly 24 May 1810
Wallace William to White Nancy 23 Mar 1819
Wallace William to Lord Nelly 12 Nov 1832
Wallace William to Nutter Catherine 21 Sep 1865 C
Wallace William D. to Slocum Mary Jane 25 Mar 1848
Wallace William D. to Shores Hettie A. 1 Aug 1871
Wallaae William H. to Dunn Julia Anne 14 Oct 1851
Wallace William R. to Kelly Anna C. 27 Jun 1866
Waller Alexander P. to Goslee Mary E. 13 Jun 1842

Waller Benjamin to Adams Mary 11 Dec 1797
Waller Benjamin to Venables Matilda B. 17 Dec 1866
Waller E. Franklin to Patterson Isabella L. 14 Jan 1862
Waller Esme M. to Vance Elizabeth E. 14 Mar 1838
Waller George to Reid Eleanor 15 Nov 1815
Waller George to Giles Elizabeth 29 Apr 1816
Waller George to Waller Julian 21 Nov 1843
Waller George to Webster Sarah Ann 18 Mar 1851
Waller George to Dougherty Amanda 8 Mar 1867 C
Waller George (of Jas) to Bratter Maria 8 Jun 1822
Waller George (of Jas.) to Brattan Mary Anne 22 May 1843
Waller George B. R. to White Isabella M. 18 Dec 1849
Waller George W. to Rowe Maria J. 22 Jul 1858
Waller Isaac to Stewart Easter A. 19 Feb 1867 C
Waller James D. to Done Henrietta 6 Nov 1816
Waller James D. to Jones Louisa 24 Oct 1866
Waller John R. to Price Sarah J. 19 Mar 1856
Waller John T. to Bailey Elizabeth 18 Nov 1845
Waller Jonathan to Wilson Rachel 26 Feb 1805
Waller Nelson to Rencher Mary 11 Feb 1817
Waller Richard J. to Goslee Zipporah 27 May 1862
Waller Robert J. to Parsons Maria 31 Oct 1843
Waller Washington to White Mary Anne 27 Mar 1834
Waller William to Leatherbury Biddy D. 15 Nov 1815
Waller William to Phoebus Elizabeth A.R. 26 Oct 1843
Waller William to Dashiell Amelia P. 16 Dec 1848
Waller William (Jr) to Jones Bridget 17 Jun 1818
Waller William L. to Jones Evaline 20 Feb 1816
Waller William S. to Phillips Jarusa 28 Jan 1845
Waller William T. to Waller Mary E. 1 Feb 1864
Waller William T. to Adams Lucinda 7 Jan 1868
Waller William Washington to Jones Mary E. 14 Apr 1857
Wallis Charles to Dorman Mary 29 Dec 1830
Wallis Severn to Williams Nancy 1 Dec 1817
Walliss Thomas to Phillips Mary Anne 22 Feb 1842
Walls George to Davy Nancy 30 Jul 1825
Walston Charles G. to Connelly Mary F. 11 Dec 1855
Walston Charles H. to Pruitt India A. 8 Aug 1871
Walston David to Davis Elizabeth 25 Jan 1820
Walston David to Riggin Betsy 21 Jan 1825

Walston David to White Becky 31 Jan 1833
Walston David to Williams Priscilla 5 Jan 1836
Walston George to Adams Leah 17 Oct 1798
Walston Isaac to Holland Amelia 17 Jul 1855
Walston John T. to Ford Louisa 13 Dec 1848
Walston Josiah to Ford Peggy 27 Nov 1801
Walston Nehemiah to Walston Milcah 16 Apr 1812
Walston Nehemiah to Ford Lotty 9 Jan 1816
Walston Nehemiah to Sterling Zipporah 26 Jan 1830
Walston Thomas to Carver Sallie A. 15 Mar 1870
Walston Thomas Henry to Evans Zipporah 22 Mar 1836
Walston Tubman to Done Anne M. 24 Jan 1812
Walston William to Cottingham Mary 24 Jul 1804
Walten Hamilton to Horner Malissa J. 9 May 1861
Walter Francis D. to Lloyd Susan 19 Apr 1814
Walter George to Bozman Bridget 22 Nov 1814
Walter George to Larmore Catey 13 Dec 1819
Walter George to Dickerson Elizabeth 26 Nov 1824
Walter George A.C. to Dunn Mary C. 9 Oct 1849
Walter George D. to Waters Mary B. 28 Sep 1814
Walter George D. to Walter Sally E. 23 Sep 1845
Walter James to Dashiell Bridget 17 Dec 1803
Walter James to Waters Sarah 8 Dec 1812
Walter Jesse to Hull Rachel 12 Oct 1819
Walter John to Kemp Anne 3 Sep 1807
Walter John to Webster Mary Anne 7 Mar 1832
Walter Joseph to Huffington Eleanor 4 Sep 1817
Walter Levin to Nelson Rosey 3 Sep 1816
Walter Robert to Mezick Margaret Jacobs 7 May 1816
Walter Robert to Walter Rosa Jane 7 Jan 1845
Walter Samuel. to Venables Sally 23 Aug 1817
Walter William to Porter Elizabeth 10 Nov 1835
Walter William James to Johnson Sarah E. 30 Jan 1862
Walters Levin A.H. to Bedsworth Williamanna 12 Nov 1860
Walton Thomas to White Leah 2 Jun 1801
Waltum William to Waltum Priscilla !3 Jun 1797
Wangeman John C. to Dashiell Virginia R. 24 Apr !862
Waples Joseph to Coulbourn Mary W. 15 Mar 1834
Ward Aaron to Newman Sally 1 Feb 1826
Ward Augustus to Lawson Mary W. 12 Jun 1866

Ward Charles to Dougherty Elizabeth Jane 7 Apr 1849
Ward Daniel to Riggin Polly 25 May 1824
Ward Daniel S. to Prewitt Julia Anne 20 Jan 1854
Ward David to Stevenson Grace 29 Aug 1868 C
Ward Elijah to Somers Eliza A. 10 Mar 1826
Ward Elijah to Parks Patty 6 Oct 1830
Ward Elijah to Hall Elizabeth L. 13 Feb 1832
Ward Elijah to Byrd Permelia 24 Jul 1838
Ward Elijah to Holland Elizabeth 10 Jul 1839
Ward Elijah S. to Adams Caroline B. 3 Nov 1863
Ward Elisha to Lawson Sally 22 May 1838
Ward Elisha E. to Saulsbury Elizabeth 9 Dec 1856
Ward Elisha E. to Evans Mary E. 6 Nov 1867
Ward George F. to Beauchamp Mary A. 14 May 1833
Ward George F. to Emory Maria Louisa 2 Aug 1851
Ward George W. to Moore Susan 28 Nov 1865
Ward Gilliss to Puzey Elizabeth 10 Sep 1825
Ward Hance to Somers Mary E. 15 Aug 1862
Ward Hance N. to Hickman Emily E. 18 Jan 1868
Ward Henry to Johnson Rachel 2 Aug 1808
Ward Henry to Sterling Milly 8 Jul 1831
Ward Henry to Sterling Mary Anne 9 Jul 1861
Ward Hope to Ward Susan 7 Aug 1849
Ward Hope to Purnell E. F. 13 May 1870
Ward Isaac to Lord Sally 27 Dec 1811
Ward Isaac to Riggen Rebecca 10 Dec 1823
Ward Isaac to Nelson Zipporah J. 19 Aug 1845
Ward Jacob to Mason Anne 19 Oct 1826
Ward James to Sterling Milcah 6 Jun 1815
Ward James to McDaniel Mary 29 Dec 1819
Ward James to Townsend Sarah 14 Dec 1824
Ward James to Dryden Jane 23 Aug 1836
Ward James to Somers Sally F. 19 Nov 1860
Ward John to Miles Betsy 22 Apr 1801
Ward John to Lankford Lucy Anne 8 May 1830
Ward John to Sterling Sally 21 May 1844
Ward John to Ward Caroline 2 Jan 1850
Ward John to Ward Marzilla 29 Apr 1859
Ward John to Haley Jane 19 Oct 1861
Ward John G. to Holland Amelia 31 Dec 1867

Ward John H. to Dougherty Sarah C. 26 Jan 1867
Ward John O.F. to Green Elizabeth E. 1 Apr 1856
Ward John S. to Holland Elizabeth J. 24 Mar 1858
Ward John S. to Miles Sarah E. 10 Mar 1870
Ward John T. to Sterling Elizabeth E. 3 May 1853
Ward John T.B. to Tull Margaret J. 28 Nov 1865
Ward Joseph to Ward Martha 29 Aug 1797
Ward Josiah J.S. to Lawson Nancy 20 Dec 1864
Ward Levi to Scott Sally 9 Dec 1800
Ward Lewis F. to Nelson Nancy 11 Feb 1862
Ward Noah to Ward Patty Anne 23 Oct 1832
Ward Noah to Dize Julia A. 17 Sep 1860
Ward Stephen to Tignal Elizabeth 1 Sep 1808
Ward Stephen to Ward Elizabeth 5 Sep 1818
Ward Stephen to Gibbons Leah 5 Sep 1818
Ward Stephen to Handy Margaret M. 22 Jan 1850
Ward Stephen W. to Nelson Rebecca 8 Jul 1856
Ward Thomas to Johnson Ritty 29 Sep 1829
Ward Thomas to Ward Mary Jane 29 Sep 1835
Ward Thomas to Ward Betsy Burton 30 Oct 1835
Ward Thomas to Corbin Margaret 14 Jun 1859
Ward Thomas M. to Handy Sarah Anne 2 Feb 1830
Ward Thomas W. to Riggin Christiner 15 May 1866
Ward Walter B. to Ward Leah 9 Jan 1849
Ward William of Ezekiel to Dougherty Patty 23 Aug 1825
Ward William to Ward Mary 13 Jul 1820
Ward William to Ward Mary 27 May 1823
Ward William to Somers Molly 13 Jan 1824
Ward William to Landen Margaret 14 Oct 1824
Ward William to Wilson Mary 22 Jan 1833
Ward William to Dryden Ann 24 Jan 1835
Ward William to Lord Sarah 21 Feb 1849
Ward William to Nelson Maria 13 Aug 1850
Ward William A. to Ford Milcah A. 13 Jun 1854
Ward William A. to Sears Mary I. 25 Jun 1867
Ward William E. to Sterling Sarah E. 26 Nov 1859
Ward William E. to Somers Mary 1 Oct 1861
Ward William H. to Laird Virginia T. 19 Jul 1860
Ward William S. to Cullen Eliza J. 11 Feb 1862
Ward William S. to Horsey Candace 2 Jan 1869

Warner Layfield to Fletcher Margaret 4 Oct 1848
Warren Henry to Dashiell Sarah Anne Jane 25 Feb 1841
Warwick James W. to Lankford Mary Grace 3 Oct 1857
Warwick John to Layfield Mary 22 Nov 1833
Warwick John to Wilson Peggy 11 Sep 1838
Warwick John to Gibbons Susan 13 Oct 1864
Warwick John H. to Parker Frances 9 Sep 1867
Warwick Josiah to Gibbons Nancy 25 Jan 1809
Warwick Levin to Matthews Anne 12 Sep 1808
Warwick Severn to Dubberly Elizabeth 1 Jan 1814
Warwick William F. to Dorsey Mary Anne 30 Nov 1841
Warwick William R. to Selby Levinia 23 Jul 1816
Warwick William T. to Beauchamp Sarah 5 Oct 1868
Washboard James to Marshall Mary 14 May 1833
Washburn George to Adams Eleanor 26 Dec 1843
Washburn Henry to Kibble Rosetta 20 Sep 1842
Washburn James to Coxe Gatty 21 May 1844
Washburn Reuben to Chatam Hetty 6 Feb 1849
Washburn Reubin to Taylor Betsy A. 19 Sep 1865
Washburn William to Windsor Sarah 10 Aug 1837
Washburn William to Bradley Rebecca 18 Jun 1862
Washburn William F. to Huston Henrietta 20 May 1862
Washington John H. to Waters Lucretia 20 Nov 1866 C
Waters Addison to Collins Jane 10 Apr 1862 C
Waters David to Dixon Sally 23 Nov 1813 C
Waters Edward D. to Tilghman Martha 25 Nov 1867 C
Waters Edward Mariott to Cottman Hannah 15 May 1803
Waters George to Boggs Sally 5 Dec 1864 C
Waters Hobart F. to Brown Charlotte F. 7 Oct 1871
Waters Horace to Elzey Annie 2 Jul 1870 C
Waters Isaac to Holland Leah 21 Mar 1871 C
Waters John to Smith Rosetta 1 Nov 1813
Waters John to Waters Harriet 27 Jan 1840
Waters John to Johnson Amanda 14 Dec 1853
Waters John to Sudler Maria 3 Jan 1866 C
Waters John to King Esther 29 Mar 1869 C
Waters John to Jones Emily 28 Dec 1869 C
Waters John to Johnson Emaline 31 Dec 1869 C
Waters John R. to Whaley Elizabeth 6 Apr 1847
Waters John W. to Copper Levina 5 Jul 1871 C

Waters Joseph to King Hannah 17 Dec 1867 C
Waters Joseph G. to Aires Betsy Jane 21 Nov 1827
Waters Joshua to Roach Teney 31 Dec 1869 C
Waters Levin L. to Hyland Eliza R.W. May 1827
Waters Levin L. to Jones Lucretia 5 Dec 1859
Waters Littleton to Boston Susan 21 Feb 1860 C
Waters Littleton to Roberts Anne M. 22 Sep 1868 C
Waters Littleton to Tilghman Lucy 20 Feb 1871 C
Waters Moses to Miles M.E. 26 Dec 1871 C
Waters Revel to Wright Harriet 30 Nov 1869 C
Waters Richard to Cheney Mary Day 21 Jun 1798
Waters Richard to Maddux Sally 20 Oct 1868 C
Waters Richard H. to Dashiell Adeline E.W. 12 Oct 1840
Waters Samuel to Dashiell Leah J. 15 Jan 1863 C
Waters Samuel J. to Sudler Caroline A. 12 Nov 1844
Waters Samuel J. to Boggs Rosanna 5 Oct 1848
Waters Samuel J. to Curtis Mary E. 26 Dec 1871 C
Waters Stephen to Lankford Lovey 3 Dec 1804
Waters Stephen to Gale Ellen 18 Sep 1858 C
Waters Stephen to Waters Elizabeth 26 Sep 1868 C
Waters Thomas to Dixon Rosina 17 May 1869 C
Waters William to Waters Fanny 17 Dec 1855 C
Waters William to Jones Nancy 17 Jun 1857 C
Waters William to Waters Laura 8 Nov 1869 C
Waters William to Netter Fannie 11 Apr 1871 C
Waters William (Jr} to Lister Julian 20 Apr 1815
Waters William C. to Jones Elizabeth 25 Jan 1814
Waters William Gilliss to Elzey Anne Glascow 29 May 1799
Waters William H. to King Charlotte W. 22 Dec 1847
Waters William U. to Jones Eleanor 20 Nov 1820
Watson Absolum to Turner Julia 23 Dec 1869 C
Watson Charles B. to Messick Julia A. 15 Jul 1870
Watson John to Griffith Martha A.B. 26 Mar 1835
Watson William to Matthews Sally A. 7 Jun 1808
Watson William to Adams Martha Anne 2 Jun 1847
Watson William to Lankford Elizabeth 20 May 1868
Watson William H.H. to Carey Rhody A. 20 Mar 1867
Watts David to Williams Margaret 4 Aug 1823
Watts David to Palmer Elizabeth A.S. 17 Dec 1833
Watts John Washington to Turner Margaret 14 Feb 1827

Way Elow J. to Walter Elizabeth H. 15 Jul 1842
Weatherly Charles to Acworth Polly 17 Dec 1801
Weatherly Constantine to Walker Leah 8 Aug 1815
Weatherly Edmond to Austin Ann Maria Aug 1830
Weatherly James to Low Elizabeth 23 Jan 1805
Weatherly Joseph to Maddox Julia 18 Feb 1815
Weatherly Joseph to Walker Catey 4 Jan 1820
Weatherly Joseph to Rider Henrietta 5 Dec 1843
Weatherly Lee P. to Jones Teresa Anne 10 Sep 1833
Weatherly Littleton to Chambers Margaret 20 Jan 1818
Weatherly Peregrin L. to Hitch Margaret 1 Nov 1803
Weatherly Perry Leatherbury to Skinner Leah 1 Dec 1801
Weatherly Peter D. to Bounds Esther 20 Feb 1844
Weatherly Royston to Russum Nancy 22 Feb 1825
Weatherly Samuel to Bradley Mary 16 Oct 1811
Weatherly William to Leatherbury Mary 11 Feb 1800
Weatherly William J. to Collins Aniyrillis 29 Jan 1855
Weatherly William J. (Capt.) to Melson Mary H. 29 Dec 1858
Weaver Lewis H. to Duncan Emily A. 8 May 1860
Webb Alfred M. to Shay Henrietta 6 Jan 1852
Webb Edward to Kelly Williamanna 4 Jul 1865
Webb George S. to Leonard Elizabeth 2 Aug 1866 C
Webb James to Walston Nelly 12 Jun 1804
Webb James to Costen Betsy 12 Jul 1808
Webb John to Collins Hetty 10 Dec 1799
Webb John to Cottman Emily 9 Mar 1858
Webb William to Scott Priscilla 14 Jun 1828
Webb William to Melvin Sarah 8 Dec 1846
Webster Alexander W. to Windsor Julia R. 23 Jan 1871
Webster Alexander W.W. to Kelly Louisa 26 Jun 1839
Webster Columbus F. to Webster Margaret W. 12 Oct 1859
Webster Daniel to Washburn Catherine 12 May 1862
Webster Daniel J. to Horner Julia C. 25 Dec 1871
Webster Daniel W. to Vetra Temperance N. 2 Apr 1857
Webster David to Parks Priscilla 7 Jul 1835
Webster Gabriel S. to Jones Mary A. 27 Jun 1849
Webster Gabriel S. to Windsor Susan A. 20 Dec 1865
Webster George S. to Webster Margaret C. 22 Feb 1866
Webster Hamilton to Parks Lucretia 3 Aug 1839
Webster Hamilton J.C. to Jones Sarah Ann 23 Apr 1850

Webster Hamilton S. to Wilson Milcah 25 Mar 1848
Webster Horatio to Shores Hester Anne 10 Jan 1840
Webster Jabus to Webster Elizabeth 27 Feb 1821
Webster Jacob to McDorman Polly 17 Oct 1809
Webster Jacob to Parks Hessa 19 Mar 1840
Webster James to Horner Lucretia 30 Sep 1824
Webster James to Webster Clarisa 31 Aug 1842
Webster James to Bozman Elizabeth 10 Dec 1851
Webster James C. to Webster Eleanora C. 16 Feb 1867
Webster Jesse to Webster Eliza 15 Jul 1835
Webster Jesse Hiram to Windsor Elizabeth 27 Jun 1849
Webster John to White Leah 6 Sep 1808
Webster John to Shores Anne Maria 26 Jun 1857
Webster John C.B. to Horner Rebecca J. 23 Apr 1861
Webster John H. to Summers Mary W. 16 Dec 1856
Webster John M. to Webster Margaret I. 18 Jan 1870
Webster John P. to Shores Martha W. 6 Sep 1866
Webster Joseph S. to Simpkins Matilda A. 10 Feb 1857
Webster Major to Harrington Elizabeth 12 Jun 1823
Webster Major Jackson to Wallace Mary J. 19 Nov 1851
Webster Major W. to Carew Smith 3 Jan 1861
Webster Mezick to Bozman Mary 11 Oct 1819
Webster Michael to Travers Betsy 9 Aug 1814
Webster Michael to Evans Mary C. 11 Mar 1845
Webster Nathaniel to White Sarah 16 Jun 1819
Webster Noah to Moore Mary Jane 18 Jun 1844
Webster Prettyman to Webster Angelina 23 Mar 1865
Webster Samuel to Shores Sarah 23 Feb 1847
Webster Silas T. to Kelly Louisa 8 Feb 1848
Webster Theolfes to Hitchens Margaret Anne 3 Mar 1859
Webster Wallace to Rowe Eliza 2 Apr 1833
Webster Wesley to Webster Drusilla R. 14 Feb 1853
Webster William to Webster Nancy 20 Apr 1830
Webster William to Webster Polly 10 Sep 1832
Webster William B. to Benton Margaret F. 14 Jun 1864
Webster William H. to Parks Martha A. 7 Feb 1854
Webster William J. to _____ Mary A. 10 Jan 1861
Webster Zacchariah to Rowe Emily 10 Aug 1847
Webster Zachariah to Jones Mary 20 Dec 1853
Webster Zachariah T. to Horner David Anna 5 Sep 1871

Webster Zachariah W. to Gibson Emma J. 9 Jun 1868
Weeks John to Black Hetty 24 Feb 1843
Wessels Ephraim to Davis Mary 26 Jun 1851
West Isaac to Horsey Nancy 18 Mar 1802
West James H. to Nicholson Sarah W. 9 Feb 1798
Whaley Calvert L. to Martin Sally 8 Dec 1829
Whaley Charles W. to Tull Mary E. 30 Oct 1854
Whalton William H. to Lawson Nelly 14 Feb 1854
Whaples George H. to Bozman Susan F. 27 Dec 1870
Whayland John to Harris Nancy 25 Oct 1825
Whayland John to Banks Mary Ann 11 Dec 1837
Whayland John to Morris Lucinda E. 25 Jun 1839
Whayland John to Jones Maria 12 Aug 1868 C
Whayland Joseph to Wilson Fanny 10 Dec 1868 C
Whayland Thomas to Fowler Nancy 22 Feb 1825
Whayland Thomas to Hitch Ann 1 Mar 1836
Whayland Thomas J. to Disharoon Columbia E. 3 Sep 1849
Whayland Thomas J. to Acworth Sally 28 Mar 1865
Whayland William to King Mary A. 9 Mar 1865
Whayland William (Jr) to Fowler Alice 4 Nov 1829
Whealton William to Ward Harriet 13 Dec 1826
Wheatley Charles H. to Fooks Mahala 25 Oct 1864
Wheatley George to Mezick Emily 8 Jan 1861
Wheatley Joseph to Bloodsworth Elizabeth 9 Aug 1836
Wheatley William M. to Williams Nancy C. 18 Feb 1857
Wheatly Joseph to Ross Rosa 26 Oct 1865
Wheatly William D. to Jones Maria E. 14 Nov 1857
Wheeler Henry to Pollitt Rebecca 11 Jun 1841
Wheeler Henry to Pusey Mary Anne 2 Mar 1847
Wheeler James to Hunt Mary 5 May 1812
Wheeler Joseph to Roach Lovey 3 Nov 1815
Wheyland William to Darby Polly 27 Jan 1801
Whister Joseph M. to Milligan Emily F. 23 Feb 1864
White Alexander to Scott Mary Anne Dine 28 Jun 1832
White Alexander to White Elizabeth 2 Apr 1855
White Arthur to Wilson Mary Ann 14 Nov 1848
White Asa to Turner Elizabeth 17 Jan 1837
White Asa to Jones Elizabeth 4 Dec 1843
White Beacham to Banks Mary 25 Jan 1848
White Beachamp to Morris Polly 19 Jun 1820

White Benjamin T. to Rowe Ellen 29 Aug 1871
White Cornelius to Harris Mary C. 26 Oct 1871 C
White Daniel James to Webster Mary Elizabeth 10 May 1870
White David to Webster Elizabeth 2 Jan 1828
White David to Webster Mary W. 15 Jul 1865
White David G. to Layfield Sally 17 Apr 1845
White David W. to Wallace Julia W. 25 Apr 1871
White Edward to Wilson Rosa 10 Jan 1870 C
White Edward A. to Price Mary F. 13 Nov 1868
White Edward J. to King Aurelia W. 13 Mar 1849
White Elisha T. to Revill Nancy E. 28 Mar 1840
White Ephraim to Cluff Elizabeth 29 Dec 1869
White Eugene T. to Johnson Sally A. 13 Dec 1848
White Francis to Furniss Arine 1 Jan 1829
White George A. to Wallace Eugena 4 Jan 1855
White George H. to Larmore Sarah A. 14 May 1844
White Gowan to Hickman Biddy 25 May 1799
White Gustavus A. to Riall Laura 6 Feb 1867
White Henry to Fowler Alice 17 Oct 1809
White Henry to McDorman Harriet 29 Apr 1812
White Henry to Bennett Louisa 23 Feb 1819
White Henry to Walston Mary 19 Dec 1821
White Henry to Ellis Sally 17 Jun 1828
White Henry to Whitlock Mary Anne 21 Jul 1834
White Henry to Crosly Maria Anne 25 Jan 1842
White Henry to Lowe Eleanor 1 Jan 1850
White Henry A. to Stone Annie M. 8 Dec 1842
White Henry B. to Wallace Rebecca N. 20 Jul 1864
White Henry H. to Kelly Sally R. 26 Dec 1871
White Henry P. to Howard Elizabeth H. 1 Nov 1842
White Henry T. to Ward Miranda T. 4 Feb 1857
White Henry W. to Reddish Eliza Jane 20 Jan 1852
White Ichabod to Cavanaugh Rebecca 20 Nov 1810
White Isaac to Robertson Julia R. 21 Mar 1870 C
White Jacob W. to Bayley Isabella 12 Oct 1838
White James to Waller Biddy 7 Jun 1815
White James to Crockett Betsy 21 Mar 1829
White James to Banks Anne 20 Mar 1838
White James to White Adeline 17 Dec 1839
White James to Cluff Sally 27 Jul 1842

White James to Elzey Matilda 24 Dec 1860 C
White James to Smith Ellen 28 Dec 1870 C
White James C. to Jones Elizabeth E. 9 Apr 1867
White James E. to Whittington Margaret O. 18 Jul 1867
White James Francis to Renshaw Sarah Chapman 24 Feb 1840
White Jeffary to Jones Sarah E. 15 Mar 1862 C
White Jerome B. to Pollitt Nancy 13 Oct 1845
White John to Dashiell Mary 2 Jan 1838
White John to Tull Susan J. 30 Nov 1841
White John to Larmore Ellen 17 Dec 1851
White John to Heath Esther E. 29 Oct 1861
White John B. to Windsor Sarah E.D. 28 Jul 1868
White John Bell to Windsor Mary Jane 23 Aug 1850
White John C. to Muir Wesley A. 12 Jun 1866
White John H. to McDaniel Sarah E. 3 Jul 1848
White John Q. to Heath Virginia W. 6 Mar 1854
White Joseph to Carmien Nancy 18 Mar 1813
White Leolin F. to Shores Estelle H. 16 Aug 1864
White Levin to Calloway Henrietta -- Jun 1850
White Levin C. to White Eliza Anne 25 Jan 1830
White Levin P. to Wallace Indianna 14 Jun 1870
White Littleton S. to Jones Mary Anne 10 Jan 1827
White Major to Kelley Leah --(?) 1837
White Major to White Harriet E. 26 Aug 1848
White Major to White Jane 30 Jan 1855
White Nathaniel W. to Shores Elizabeth A. 24 Jun 1845
White Samuel to Walston Margaret 8 Aug 1820
White Samuel to Ellis Esther 16 Dec 1828
White Samuel to Wainright Betsy Ann 29 Jan 1838
White Samuel to Hughes Mary E.A. 11 Jan 1847
White Samuel W. to Jones Leah E. 25 Feb 1864
White Stephen to Adams Margaret 22 Jan 1829
White Stephen P. to Kirby Charlotte 2 May 1837
White Tembroke to McClain Harriet A. 10 Sep 1866
White Thomas to Wright Anne 16 Jan 1798
White Thomas to Kelly Sarah 4 Jul 1825
White Thomas to Hughes Sallie 12 Oct 1854
White Thomas A. to Dashiell Mary E. 21 Jan 1862
White Thomas W. to Jones Mary E. 21 Sep 1849
White Titus to Coulbourn Letitia 9 Nov 1864 C

White Titus to Ward Hetty 7 Mar 1867
White Tubman to Walston Peggy 20 Jun 1820
White William to Dove Anne 24 Dec 1798
White William to Wallace Rebecca 9 Nov 1812
White William to White Elizabeth 10 Dec 1823
White William to Broughton Ann 31 Jan 1826
White William to Dorman Peggy 1 Jul 1834
White Willia to McDorman Eleanor 28 Dec 1836
White William to Schoolfield Elizabeth 22 Nov 1856 C
White William B. to Maddux Elizabeth 22 May 1855
White William J.C. to Reese Mary A. 23 Jan 1844
White William J.C. to Kelly Eliza E. 15 Oct 1844
White William L. to Barkley Angelina 20 Oct 1847
White William R. to Tignor Sarah L. 12 Jun 1866
White William R. to Holland Sarah M. 29 Dec 1868
White William S. to Evans Maria Ann 5 Jun 1849
Whitelock Edward to White Polly 7 Dec 1835
Whitelock Elisha to Adams Susan 30 Jan 1811
Whitelock Elisha to Waller Sally 31 Oct 1816
Whitelock Elisha to Broughton Maria 29 Apr 1823
Whitelock James to Costen Harriet 10 Oct 1811
Whitelock James A. to Tignor Malissa E. 15 Dec 1868
Whitelock Joshua to Jones Martha 24 Feb 1836
Whiting James to Kelsick Ann 14 Jul 1832
Whitney Alfred to Pusey Mary Ellen 20 Nov 1844
Whitney Benjamin F. to Barnes Catherine 3 Mar 1868
Whitney Daniel to Hariss Sally 15 Jan 1811
Whitney David to Evans Rachel 21 Jan 1799
Whitney Henry to Bowen Mary 1 Nov 1831
Whitney Isaac to Gurney Betsy 29 Mar 1804
Whitney Jesse to Reed Matilda 18 Apr 1843
Whitney Samuel C. to Williams Lizzie 17 Apr 1867
Whitney Sidney to Lawrence Mary E. 11 Feb 1862
Whittington Alfred to Donoho Rozina 23 Jan 1854
Whittington Algernon to Miles Sarah Jane 5 Mar 1849
Whittington Benjamin to Coulbourn Esther A. 11 Jun 1844 C
Whittington Edward to Carroll Lucy 30 May 1871 C
Whittington George to Johnson Henrietta 9 Jul 1870 C
Whittington George E. to Handy Mary 28 Jun 1859
Whittington Henry to Dougherty Roxy Ann Jane 2 May 1848

Whittington Isaac to Coulbourn Sally 2 Aug 1830
Whittington James to Coulbourn Sarah 18 Dec 1799
Whittington James (of Wm.) to Lawson Sarah 21 Nov 1814
Whittington John to Polk Sally 14 Jun 1814
Whittington John to Milbourn Sally 10 Mar 1825
Whittington John to Stevenson Sarah V. 28 Nov 1854
Whittington John to Cottman Leah 2 Jun 1863 C
Whittington John A.F. to Beauchamp Susan E. 17 Nov 1857
Whittington Joseph C. to Marshall Virginia G. 31 May 1871
Whittington Littleton to Handy Hannah A. 22 Dec 1846
Whittington Littleton to Handy Julia 26 Jun 1855
Whittington Luther A. to Garrison Mary J. 12 Nov 1856
Whittington Matthias to Dorman Polly 23 May 1812
Whittington Robert B. to Handy Elizabeth H. 25 Nov 1856
Whittington Robert E. to Handy Caroline 12 Feb 1850
Whittington Robert H. to Lankford Levitha J. 25 Apr 1865
Whittington Samuel to Broughton Elizabeth 14 May 1869
Whittington Southey to Rider Sarah Anne --(?) 1838
Whittington Southey to Rider Jane L. 5 Mar 1839
Whittington Southy to Coulbourn Mary 3 Jul 1804
Whittington Southy F. to Marshall Mary W. 13 Mar 1832
Whittington Stephen to Miles Ritty 7 Apr 1828
Whittington Stephen to Dewey Mary Jane 15 Jul 1862 C
Whittington Stephen to Jones Eliza J. 8 Feb 1870 C
Whittington Stephen H. to Handy Eliza J. 27 May 1862
Whittington Stevenson to Tull Jane 2 Oct 1839
Whittington Thomas E. to Polk Rebecca 28 Nov 1851
Whittington William to Handy Anne 13 Feb 1821
Whittington William to Polk Sarah Elizabeth 23 Mar 1847
Wiett Lemuel to Roach Polly 29 Dec 1810
Wigfall Henry to Stewart Emily 2 Feb 1869 C
Wilkenson Isaac to Bennett Margaret A. 23 Dec 1852
Wllkerson Isaac to Wallace Eliza E. 14 Aug 1870
Wilkins John to Bell Mary 6 May 1800
Wilkins Ogden to Moore Sarah A. 22 Jun 1870
Wilkins Ogden H. to Broughton Texina C. 27 Jan 1868
Wilkins Phineas to Smith Mary E. 10 Dec 1855
Wilkins Seth to Beachamp Martha 4 Apr 1827
Wilkins Thomas W. to Lankford Henrietta 28 Oct 1812
Wllkinson Isaac to Wallace Everline 2 Aug 1866

Wilkinson Sewell to Stant Sarah J. 10 Feb 1863
Wilkinson Washington to White Elizabeth 13 Nov 1832
Willey Jabez to Bradley Rachel A. 3 Mar 1862
Willey Solomon to Kelly Maria 3 Jun 1862
William Tubman to Larramore Martha 27 Sep 1808
Williams Aaron to Pollitt Mary 5 Feb 1867 C
Williams Arthur to Jones Rebecca 18 Jul 1868 C
Williams Benjamin to Beauchamp Tabitha 2 Jul 1808
Williams Benjamin to Townsend Sarah Ann 1 Jan 1850
Williams Benjamin C. to Townsend Amanda F. 16 Nov 1869
Williams Benjamin F. to Green Amelia C. 17 Mar 1869
Williams Edward to Wyatt Sarah J. 29 May 1860
Williams Elijah to Ingersoll Rachel 25 Apr 1815
Williams Elisha to Seabreeze Theresa Anne 28 Jan 1845
Williams Elisha to Anderson Louisa 24 Dec 1858
Williams Elisha to Curtis ___cy 21 Sep 1871 C
Williams Emory L. to Shipley Kate Q. 18 Nov 1862
Williams George to Horsey Henrietta 9 Feb 1870
Willis George W. to Wainright Mary T. 11 Jun 1861
Williams Hiram T. to Jones Mary E. 1 May 1866
Williams Hugh to Lankford Sally 11 Sep 1821
Williams Isaac to Ingersoll Ann 30 Jun 1819
Williams Isaac to Howard Henrietta 13 Nov 1821
Williams Isaac to Prettyman Louisa 21 Dec 1868 C
Williams Isaac to Robins Susan 15 Nov 1870 C
Williams Isaac F. to Stuart Rebecca R. 4 Sep 1819
Williams James H. to Moore Mary C. 7 Nov 1848
Williams James P. to Boston Harriet E. 10 Feb 1868
Williams Jeremiah M. to Robertson Mary Jane 27 Apr 1846
Williams Jesse to Simms Lucy 26 Sep 1871
Williams John to Crockett Mary 16 Jan 1801
Williams John to Taylor Charlotte 11 Jan 1823
Williams John to Walker Nancy 23 Jul 1839
Williams John to Blades Sarah Anne 3 Jun 1840
Williams John to Miles Milly 11 May 1871 C
Williams John Henry to Rider Matilda C. 23 Nov 1852
Williams John P. to Fooks Anne E. 26 Nov 1849
Williams John Wesley to Majors Sarah L. 30 Jul 1867
Williams Joshua to Willin Mary 24 Oct 1810
Williams Joshua to Hines Milcah 18 Apr 1860 C

Williams Levin to Travers Arietta 12 Oct 1818
Williams Levin H. to McDaniel Margaret E.J. 3 Sep 1851
Williams Matthias D. to Allen Mary J. 20 Jul 1852
Williams Moses to Hayward Sarah 26 Dec 1871 C
Williams Panner to Street Sally 26 Oct 1808
Williams Peter to Rose Nancy 19 May 1852
Williams Planner to Willing Sally 21 Nov 1810
Williams Planner to Willin Elizabeth 2 Jul 1816
Williams Robert to Disharoon Mary 6 Aug 1838
Williams Samuel to Moore Margaret 12 Mar 1822
Williams Samuel to Turner Charlotte 22 Aug 1855
Williams Samuel P. to Larmore Mary W. 27 Feb 1860
Williams Stephen to Taylor Mary Elizabeth 22 Jan 1853
Williams Thomas to Riggin Patty J. 6 Jun 1856
Williams Thomas J. to Coxe Esther A. 20 Dec 1842
Williams Thomas J. to Jones Mary E. 11 Feb 1864
Williams Thomas W. to Ward Milcah A. 1 Mar 1864
Williams William to Killum Anne Maria 21 Dec 1812
Williams William to Cantwell Rachel 20 Apr 1830
Williams William to Corbin Polly 13 Jun 1833
Williams William to Roberts Mary A. 15 May 1849
Williams William to McGrath Sally 28 Aug 1862
Williams William (of Jno) to Barkley Gatty 2 Jul 1816
Williams William (of Sam'l) to Crouch Mary W. 2 May 1849
Williams William (of Wm) to Disharoon Molly 20 Jan 1818
Williams William S. to Lowes Esther E. 26 Apr 1836
Williams Zedekiah H. to Travers Priscilla C. 29 Dec 1828
Willie Jabez to Elliott Mary Jane 18 Jan 1853
Willin Charles to Dove Jane 7 Dec 1848
Willin George to Insley Dolly 7 Jun 1826
Willin Isaac to Bozman Emeline 11 Jun 1851
Willin James to Insley Susan 4 Jun 1850
Willin John L. to Evans Esther 26 Jun 1866
Willin Robert to Windsor Leah 9 Jan 1821
Willing Aaron to Simpkins Sinah 19 Jan 1813
Willing Charles to Kebble Henny 10 Jun 1823
Willing Charles to Hitch Eveline 23 Oct 1844
Willing David to Evans Polly 19 Jul 1819
Willing George to Hopkins Esther E. S. A. 14 Nov 1820
Willing George to Moore Eleanor 3 Oct 1840

Willing George M. to Aikman Sally S. 2 Nov 1819
Willing George W. to Somers Mary Olivia 29 May 1865
Willing Hezekiah H. to Parks Margaret W. 5 Nov 1850
Willing Isaac A. to Curtis Charlotte 11 Jan 1843
Willing Isaiah to Cullen Mary 10 Jan 1820
Willing James (Jr) to Dickerson Sarah 29 Nov 1814
Willing James A. J. (Doctor) to Willing Mary Elizabeth 15 Feb 1859
Willing James R. to Shores Anna 17 Apr 1867
Willing John E. to Langsdale Mary J. 1 Mar 1853
Willing John W. to Willing Georgia A. 8 Sep 1866
Willing Matthias to Willing Nancy 29 May 1821
Willing Thomas to McDorman Priscilla 19 Jan 1847
Willing Tubman to Adams Bridget 18 May 1826
Willing Ware C. to Turner Rebecca 8 Jun 1840
Willing William to Bozman Rebecca 4 Jul 1811
Willing William to Robertson Rachael 27 Dec 1831
Willing William J.S. to Walter Anne M. 10 Feb 1853
Willis Charles T. to Fontaine Mary E. 4 Mar 1852
Willis Henry to Dryden Eliza 25 Nov 1824
Williss Hiram to Elliott Miranda 20 Jan 1840
Wilson Abraham to Conner Ann 1 Mar 1825
Wilson Albert R. to Riggin Mary C. 1 Apr 1862
Wilson Bnjamin to Conway Sarah 12 May 1855 C
Wilson Charles to Johnson Araminata 8 Dec 1863 C
Wilson Covington to Bradley Isabella 9 Jan 1861
Wilson David to Covington Priscilla 3 Sep 1799
Wilson David to Polk Mary 17 May 1804
Wilson David M. to Waller Bridget 5 May 1821
Wilson Denard to Miles Hannah Anne 1 Jun 1855
Wilson Denwood to Stevens Elizabeth 26 Jul 1803
Wilson Denwood to Sterling Laney 16 Jan 1829
Wilsosn Dinard to Dougherty Pearey 24 May 1831
Wilson Elijah to Sterling Patty 19 May 1846
Wilson Ephraim to Orton Betsy 26 Dec 1866 C
Wilson Ezekiel. to Lloyd Deliah 13 Nov 1820
Wilson Francis to Wesley Mary 29 Dec 1869 C
Wilson George to Elliott Dolly 10 Feb 1824
Wilson George to Tully Margaret 8 Sep 1831
Wilson George to Byrd Mary 10 Apr 1852
Wilson George to Riggin Nancy J. 2 Jul 1855

Wilson George R. to Somers Sarah E. 27 Oct 1863
Wilson George T. to Garrison Emma L. 2 May 1860
Wilson Harry to Hurst Harriet 5 Jun 1824
Wilson Hezekiah to Hall Polly 12 Jan 1819
Wilson Isaac to Shipham Peggy 4 May 1802
Wilson Isaac to Phobus Miranda 19 Jan 1842
Wilson J. Henry to Wainright Rebecca J. 30 May 1866
Wilson James to Bell Elizabeth 20 Dec 1831
Wilson James to Polk Elizabeth 18 Dec 1843 C
Wilson James to Atwood Susan S. 8 Apr 1862
Wilson James to Marshall Margaret A. 6 Jan 1863
Wilson James L. to Horner Margaret T. 5 Sep 1848
Wilson James L. to Webster Mary J. 11 Jul 1856
Wilson James M. to Wallace Margaret E. 29 Apr 1857
Wilson James W. to Dougherty Esther E.J. 23 Jan 1841
Wilson James W. to Dickerson Mary V. 15 May 1866
Wilson Jesse to Betsworth Betsy 29 Jul 1800
Wilson Jesse to Cottingham Nancy 15 Jun 1824
Wilson Jesse to Riggin Charlotte --- Jan 1833
Wilson John to Trader Betsy 5 Mar 1811
Wilson John to Summers Sally 3 Jun 1820
Wilson John to Somers Sally 3 Jun 1837
Wilson John to Brown Ann 21 Feb 1842
Wilson John to Ward Adaline 4 Jul 1848
Wilson John (Jr) to Norwood Elizabeth 18 Jul 1818
Wilson John C. (Jr) to Jones Sally E. 25 Mar 1830
Wilson John M. to Blake Elizabeth S. 30 May 1854
Wilson John W. to Rowe Serrepta Jane -- Jul 1850
Wilson John W. to Williams Ellin P. 13 Sep 1859
Wilson John W. to Wainright Esther A. 17 Oct 1864
Wilson Joseph to Turpin Mary 13 Feb 1809 .
Wilson Joshua to Jones Ann Maria 18 Jan 1870 C
Wilson Lambert to Turpin Mary 26 Nov 1867 C
Wilson Levi to Adams Amy E. 8 Aug 1871
Wilson Levin to McDorman Sally 3 Nov 1807
Wilson Levin to Walter Nancy 18 Aug 1813
Wilson Levin to Cluff Sarah Purnell 21 Apr 1819
Wilson Levin to Mazick Anne 14 Mar 1828
Wilson Levin J. to Layfield Drucilla 16 Jul 1861
Wilson Levin S. to Ballard Leah 31 Jan 1865

Wilson Michell to Turpin Priscilla 5 Jan 1820
Wilson Moses to Waller Ellen 10 Dec 1868 C
Wilson Nero to Miles Anne 30 Dec 1864 C
Wilson Noah to Hobbs Mary 11 Aug 1824
Wilson Rider to Mezick Medea 17 Apr 1830
Wilson Samuel to Russell Eleanor 12 Feb 1829
Wilson Samuel to Layfield Sally W. 30 Jan 1847
Wilson Samuel to Perry Jane 7 Mar 1848
Wilson Samuel to Evans Keziah 10 Jul 1849
Wilson Samuel to Evans Mary Jane 26 Jul 1859 C
Wilson Samuel W. to Hitch Olivia M.E. 11 Jan 1859
Wilson Stephen H. to Catlin Cornelia A. 16 May 1859
Wilson Washington to Larmore Sarah Ann 19 Oct 1847
Wilson William to Johnson Deborah 19 Jan 1799
Wilson William to Riggen Leah 7 Jan 1803
Wilson William to Whittington Elizabeth 17 Jan 1817
Wilson William to Dise Mary 3 Feb 1847
Wilson William F. to Wright Elizabeth B. 20 Jan 1840
Wilson William H. to Shores Nelly 13 Nov 1828
Wilson William H. to Green Hester A. 11 Jan 1859
Wilson William H. to Waller Mary V. 21 Feb 1866
Wilson William H. to Byrd Sally A. 29 May 1866
Wilson William H. to Pusey Elizabeth E. 5 Jun 1866
Wilson William J. to Goslee Susan 29 May 1866
Winder Charles to King Esther W. 19 Jan 1804
Winder William H. to Polk Gertrude 7 May 1799
Windson John to Redden Milly 12 Jan 1802
Windsor Alfred M. to Dashiell Cella E. 7 Apr 1858
Windsor Benjamin to Windsor Jane 29 Jun 1824
Windsor Eldridge to Webster Mary 5 Apr 1860
Windsor Elijah E. to Davis Charllotty 8 Feb 1849
Windsor George W. to Webster Sarah B. 3 Apr 1868
Windsor Hamilton to Wallace Ann 11 Oct 1855
Windsor Henry to Webster Betsy 10 Sep 1832
Windsor Hiram to Dove Milcah 3 Feb 1870
Windsor Isaac to Porter Matty 16 Feb 1825
Windsor Isaac to Badley Nancy 18 Jun 1833
Windsor Isaac J. to Brown Eleanor 1 Feb 1861
Windsor Isaac J. to Ford Susan Vaughn 24 Dec 1862
Windsor James to White Hetty 19 Jan 1836

Windsor James H. to Robinson Phobe C. 23 Jun 1841
Windsor John to Jones Rebecca 24 Jul 1827
Windsor John to Landen Polly 3 Aug 1841
Windsor John to Webster Levinia 4 Jun 1850
Windsor John to Donoho Jane 20 Nov 1855
Windsor John to Landon Leah 4 Mar 1862
Windsor John Henry to White Kezia V. 1 Mar 1858
Windsor John K. to Byrd Sally A. 24 Mar 1852
Windsor John W. to Adams Emily C. 11 Aug 1868
Windsor Joseph to Huffington Sally 16 Jul 1808
Windsor Joseph to Robertson Anne 14 Mar 1828
Windsor Lazarus W. to Abbet Sophia 30 Mar 1802
Windsor Robert C. to Stanton Mary 3 Apr 1844
Windsor Samuel J. to Evans Adaline D. 17 Jan 1861
Windsor Samuel R. to Bailey Elizabeth A. 22 Feb 1864
Windsor Severn to Austin Betsy 8 Sep 1829
Windsor Thomas to McGrath Mary 19 Feb 1822
Windsor Thomas to Seabreeze Eleanor 7 Feb 1832
Windsor Thomas to Leonard Jane 16 Dec 1856
Windsor William to Nichols Keziah 13 Feb 1816
Windsor William to Ellis Elizabeth 27 Mar 1821
Windsor William to Jones Susan 26 Mar 1836
Windsor William to Webster Priscilla 28 Jun 1853
Windsor William John to Washboard Nancy 30 Sep 1856
Windsor William R. to Horner Tabitha S. 4 Jan 1862
Windzor James to Hopkins Leah 30 Jun 1803
Wingate Aaron to Jones Rachel 27 Jan 1818
Wingate David to Swift Anne 24 Dec 1834
Wingate George E. to Hughes Arianne A. 19 Dec 1849
Wingate Lemuel to Bailey Nancy 24 Jan 1838
Wingate William to Maddux Eleanor 3 Oct 1827
Wingate Wm. to Dorsey Mary 21 May 1835
Winget Matthias to White Peggy 19 Apr 1803
Wingit Evans to Layfield Jenny 4 Jan 1802
Winright Hamilton to Matthews Elizabeth 6 Sep 1803
Winright Jesse to Heath Eleanor 18 Jan 1804
Winright John to McIntire Peggy 10 Aug 1799
Winright John to Douglass Elizabeth 31 Aug 1808
Winright Joshua to Street Polly 28 Mar 1810
Winright Levin to Daugherty Hetty 16 Jun 1801

Winright Stephen to McIntire Temperance 20 Aug 1799
Winright Stephen to Winright Leah M. 23 Mar 1841
Winright William to Winright Eliza Anne 10 Mar 1830
Winright Zadoc to Winright Jane 18 Nov 1800
Winsor Elijah to Douglass Biddy 11 Dec 1800
Wise Jacob to Burnett Emily 4 Dec 1867
Wise John R. to Johnson Annie M. 23 Aug 1871 C
Wise William to Wilson Anne C. 10 Dec 1811
Wood James D. to Dashiell Henrietta 24 Jun 1857
Wood Joshua to Jones Betsy 6 Jul 1802
Wood William T. to Maddux Sarah 13 Feb 1828
Wood William T. to Tull Elizabeth M. 26 Oct 1830
Wood William T. to Johnson Julia Anne 19 Dec 1833
Woodcock Amos W. to Wright Julia 25 Aug 1862
Woodland Benjamin to Wilson Laura W. 7 Jul 1868
Woolford Alison H. to Anderson Margaret L. 31 Aug 1858
Woolford Arthur G. to Polk Annie C. 30 Sep 1868
Woolford George H. L. to Wailes Eleanor 30 May 1826
Woolford John to Polk Ellen G. 31 Oct 1837
Woolford John to Polk Caroline E.G. 23 Nov 1852
Woolford Levin to Handy Prissy 7 Feb 1800
Woolford Levin to Waters Annie E. 8 Oct 1849
Woolford William G. to Holbrook Matilda C. 22 Apr 1839
Woollen Levin to Dickerson Eliza 21 Sep 1848
Wright Boaz to Dutton Leah 21 May 1832
Wright Clement M. to Weatherly Elizabeth 10 Nov 1846
Wright Cylus to Newnan Margaret 26 Aug 1871 C
Wright David to Lewis Elizabeth 6 Jul 1866 C
Wright Gabriel to Wilson Lovey 9 Nov 1871 C
Wright George to Simpson Bridget 3 Jan 1797
Wright George Stanley to Wright Catherine 23 Jan 1828
Wright George W. to Phillips Alsey J. 16 Feb 1863
Wright Henry to Lenon Louisa 12 Apr 1870 C
Wright Jacob P. to Bennett Anne M. 21 Mar 1864
Wright James to Phillips Julicom 17 Jan 1835
Wright Jesse to Hill Mary 10 Jan 1844
Wright Joseph to Harris Sarah P. 10 Dec 1838
Wright Levin to Robertson Rachael --(?) 1838
Wright Levin to Conway Eleanor 5 Apr 1853
Wright Morris to Black Sarah Jane 1 Aug 1854 C

Wright Morris to Dashiell Sally 18 Oct 1859 C
Wright Noah to Wright Mary 5 Jun 1821
Wright Noah to Hopkins Henrietta 26 Jan 1848 C
Wright Rufus to Colmon Leah 21 Jan 1871 C
Wright Samuel to Prettyman Martha E. 9 Jan 1868
Wright Thomas to Glaster Nancy 19 Mar 1804
Wright Tubman to Goslee Nelly 21 Jan 1814
Wright Warren W. to Thompson Caroline 23 Feb 1866 C
Wright William to Townsend Nancy 10 Aug 1852 C
Wright (Dr.) Archibald Wesley to Gardner Elizabeth E. 30 Apr 1856
Wrink William (Revd.) to Ballard Amanda E. 13 Mar 1850
Wroten Thomas H. to Rock Mary E. 6 May 1867
Wroten Tubman to Philips Nelly 4 Jun 1807
Wrotten John to Darby Katharine 10 Oct 1797
Wyatt Charles W. to Walker Sarah Jane 5 May 1869
Wyatt Edward to Cox Polly 25 May 1812
Wyatt George to Walker Lyssia 5 May 1866
Yerby Lemuel to King Sally E. 28 Jun 1855
Yerby Lemuel (Dr.) to Waters Susan Jane 13 Aug 1834
Young Andrew J. to Butler Sarah E. 20 Nov 1856
Young James to McIntyre Rhoda 31 Mar 1804
Young James H. to Stevenson Sally E.M. 28 Sep 1841
Young James H. to Stevenson Emeline 17 May 1855
Young John to Adams Mary 27 Dec 1803
Young John to Evans Charity E. 2 Jul 1829
Young Littleton to Taylor Jane 11 Apr 1800
Young Louis R. to Bloxsom Mary 19 Feb 1866
Young Nicholas to Gravenor Jane 13 Jan 1837
Zollicoffa Henry to Turner Julia S. 24 Jan 1860

www.ingramcontent.com/pod-product-compliance
Lightning Source LLC
Chambersburg PA
CBHW061722270326
41928CB00011B/2077